A history of the

BERKS and HANTS line

Reading to Westbury

Peter Simmonds

 Noodle N.B. Books

A history of the

BERKS and HANTS line

Reading to Westbury

Peter Simmonds

© Peter Simmonds and Noodle Books 2014

ISBN 978-1-906419-88-2

First published in 2014 by Kevin Robertson
under the **NOODLE BOOKS** imprint
PO Box 279
Corhampton
SOUTHAMPTON
SO32 3ZX

www.noodlebooks.co.uk

Printed in England by Berforts, Information Press..

Front cover - *An unidentified "Warship" diesel-hydraulic takes a down West of England express past Crofton Pumping Station. The Kennet & Avon canal can just be glimpsed to the right of the train. (Amyas Crump collection)*

Frontispiece - *Newbury in transition. Soon after the remodelling of Newbury station's track layout one of the first High Speed Trains, recently introduced on West of England services, calls with an up train. (Author)*

Page 2 - *No 6820 'Kingstone Grange' climbing hard past East Grafton junction on a down freight, 6 June 1961 (Donovan E H Box)*

Page 3 - *Staff at Pewsey.*

CONTENTS

The Berks and Hants Railway and associated lines

This map defines, by solid lines, the sections of railway described in detail in this book. Each section is defined by its ELR (Engineers' Line Reference) e.g. BHL = Berks & Hants Line

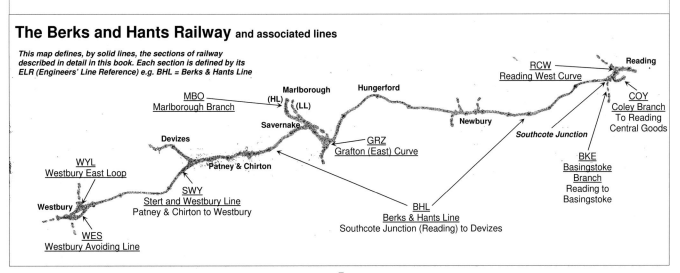

RCW
Reading West Curve

Reading

COY
Coley Branch
To Reading
Central Goods

MBO
Marlborough Branch

(HL)

Marlborough

(LL)

Hungerford

Newbury

Southcote Junction

Savernake

Devizes

GRZ
Grafton (East) Curve

BKE
Basingstoke
Branch
Reading to
Basingstoke

WYL
Westbury East Loop

Patney & Chirton

SWY
Stert and Westbury Line
Patney & Chirton to Westbury

BHL
Berks & Hants Line
Southcote Junction (Reading) to Devizes

Westbury

WES
Westbury Avoiding Line

PUBLISHER'S NOTE

It was with immense pleasure that I first learned of the efforts of Peter Simmonds in researching and recording the history of the Berks and Hants Railway. To one whose youngest times were spent at Newbury the railways of the area have long held a particular fascination, initially it must be said for the Didcot, Newbury and Southampton route, a line I recall travelling on numerous times as a child.

A subsequent move of home to Winchester did not diminish that interest. Relations at Thatcham meant there would be many subsequent visits to the area and where, whilst my cousins might be cajoling me to join them in more healthy outdoor pursuits in the area known as 'the Moors', I recall standing spellbound on occasions to watch a shining green engine with burnished copper and brasswork pass by. (I know now these would have been on the Race Day trains.)

Years later the railway interest had not altered, increased if anything, and it was with great pleasure that from the late 1960s onwards I embarked on the research that would eventually lead to books on the 'DNS' and Lambourn lines.

One of the pleasures of these studies were the opportunities to talk to former railwayman, without exception all so willing to recall their stories. Indeed it was in consequence of these discussions that the Lambourn book came about.

Having, in the course of this research, obtained much information on the Berks and Hants line, my avowed intention was to progress a book on this line. For a variety of reasons that volume never materialised, although the material gathered was retained.

Upon meeting Peter Simmonds the opportunity to finally produce the story of the railway was at last available. Peter has covered the ground thoroughly and it is thus a privilege to be involved with this work and present what I sincerely believe will be the definitive work on the Berks and Hants line.

Kevin Robertson

Corhampton 2014

*Pre-war calm at Newbury as two very different trains await their departure times. In the Winchester bay, the Southampton train is headed by GWR 'Duke' class 4-4-0 No 3256 'Guinevere', built at Swindon in 1905. The leading coach is a clerestory composite (first and third class) vehicle that was once a slip coach (see **Glossary**). In the Lambourn bay is the GWR diesel railcar No 18, built especially for the Lambourn branch and capable of hauling a trailing load such as horse boxes. Photograph dated April 1938 (Author's collection - original slide from ccq)*

FOREWORD

The intention of this book is to describe in detail the history of the line from Reading to Westbury and, at the same time, bring together information currently scattered amongst thousands of sources, not all of which are readily available to the public.

Although comprehensive histories have been published of other railways in the vicinity of the line, no history has previously been published of the Berks and Hants Railway (incorporated 1845), the Berks and Hants Extension Railway (incorporated 1859) and the Stert and Westbury Railway (incorporated 1894), the surviving sections of which are known today as **"The Berks and Hants line"**.

I am proud to present this history based on over 20 years of research and having referenced countless sources including the submissions for all projected railways, which during the years of the railway mania were manifold. I have taken a chronological approach as much as possible and hope this will benefit the reader in understanding the sequence of events which shaped the railway we know today.

Sources with particular reference to each chapter are listed at the end of each chapter; other sources are included under "Further Reading" at the back of the book.

In conjunction with the publication of this book, an archive has been prepared which will be made available, in due course, at the principal public libraries along the route.

In a comprehensive history of this nature, and one which relates significant events from the 1820s onwards, omissions and errors are bound to occur. The publisher would be pleased to be advised not only of any such items but of any new information which may be relevant to this history.

Peter Simmonds

Newbury 2014

A number of people have been of considerable help to me in the preparation of the text, appendices and photographs and I would particularly like to mention:

Ben Andrews
Nigel SM Bray
David Canning
The late Larry Crosier
David Fox
The late John Gould
Christopher Hall, RA
Mary Harper
Dave Hazell
Dave Parsons
Malcolm Pearce
Rodney Pinchen
Alex Sankey
Stuart Wise

I would also like to thank the staff of the following archives, museums, libraries and other organizations that have helped me with research and the provision of photographs:

Berkshire Record Office
Great Western Trust
Hampshire Record Office
Newbury Library
Parliamentary Archives
Pewsey Heritage Centre
Railway Correspondence and Travel Society
Reading Borough Library
STEAM: Museum of the Great Western Railway
Swindon Central Library
West Berkshire Museum
Wiltshire and Swindon History Centre
Wiltshire Museum Devizes

This book is for Colin, Rory and Hugh and is dedicated to the memory of Kevin and Alan and also to all those who have met with misfortune on the line.

All things good to know are difficult to learn.
GREEK PROVERB

Page 8 upper - *At this much-photographed location at Little Bedwyn, the Berks and Hants line runs close to the Kennet and Avon canal. Before the doubling and upgrading of the line in the 1897-98 period, a level crossing existed here and a bridge over the canal. These were replaced with footbridges as seen in the photograph; the three spans of the railway footbridge have subsequently been replaced with precast concrete sections. Behind the photographer are the bridges carrying the diverted road over the railway and the canal. Photograph dated 29 March 2012 (Author)*

Page 8 lower - *The Great Western sign at Midgham, similar to those erected at several stations down the line, bears an additional board for Douai School. This school was the public (independent) school that was run by the Douai Abbey Benedictine community at Woolhampton until it closed in 1999. As explained later in the text, Midgham station is located in the village of Woolhampton (Author)*

DESCRIPTION OF THE LINE
Reading to Devizes 1865

The year 1865 has been chosen to illustrate the full extent of the Railway which is the principal subject of this book as by then the Berks and Hants Extension Railway was open, connecting Hungerford with Devizes, and the Marlborough Railway was in use having been opened in 1864; also a timetable is available for 1865.

Description of the Line: Reading to Devizes 1865

Our journey starts in the down bay platform at Reading, which is a one-sided station. Having perhaps arrived from Paddington at the down platform, we find our train on the opposite side of the platform at the forward end of the train. Consisting of a small steam locomotive and a string of four- and six-wheeled first and second class carriages, our train is scheduled to leave at 12 noon for all stations to Devizes, continuing thence to Trowbridge.

This is the second train of the day, the first having left Reading at 8.50am. That train had also provided accommodation for third class passengers; the company was required by Act of Parliament to provide at least one train a day for third class passengers, calling at all stations and charging the statutory penny a mile.

On departure, we soon reach the junction for the Berks and Hants line, without needing to enter the main line. The line as far as Hungerford is double track and was opened on 21 December 1847, some seven years after trains reached Reading from London. The broad gauge track (see Glossary) curves to the left towards Oxford Road Junction and we see the streets of Reading on our left and Reading Engine Shed on the right. At the junction, we are joined by the double-track connection with the main line in the Bristol direction, which was opened in 1856. This connecting line has mixed gauge track (see Glossary), as does the line on which we are now travelling. Just after the junction, we cross

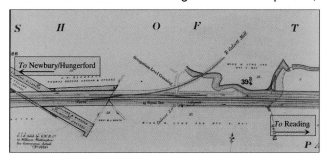

the Oxford Road on a shallow brick arch bridge and pass the site of the future Reading West station. As we enter a deep cutting, our driver will see ahead two high brick three-span bridges, the first carrying the Tilehurst Road and the second the Bath Road over our line.

At the end of the cutting, we reach Southcote Junction, where the Basingstoke Branch (the "Hants" section of the Berks and Hants Railway), also a double line, proceeds straight ahead, whilst we take a long right-hand curve onto an embankment on the River Kennet flood plain. Not far from here, on the left, is the Kennet and Avon Navigation, running from the River Thames at Reading to Newbury

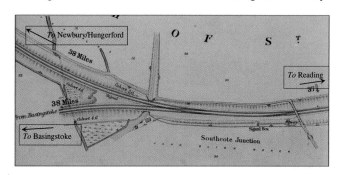

(simply referred to henceforth as "the canal"). From the junction onwards, the track is broad gauge only, the mixed gauge track having been provided only on the Basingstoke Branch, to enable through freight trains to be worked from the Midlands and North to Southampton. No habitation is visible, only the attractive scenery of the flood plain and the numerous mills in the area taking advantage of the river and the Holy Brook, which we cross several times. Soon after passing the Burghfield Road Crossing, the line to Calcot Mill can be seen on our right curving away towards the Holy Brook **(Note 1)**.

The first station, Theale, is reached at the end of a long straight, not a common feature of this line which follows the river and canal to Hungerford. By the time we reach Theale, we observe that the area to our right is arable and pasture,

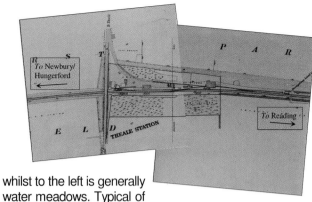

whilst to the left is generally water meadows. Typical of other stations on the line, two short low platforms are provided, with the main station buildings, in the "Brunel chalet" style on the "town" side, whilst our platform has a shelter in a similar style. There is no footbridge; passengers cross the line by the road bridge, whilst a board crossing (timber level crossing) at the end of the platforms enables staff to cross the line to deal with the trains and to convey parcels, mail bags and milk churns between platforms. Also typical, and again on the "town side", a small goods yard is provided with a goods shed, cattle dock and sidings, and a crane for loading and offloading. At the far end of the station is a spur giving access by a wagon turntable (see Glossary) to a short platform, probably used for loading horses and carriages.

Signalling is rudimentary, with disc and crossbar signals at the entrance and exit to each station and at the junctions. Between stations, trains are operated on the time-interval system. There is no signal box; the signals being operated by a "bobby" standing beside the post, or from levers in a ground frame at the larger stations **(Note 2)**.

We leave the station under a bridge carrying a road which also leads to Burghfield. Continuing westwards, we see on the left the line to the Tile (Tyle) Mill on the Kennet, with its siding, and then the canal can be seen as we follow its course and cross the minor road to Ufton Nervet on the level. Approaching Aldermaston Station, we pass under a bridge carrying the road to Padworth. On each side of the station are further overbridges, each consisting of brick side

arches and brick abutments, with a main span over the tracks of wrought iron. Perhaps Aldermaston Road would have been a more appropriate name, the village being

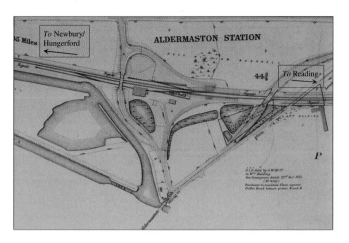

some 2 miles away, on the far side of the valley. The station buildings are of a similar type to those at Theale. Like all the minor stations, the arrangement of the station and goods yard would be similar to that at Theale, with variations at each location to suit the expected traffic.

Never far from the canal, the line continues its sinuous and gently rising course, passing under a minor road bridge, to cross the road to Brimpton and Wasing on the level at Woolhampton station. This station is very well situated for the village, which is centred on the Bath Road, a few hundred yards on our right. The level crossing gates here

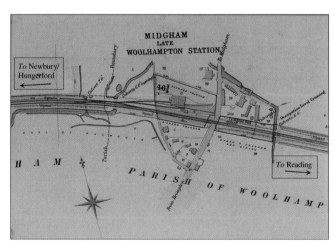

are worked manually by the station staff. The station building, on our right, is of wooden construction unlike the previous stations and there is a small shelter on our platform. The small goods yard is also on our right, at the Newbury end of the station, the goods shed being close to the station building **(Note 3)**.

Beyond the platform ends, the line immediately curves to the left and then to the right. We keep close to the canal, passing under the road leading to Brimpton and a crossing leading to Colthrop Mill and reach Thatcham station. This is some distance south of the village and is situated by a level crossing of the road to Crookham and Headley. The nearness of the bridges taking the road over the canal and

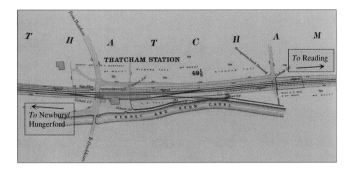

river, and the continuing location of the line on the flood plain, reminds us that the area is prone to flooding. The main building is again on the right - it is a modest affair like that at Midgham. The goods yard is on the left on the narrow strip of ground between the canal and the railway; the goods shed abuts the back of the platform. The one siding to the east of the goods yard terminates adjacent to the canal and would have been suitable for transhipment. As we leave the station we see that the line from the goods shed continues across the road before joining our line and that the crossing gates are arranged accordingly.

As the line continues towards Newbury, extensive reed

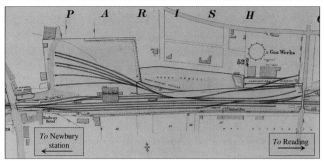

beds can be seen either side of the line, now elevated well above them. We cross the river and canal near Bull's Lock at a place where they are combined. This bridge has spans and intermediate supports of timber, the abutments being of brick. Boats have to navigate between the supports on the fast-flowing river. Now on the south side of the river and canal, the line continues across reed beds and meadows, passing under several bridges before entering Newbury Station.

This simply consists of two platforms, with a short overall roof typical of stations of the period. Modest as this seems, the 1865 passenger train timetable shows only four weekday trains each way, none of which started their journeys here. Also typical of the period, some short bay platforms are provided for activities such as horse and carriage landing (see reference in the following timetable notes to the conveyance of horses and carriages by train).

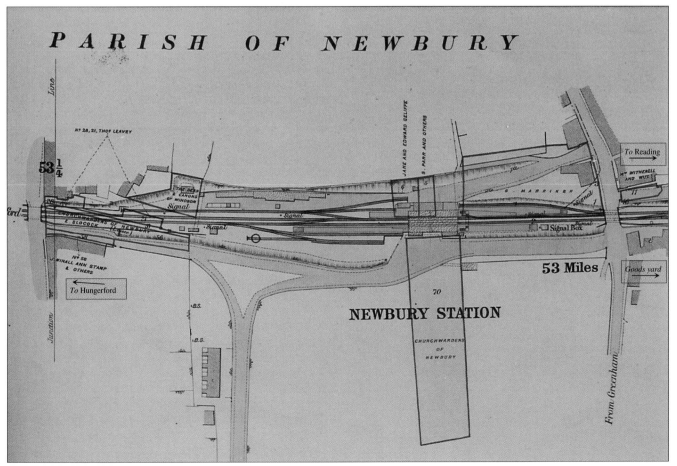

Approach roads give access to each side of the station. We have already passed, on our right, the large goods yard, with its fan of sidings and commodious goods shed with two tracks under cover. We may see a small steam engine shunting here.

To the east of the station, the line passes under three road bridges; to the west three more at Bartholomew Street, Rockingham Road and Enborne House. The first four of these bridges are metal spans on brick abutments, whereas the Rockingham Road and Enborne House bridges consist of graceful brick arches. The railway through the town centre of Newbury, as indicated by the number of bridges, is in cutting throughout, the station area being prone to flooding after heavy rain **(Note 4)**.

The double line of the Berks and Hants Railway continues to Hungerford. Soon we cross the canal on a bridge similar to that described at Bull's Lock, before Newbury, and are now on the flood plain between the canal and the river. This is the Kennet and Avon Canal, linking Newbury with Devizes and Bath and opened in stages between 1797 and 1810. We cross the River Kennet on a long, sweeping reverse curve which takes us to Hamstead Crossing, passing over a minor road linking the village of Hamstead Marshall, a mile to our left as the crow flies, and the Bath Road, out of sight but running parallel to us on our right. Like all others, this crossing is manned whilst trains are running, but unlike the others already passed, is remote from any station.

The scenery on either side, consisting of water meadows, streams and stands of trees, is very attractive. A feature of this area, and of several others in the Kennet Valley, is the intricate system of channels connecting the river and canal ensuring that the level of the latter is maintained at the correct level. Irish Hill is prominent on our left and we cross the main river again and other waterways. Kintbury station is reached adjacent to the crossing of the road which links the adjacent village, on our left, with the Bath Road. The goods yard lies entirely beyond the crossing, on the village side, like that at Thatcham being squeezed between the railway and the canal.

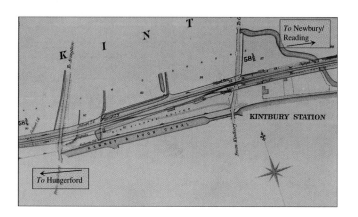

Leaving Kintbury, we pass under an accommodation bridge and then enter a long reverse curve, in doing so crossing on a metal bridge one of the channels that link the canal and the river. The line sweeps away from the canal and climbs up to cross it on a 3-span bridge, again similar to that at Bull's Lock, keeping to higher land as it runs roughly parallel with the canal to Hungerford. Running close to the canal, we see Hungerford Common on each side as we reach the minor road joining the Bath Road and the common and see Dun Mill on our right. The final section of the line into Hungerford continues on a narrow strip of land between the main part of the common on our left and the canal until the first of the town's buildings appears on our left. The station is soon reached, without crossing any further roads.

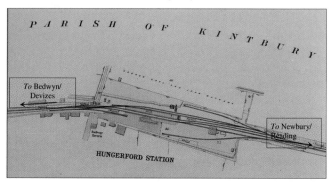

Hungerford Station was the terminus of the "Berks" section of the Berks and Hants Railway (the "Hants" section, as already mentioned, going to Basingstoke) until the Berks and Hants Extension Railway (B&HER) was opened through to Devizes on 11 November 1862. We have already passed, on our left, the large goods yard, which has facilities to deal with a large range of commodities. The track arrangements are quite complex, and no doubt have developed from Hungerford's original role as a terminus, with the need for the turning and servicing of locomotives here. Furthermore, as the Great Western Railway always intended to extend the line to Westbury to connect with the Wilts, Somerset and Weymouth Railway at the latter place, the layout of the original station, and the recent changes thereto, would have taken those plans into account.

Leaving Hungerford on the "Extension" line, we switch to the single, broad gauge track before crossing on the level a minor road which gives access to the area between the railway and the canal to the right. As at Thatcham, one short goods line also crosses this road on our left. Passing over the High Street on a single-span bridge fitted into a narrow gap between the buildings lining each side of the street, we can see a busy street scene, maybe with a market in progress. This section of line, through to Devizes, was built as a single line. Threading our way through an old and attractive part of the town and crossing several minor roads, we reach open country, passing along a hillside with the canal and the river below to our right. Here is the first bridge over the Extension line, built for double track as were all overbridges on the B&HER.

From here onwards we will keep in close touch with the canal but rather than follow the course of the River Kennet towards Marlborough, we follow one of the river's tributaries, the Dun, until we reach the highest point of the line at Savernake. Leaving the higher land on which we passed through Hungerford, we pass through water meadows, keeping contact with the canal and the river and at a level high enough above them to prevent the line being subject to the annual winter floods. We cross the river and then the canal, the latter on a bridge of two wrought-iron spans supported by an intermediate pier and brick abutments. Now the Bath Road comes into sight on the right before turning away to run due west through the nearby village of Froxfield and on to Marlborough. A bridge over the line carries a minor road but there is no station here. We soon pass our first level crossing, over another minor road at a place called Fore Bridge. As there is no station to provide staff for manning the crossing, a crossing-keeper's cottage is provided close to the line on the left hand side. Passing the hamlet of Little Bedwyn close to the canal, and our first crossing of a public road on the Extension, we once again note the absence of a station; a crossing-keeper's cottage is provided close to the line on the right-hand side. With the village of Great Bedwyn visible on our right, we reach

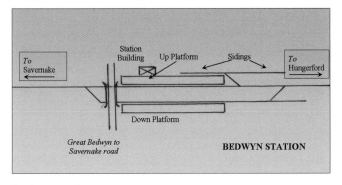

Bedwyn station.

Station buildings on the Berks and Hants Extension Railway were built in a particular style which we shall also see at Savernake, Pewsey and Woodborough. At Bedwyn, the building is on the village side; a siding and small bay platform can also be seen on our right. There is a crossing loop here, with two platforms. The loop and second platform were not provided at the opening of the line and were added later. There is a short siding but no goods shed. Passing under the Great Bedwyn – Shalbourne road and then a level crossing of the road to Wilton, we continue our steady climb to the summit at Savernake, keeping the canal and the river, which is now just a stream, on our left. On our right are the fields and woodlands on the edge of Savernake Forest, which are visible all the way to Savernake station. Ahead of us are two minor level crossings, the second, at Crofton, being on the line of the Roman Road which ran from Marlborough south-eastwards towards Haydown Hill, a high point on the Hampshire Downs (835ft) some distance to our left, and onwards to Winchester. Being a public road, there is a crossing-keeper's cottage here, too.

Our driver will now be able to see the tall chimney of the Crofton Pumping Station, designed by John Rennie, just to the right of the line. The station contains two steam engines, installed in 1812 and 1843, which pump water from the reservoir we can see on our left (Wilton Water) by means of a leat (small channel) for a distance of about 1500 yards to the summit section of the canal. Our line curves sharply to the right as it passes the pumping station to pass under the Burbage - Bedwyn Road and follow the canal again towards Savernake station. The Extension line has not been built to a very high standard, with many tight curves and short gradients, but the curve at the pumping station was unavoidable if the canal, which arriving first and thus adopting the best route in the area, was to be followed. Beyond the locks we see on our left is the summit section of the canal. The railway continues to climb as it approaches Savernake station, where it will cross this section of the canal at a location where it is in tunnel. Bruce tunnel, whose portal can be seen on our left, therefore not only passes under the railway but under Savernake Station too.

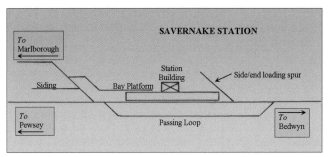

Savernake station is situated in a cutting through a ridge, the road from Burbage to Durley and The Warren crossing the line on a brick arch bridge. The track layout on the main line consists of a single through platform and a crossing loop at the east (Reading) end of the station. Surprisingly, we will cross the up train to Reading here. This means our train must wait in the loop while the other train uses the platform and then take its turn at the platform. Both trains are due to leave Savernake at 1.30pm, clearly this is unlikely unless the Reading train carries out some shunting before departure.

As Savernake is a junction with the Marlborough Branch, opened on 4 April 1864; it can be seen that the track and platform arrangements are very rudimentary and inadequate for a junction station. The branch platform is a bay platform beyond the bridge, where the Marlborough train is waiting, consisting of a small number of similar carriages to our train hauled by a small tank locomotive.

The station building is of the type already seen at Bedwyn and is the largest on the Extension; there is a small refreshment room under the management of the nearby Forest Hotel, which itself has just been opened. There are short sidings at each end of the station, both on the right side and no goods shed. Water for the station and engine purposes is taken from the canal at the east end of the tunnel.

Control of trains on the single line between stations on the Hungerford and Devizes section is by a primitive system known as Disc Telegraph; between Savernake and Marlborough, the single line is worked by train staff **(Note 2)**.

Leaving Savernake, we first see on our right the Marlborough Branch curving away and then immediately the canal again as it emerges from the western portal of the canal tunnel. Initially the canal and railway remain close, however although both railway and canal continue to Pewsey and Devizes, the railway is generally a little to the south of the canal. The summit of the line, being at the crossing of the canal, is now behind us as we pass under the Marlborough – Burbage road bridge, a wrought iron span between stone abutments, and see the Burbage Goods Depot. The depot consists of a simple loop serving a goods shed with a siding at each end of the loop, sited adjacent to the canal for transhipment purposes.

The line falls on varying gradients to Pewsey, passing through many curves but none of any severity. The scenery on either side can be described as typical rural England, with occasional views of the canal on our right and, as we near Pewsey, distant views of Salisbury Plain on our left. The village of Wootton Rivers is on our right and we pass over or under a number of minor roads before reaching Pewsey.

Pewsey station is reached immediately after crossing the Salisbury – Marlborough road and the station building, like the town itself, is on the left. As at Bedwyn, the crossing loop and second platform have recently been added. The railway was very welcome in the "richly agricultural" Vale of Pewsey and the station is well sited to serve the town and the

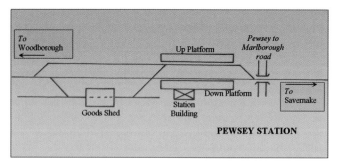

PEWSEY STATION

surrounding area. The small goods yard and goods shed are seen on the left as we leave the station.

Our journey to Devizes continues without reaching or passing near to any communities of any size, the scenery still agricultural, arable and pasture. An attractive range of hills may be seen to the right, on one of which is a white horse cut in the chalk, whilst the skyline of Salisbury Plain is

ever present on our left. On our way a number of minor roads will cross over or pass under the line; there are no public road level crossings between Crofton and Devizes. We are passing through an area with many tributaries of the River Avon, the Avon that passes through Salisbury to reach the English Channel at Christchurch.

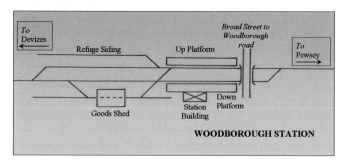

WOODBOROUGH STATION

The final intermediate station is Woodborough where the platform and goods yard are on our left, unusually on the opposite side to the nearby village. In most respects, the station and its layout are similar to those at Pewsey. The station is located just beyond the bridge carrying the Broad Street to Woodborough road across the line. As we leave for Devizes, we note that generally the land is flatter in this area, and the line is built at just above ground level, with the occasional short cutting. There are no major rivers or other features, and the canal is now some distance to the north. As the line turns slightly towards the north-west, we pass over the Devizes – Andover Road on a wrought iron span on brick abutments.

Approaching Devizes, the line crosses a ravine on an embankment which at the time of construction caused some concern due to its height of 60ft and its foundation of peaty soil; however a system of drainage had been installed in advance of the embankment construction and no problems occurred. The line then passes through a deep cutting before arriving at the mound on which Devizes Castle was built. The attractively castellated portal of the tunnel can be seen ahead; in fact the first part is a covered way (artificial tunnel provided to conceal the railway) followed by a short tunnel, the distance between portals being 190 yards.

Immediately on leaving the tunnel the line enters Devizes station on a sharp left-hand curve. The line from Holt Junction, on the Wilts, Somerset and Weymouth line between Trowbridge and Melksham, reached Devizes in 1857 and we make a "head-on" junction with this line. Devizes station is comparable in size with Newbury, with two platforms under an overall roof and a range of buildings, all constructed in timber. The goods yard is adjacent to the station, on the north side, and a small engine shed and turntable is seen on the south side.

Our train will continue to Trowbridge.

The Train Service June 1865

Weekdays: Four trains a day between Reading and Devizes and vice versa.

In the down direction (from Reading) the 7pm departure is described as an Express and may have been a through train from Paddington (dep 6.15pm). A connection to and from Marlborough was provided on the first three trains but not to/from the Express! All trains called at all stations Reading – Devizes and continued to Trowbridge.

In the up direction (to Reading) the first train, starting from Devizes, is described as "Express from Reading" so is clearly a through train; this train called at all stations to Reading but did not have a connection to/from Marlborough! The second train started at Trowbridge and was semi-fast to Reading. A note stated that "Carriages and Horses are not conveyed by this Train" (thus implying that they could be carried by other trains, including the expresses!). The third and fourth trains started at Trowbridge and called at all stations between Devizes and Reading.

Sundays: two trains each way, all stations Reading – Devizes and vice versa. The first up and second down trains started/terminated at Devizes; the other trains started from/ continued to Trowbridge respectively. There were no services on the Marlborough Branch.

Crossing/Passing Arrangements in June 1865 timetable

Weekdays

8.50am ex Reading passes 7.30am ex Devizes (Exp) between Theale and Aldermaston and the 8.22am ex Trowbridge between Newbury and Kintbury

12 noon ex Reading crosses 12.10pm ex Trowbridge at Savernake (Branch train also present)

4.38pm ex Reading crosses 5.10pm ex Trowbridge at Pewsey

7.5pm ex Reading (Exp) crosses 5.10pm ex Trowbridge between Aldermaston and Woolhampton

Sundays

None

NOTES

NOTE 1: BURGHFIELD ROAD CROSSING

On the plans submitted to Parliament, a level crossing was shown at Burghfield Road; it is not known when the bridge was provided, but it certainly would have been before the general improvements to the line at the end of the nineteenth century.

NOTE 2: SIGNALLING

See Glossary for explanation of signalling terms. Information on the methods of working the single lines is shown in the footnotes to the 1870 timetable; for the double line section, information on the time interval system is given in the History of the Great Western Railway Volume 2 1863-1921.

NOTE 3: WOOLHAMPTON

The name of the station was later changed to Midgham to avoid confusion with a large Midlands town, whose name was probably abbreviated to sound very similar at the time.

NOTE 4: NEWBURY

The names of the roads or streets on the bridges east of Newbury at the date in question are not known for certain. The first in the direction of travel was described as 'Greenham' on the parliamentary plans and gave access to the farms and houses to the south of the line; it is now used for access to the racecourse. The second is the road now known as Boundary Road, whilst the third was the continuation of Cheap Street and would probably have been known then as Greenham Road.

ADDITIONAL NOTES

The date of the maps included in this narrative is not known. With the exception of the two at Newbury the maps are believed to be a reasonably accurate representation of the situation at each location in 1865. At Newbury the maps show the station after bay platforms were added in 1882.

Stations now closed: Savernake, Woodborough, Devizes (all 1966)

Stations since opened and remaining open: Reading West (1906), Newbury Racecourse (1905 – Race traffic, 1988 – all traffic (initially experimental))

Stations and halts since opened and closed in 1966: Wootton Rivers Halt (1928) (Savernake – Pewsey); Manningford Halt (1932) (Pewsey – Woodborough); Patney and Chirton (1902) (Woodborough – Devizes); Pans Lane Halt (1929) (Patney and Chirton – Devizes)

REFERENCES

GWR Timetable June 1865

p40 "London, Reading, and Newbury, Hungerford, Devizes, and Trowbridge; To Bath, Bristol, Salisbury, and Weymouth".

Maps and plans, published and in local study libraries, county record offices and history centres

Berkshire Chronicle

25 December 1847

Devizes and Wiltshire Gazette

23 December 1847, 6 November 1862

Reading Mercury

24 December 1847; 8, 15, 22 and 29 November 1862

STEEL YARD, Upper Thames Street.

KENNET & AVON
CANAL CONVEYANCE
TO AND FROM
LONDON & BRISTOL;
AND BY STEAM TO
Dublin, Cork, and Waterford.

BETTS and *DREWE* return their acknowledgments for the Favors they have received, and beg to apprize the Public, that they have established FLY BARGES, which leave the STEEL YARD, Upper Thames Street, London, and QUEEN STREET WHARF, Bristol, daily; *and will perform the Passage in Four or Five Days, and all intermediate places in proportionate times—unavoidable detentions excepted.*

B. and D. hold themselves responsible for Goods committed to their care, according to the NOTICE and CONDITIONS SUBJOINED, which are publicly exhibited at their Offices and Wharfs; where they receive and deliver Goods.

The Proprietors give PUBLIC NOTICE, that they will not hold themselves answerable or accountable for Fire, or for any Loss or Injury the Goods may sustain, by any accident to their Barges on the Rivers, and Navigation of whatever Nature or Kind soever, (*neglect excepted,*) or for any Article, unless the same shall be entered by the Book-keeper, or marked, as received by one of them, on the Book or Paper of the Porter or other Person who may deliver it.

They will not be accountable for any Money, Plate, Watches, Rings, Jewels, Writings, Glass, China, Marble, Prints, Paintings, or other Valuables, unless entered as such, and an Insurance paid above the common rate of carriage, according to the Value, upon delivery to *them.*

Any Claim for Loss or Damage, that is not made within three Days after the Delivery of the Goods, will not be allowed.

Leakage arising from Bad Casks or Cooperage will not be accounted for.

All Goods which shall be delivered for the purpose of being carried, will be considered as *general Liens,* and subject, not only to the Money due for the Carriage of such particular *Goods,* but also to the *general Balance* due from the respective Owners to the Proprietors of the said Conveyance.

Further particulars may be obtained by applying as above, or to R. PARKER, *Darlington Wharf,* Bath ; JAMES LONG, Bradford, Wilts ; D. PHIPPS, Devizes; BETTS and DREWE *Wharf,* Newbury ; and *Gas Wharf,* Reading ; and Mr. MASON, Windsor.

LONDON, January, 1827.

N. B.—*The above Wharfingers are not accountable for Fire, or Damage arising from High Tides.*

16

1

THE DAYS BEFORE THE RAILWAY

1824 – 1829 Background

In the 1820s, the area between Reading and Hungerford was served by the Bath Road turnpike, the Kennet and Avon Canal west of Newbury and the Kennet Navigation between Newbury and Reading, where a link was made to the River Thames. West of Hungerford, the turnpike and the canal went their separate ways, the road taking a more north-westerly course via Marlborough, Chippenham and thence Bath to Bristol. The canal was routed to Bath via Devizes and Bradford-on-Avon.

The origin of the turnpikes can be traced back to the Eighteenth Century, when fast coaches started carrying passengers and mail. Newbury had been linked to Reading and the River Thames by the Kennet Navigation since 1723; the Kennet and Avon Canal was started in 1794 and completed in stages, being opened throughout to Bath in 1810.

The subsequent histories of both the turnpike and the waterways are very well documented; they are of significance as being the only direct routes from London and Reading to Bath and Bristol (then the second town in the Kingdom) that existed in the early years of the Nineteenth Century. The Bath Road was plied by a variety of coaches, the most important being the Royal Mail, whilst many of the numerous coaching inns along the route have survived to this day. Goods were carried by pack-horse or in slow, cumbersome carts.

Both these methods of transport, the turnpike and canal, had their drawbacks. Before the widespread use of tarmac, roads were waterlogged in winter and dusty in summer. Horses had to be changed frequently and the capacity of the coaches was severely limited. The canals and rivers were subject to flooding and in those colder times, ice was a frequent and severe problem. The twists and turns of the canal added to the distance to be travelled and it is worth noting that the distance from the Wharf at Newbury via the Kennet and Thames Navigations to London Bridge was almost 93 miles. A summary of the early history of the Kennet Navigation and Kennet & Avon Canal is given at **Note 1**.

The first proposal for a railway to be worked by locomotives between London and Bristol was made in 1824, by the 'London and Bristol Rail-Road Company'. John Loudon Macadam, at that time Surveyor to the Bristol Turnpike Trust, was employed to lay out the line and quickly produced plans for two routes, both north of the Marlborough and Berkshire Downs and with a terminus on the Thames at Brentford. At the time the most urgent need was for an improved method of carrying goods; the restricted carrying capacity of the canal, the journey times and the delays acting as a barrier to increased trade. In February 1825 the directors decided to adopt Macadam's scheme for the railway together with a parallel turnpike road serving the towns missed by the railway. They also announced the intention to apply for the necessary Act of Parliament; however, although the shares were stated to have been taken up, no such application was ever made and the scheme died a natural death.

In the same year there was a rash of other schemes, including 'The General Junction Railroad from London to Bristol' and 'The Taunton Great Western Railroad'. None of these schemes bore fruit.

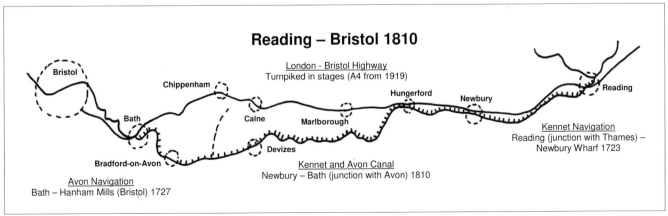

1830 - 1833 The rivals promote their schemes

In October 1830, a prospectus was published for a 'Southampton, London and Branch Railway Company' following interest in a railway from the Hampshire port and county town to London. At a meeting at Southampton on 6 April 1831, the company was formed. The 'Branch' in the title was intended to be from Basing (near Basingstoke) to Bath and Bristol via Newbury, Hungerford, Devizes, Trowbridge and Bradford-on-Avon. To form the branch junction, the Southampton line took the longer way round the "great bend of Basingstoke"; a study of a map shows a far more direct route between London and Southampton would have been via Alton. Thus, it was said, "would the English and Bristol Channels be united, and both with the metropolis".

A survey of the proposed main and branch line was made by Francis Giles in 1831 and plans were deposited. However, the directors decided not to seek the Act in the 1832 session but to allow potential proprietors time to consider carefully before subscribing. This delay enabled the London and Birmingham Railway to become the first trunk railway out of London and is said to have made easier, if not actually possible, the eventual birth of the Great Western Railway.

The prospectus of the renamed Southampton and London Railway was published in January 1832. In April, Henderson, chairman of the Southampton Committee, went to Bristol to see several influential persons, one of whom suggested William Brunton as engineer. In May 1832, Bristol supporters published a prospectus, but with unrest still simmering over the rejected Reform Bill, Henderson left Bristol.

In July 1832, Southampton and London promoters decided to get powers for the Southampton line before presenting a Bristol Bill. Following re-survey of the London and Southampton route in 1833, a further prospectus was published in December 1833 and the Bill reached Parliament in the 1834 Session. The description of the line included a reference to the branch for Bath and Bristol leaving the main line on the north side of Basingstoke, to be known as the 'Basing and Bath Railway'.

Several distinguished engineers, including George and Robert Stephenson, Isambard Kingdom Brunel (see below) and Joseph Locke, gave engineering evidence for the opponents of the line. These included supporters of what was then the embryonic Great Western Railway, who opposed the line as being the first step towards a branch from Basing to Bath and thence to Bristol.

Meanwhile, in May 1832, a practical scheme had been made for a railway between Bristol and London by way of Bath, Bradford-on-Avon, Trowbridge, near Devizes, through the Pewsey Vale to Hungerford, Newbury and Reading. The scheme, known as the 'Bristol and London Railway', was proposed by two engineers, William Brunton and H.H. Price, and estimated to cost £2.5 million. This scheme appears to have died in 1833 through lack of funding.

Despite several false starts, interest in rail communication between the first and second cities of the kingdom had been created in both commercial circles and the press. Consequently a committee of prominent merchants and others, representing the five corporate bodies of Bristol, was appointed to investigate the practicability of a more direct railway to London.

1833 – 1834 The Great Western Railway

Early in 1833 the committee decided that they should proceed with a survey and estimate. As Engineer they appointed 27 year old Isambard Kingdom Brunel, son of Marc Brunel, engineer of the Thames Tunnel, and in his own right author of the design chosen for the Clifton Suspension Bridge and Engineer to the Bristol Dock Company.

Brunel was appointed Engineer on 7 March and at once set about surveying the country between London and Bristol in company with W.H. Townsend, a land surveyor and valuer. Between Bath and Reading, intermediate towns which the railway could not afford to miss, they first inspected the route by Bradford-on-Avon, Devizes, the Pewsey Vale and Newbury. They then looked at the route north of the Marlborough Downs by Chippenham, Swindon, the Vale of White Horse and the Thames Valley and soon decided to recommend the northern route.

Following a public meeting held in Bristol in July 1833, it was resolved to form a company for the establishment of railway communication between London and Bristol. Bodies of directors were set up in each city to secure subscriptions and to obtain an Act of Parliament.

At the first joint meeting of the two committees held in London in August 1833, the title 'Great Western Railway' (GWR) was adopted. The Board of Directors consisted of two committees of twelve directors each, representing each city. The 120-mile line was estimated to cost over £2,800,000 with a prospective annual revenue to be almost £750,000. A map issued with the prospectus shows the proposed railway between Bristol and Reading to have been very similar to that which was eventually built and also shows "probable branches" from Didcot to Oxford, Swindon to Gloucester and Chippenham to Bradford-on-Avon.

As insufficient capital for the whole scheme had been subscribed at the time, the directors deposited plans in November 1833 for two separate railways covering parts of the route. These were for the sections between London and Reading and from Bristol to Bath.

The second reading of the Bill was carried in the House of Commons in March 1834 and passed to a parliamentary committee for consideration. This took 57 days and started with the public advantages of the proposed railway. For passengers, these were generally accepted, the only alternative being the stagecoaches; for goods, the inadequacies of the waterways between Bristol and London were described. Goods traffic between these places was then chiefly conducted by the River Avon, the Avon Navigation, the Kennet and Avon Canal and the Kennet and Thames Navigations; together these waterways formed a continuous route between the two

cities. As previously described, ice closed the canal whilst winter floods and summer droughts, particularly between Reading and London, caused delays on the rivers. Such delays could stretch to weeks and resulted in goods having to be sent by road at greater expense. Even under favourable conditions, the greater distances by canal and river and slower speeds of the traffic meant that, by railway, transit times would be drastically reduced. Between Reading and London the time would be reduced from three days to three hours.

1834 Defeat for the Great Western

For the new railway Brunel was the chief engineering witness and was extensively cross-examined. George Stephenson, Joseph Locke, James Walker and H.R. Palmer gave evidence in favour of the route proposed by Brunel. It was established that the line through the Thames Valley and north of the Marlborough Downs was the best course for a railway from London to Bristol. The levels were much better than any route south of the Downs and it also provided for better communication with Oxford, Gloucester and South Wales, which the southern route did not.

Opposition to the Bill came from many quarters:

Sketch of 'Newbury from the South' (Newbury during the Victorian Era 1837-1893)
F H Stillman published by W J Blackett (1893)

landowners opposed it for various reasons whilst those with a vested interest in the canals, rivers and stagecoaches opposed it for fear of competition. It was also opposed by the promoters of the London and Southampton Railway (as the Southampton and London Railway was by this time known), who were seeking their own Act of Incorporation in the same session. They went out of their way to attack the Great Western Bill, alleging that Bristol and the West of England could be equally well served by a branch from their own line. It was the beginning of long and bitter hostility to the GWR by the London and Southampton Railway (L&S).

The committee finally declared their approval of the Bill and it passed a further reading in the House of Commons. The Lords, however, rejected the Bill outright in July 1834. The truncated scheme, described by an opposing Counsel as neither "Great" nor "Western" nor even a "Railway", had perished. Despite the setback, the lengthy time before the committee had not been completely wasted and the Directors, undaunted by this defeat, began preparations for the bringing in of a new Bill for the whole line in the following year, 1835.

1834 The rival moves ahead: The London and Southampton Railway Act

Royal Assent was obtained for the London and Southampton Railway on 25 July 1834, ironically the same day the Lords rejected the truncated GWR scheme. Anticipating these events and alerted by GWR activities, the L&S Bristol line supporters resolved at Basingstoke on 16 July 1834 that "the Basingstoke and Bath" be formed, that Giles and Brunton be appointed engineers, and that the necessary steps be taken immediately for raising the subscriptions and completing the capital.

During July 1834, meetings at Devizes, Trowbridge, Bradford, Hungerford and Newbury approved the Basingstoke decision and formed local committees. However, at a public meeting held in Bath in September 1834 to consider the rival schemes, the Basingstoke and Bath scheme found little support. A prominent member of the London and Southampton committee scorned the GWR for taking its line to London instead of Basingstoke and criticised the exclusion of Newbury and Devizes from its scheme. But at that time, the sympathies of Bath and Bristol were with the GWR whose failure to obtain their Act was blamed on the London and Southampton. After hearing from Saunders (Secretary to the London Committee) and Brunel, the meeting declared support for the GWR against all rivals.

Despite this setback, at a meeting in Frome in December 1834, possible extensions of the Basingstoke and Bath through Frome, Bruton and Taunton to Exeter were hinted at.

1834 A new Great Western Railway Bill is promoted

Meanwhile, in September 1834, a Supplementary Prospectus had been issued for the GWR, inviting subscriptions for further shares. These, together with those already subscribed, would enable the Directors to carry a Bill for the whole line through Parliament in the next session.

The following passages in the prospectus describe the basis of the scheme; the first three passages also explain why the route via Newbury and Hungerford was not chosen:

"The proposed line will pass through or near to Slough, Maidenhead, Wantage, Wootton Bassett, Chippenham and Bath, and thus intersect the South of England from East to West in the manner of a main trunk, calculated to send branches to each district, North and South.

"The line has been preferred on account of the superiority of its levels and the ultimate economy of working steam power on it, as well as offering the greatest facilities for a junction with Oxford, Cheltenham and Gloucester, the manufacturing districts of Gloucestershire and Worcester, and through Gloucester with South Wales.

"A reference to a map might lead to an enquiry why a railway by way of Hungerford, Devizes and Bradford was not chosen. It is right to say that a survey of that district was in the first instance made, but the difficulties and expence (sic) of such a Railway, owing to the altitude of the general levels of the country, were found to be so considerable that, even without reference to the reasons alluded, the Directors cannot fail to prefer the northern line, which will scarcely exceed the other in length and which embracing Oxford, the clothing districts of Gloucestershire, the important towns of Stroud, Cheltenham and Gloucester; and thence leading eventually to Wales may also be made to communicate, by a short branch as before stated, with Bradford, Trowbridge and other manufacturing towns on the southern line.

"The expense of travelling and of carriage of goods by railway will not exceed half the present charge; and the time occupied in passing from the Metropolis to Bristol will be about four hours and a half.

"The sum required for the construction of the entire line of 116 miles, including depots, Locomotive Engines etc., will be £2,500,000".

The saving on previous estimates was due to a change in the direction of the line in the London area and to the Engineer having more data, thus enabling a more accurate estimate to be made. An eastern terminus was not specified and so presumably had not been fixed at this date.

A new edition of the GWR prospectus was issued in November 1834, in which the total length was given as 114 miles. A junction was to be made with the London and Birmingham Railway near Wormwood Scrubs - the station for passengers at the London end was intended to be Euston. The route was the same as that proposed in August 1833 except at the London end and between Bath and Bristol. The "probable branches" referred to in the 1833 prospectus were identical in the new prospectus except for that to Bradford which acquired a fork to Trowbridge.

During the autumn and winter of 1834, the promoters were busy stirring up support all over the West of England and South Wales. The interval between the 1834 and 1835 Bills was used not only for securing support and funds, but also for intensive design work, and it is of interest to note that surveys of actual road traffic were made at Oxford, Witney, Newbury, Reading and Maidenhead. By the end of February 1835, the whole of the shares required by parliament for the entire railway from London to Bristol had been taken, making with the shares previously taken, a capital of £2,000,000. The petition for the Bill was accordingly presented to the House of Commons.

1834 - 1835   The new scheme faces the competition

One of the proposed railway's greatest adversaries would be the London and Southampton Railway. Having obtained their Act, they began an active aggression on the Great Western Railway by again promoting a rival line from Basingstoke to Bath and Bristol through Newbury, Hungerford, Devizes, Trowbridge and Bradford. Plans for a Basing, Bath and Bristol Railway were deposited in November 1834. The Basing and Bath prospectus of 9 February 1835, capital £1,000,000, had a general committee of 88 persons, including the mayors of Newbury and Basingstoke, Lord Bolton, the Earl of Carnarvon and other revered gentlemen.

The 106-mile route from London to Bath, claimed to be the shortest, would pass near or through the towns listed in the previous paragraph and by curving between Devizes and Bath, the projected extension to Frome, Taunton and eventually further west would be facilitated. Although the scheme met with some support from these towns, it met with little or none from Bath and Bristol. The only tunnels would be at Bradford and on the approach to Bath. The junction at Basing with the London and Southampton Railway would reduce the mileage of new railway to 62, minimising property disturbance and the need for capital. It was intended that the completed Basing and Bath would merge with the London and Southampton, but the latter's funds would not be involved until the Basing and Bath got its Act.

Despite many rebuffs, the Southampton Company proceeded with their Bill for the Basing, Bath and Bristol Railway. It was in order to block the route that the Great Western added the forked branch to Bradford and Trowbridge to their own Bill.

The GWR Bill was read a second time, without opposition, in the Commons in March 1835 and forwarded to the select committee together with the report of the previous year's proceedings. The Chairman of the committee, Charles Russell (Member for Reading), announced that, as the public advantages of the railway had already been established in the previous year's Report, the Counsel could confine the case to the merits of the line proposed. The opponents therefore had to try and show the superiority of the proposed Basing, Bath and Bristol Railway, a hopeless task.

A report by George Stephenson and H.R. Palmer commissioned by Brunel stated that "The levels of the proposed line are undoubtedly superior to those of the Southampton or the Basing and Bath, or any of the extensive lines with which we have an acquaintance, and are therefore better adapted to the working of the locomotive engine both as regards economy and expedition". This was despite the inclusion by Brunel of a 1:100 gradient at Box Tunnel, which was planned to concentrate the rise from Bristol at one point to allow working by "a stationary or assistant engine".

The opponents were obliged to admit that the gradients of the Basing and Bath were generally steeper than those of the Great Western, but maintained that they were so balanced that the rises and falls compensated one for another so as to render the line practically level. The Chairman remarked that, on this principle, the Highlands of Scotland were as good a district as any other for the construction of a railway.

1835 Success at last: the Great Western Railway obtains its Act

The committee eventually decided in favour of the Great Western Bill reporting thus to the House, where it was read for a third time on 28 May 1835 - this after a proposal by a sabbatarian that no engine or carriage should move on the Lord's Day had been heavily defeated. Next day it was introduced in the Lords and read for the first time. On 6 June, despairing Bath and Basing promoters wrote to GWR chairman Benjamin Shaw offering to surrender their project if the GWR would adopt their line from Basing to Bristol in lieu of its own. On 12 June Shaw refused the offer.

The second reading was carried on 10 June and the Bill referred to a committee. Although this Committee soon came to the same decision as the Commons that no more evidence of the need for a railway to Bristol was called for, arguments continued for forty days, concentrating on the alleged dangers of the incline in Box Tunnel. George Stephenson, Joseph Locke and Messrs Palmer, Price and Vignoles, called as engineers by the promoters, expressed their unqualified approbation of the line chosen by Brunel,

and of his estimates. On the other side, the presence of William Brunton, the pioneer of 1832, is of interest.

Towards the end of August, the Committee declared the preamble proved by a clear majority and reported the Bill for third reading. The Bill was carried by a majority of peers and received royal assent on 31 August 1835. The Act contained 251 sections, many of them for the protection of individual landowners, canal companies and turnpike trusts.

So the Great Western Railway was at last incorporated and empowered to make a railway from Temple Meads in Bristol, passing through specified parishes in the counties of Gloucester, Somerset, Wilts, Berks, Oxford, Bucks and Middlesex, terminating by a junction with the London and Birmingham Railway in the Parish of Hammersmith; also a branch line to Trowbridge from near Thingley Farm and another branch from near Holt to Bradford.

The first general meeting of the new company took place in London in October 1835, when the directors reported that they proposed to push on at once with the sections of the railway between London and Maidenhead and Bath and Bristol; also that they were negotiating with the London and Birmingham Railway Board for use of their railway into London.

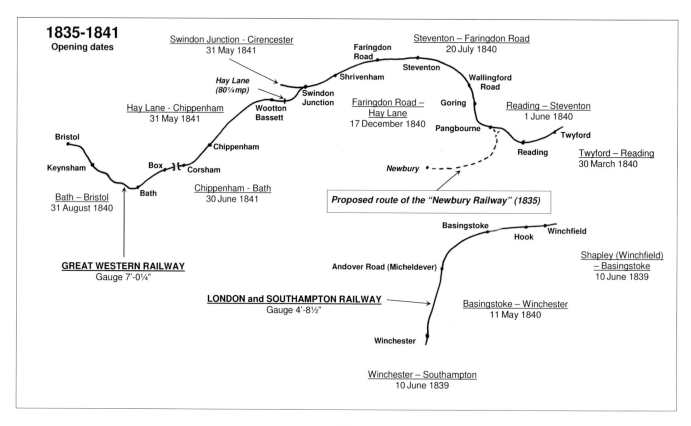

1835 Newbury seeks a link with the new Great Western Railway

The people of Newbury, having missed out on the opportunity to be on the GWR main line, were presumably anxious to be connected to that line. Plans were deposited in 1835 for a "Proposed Railway from Newbury to join the GWR at Pangbourne". The planned route commenced on the east side of Newbury to the north of the canal, and after a short distance adopted a route as far as the west side of Theale that was similar to that eventually built, the one exception was that the proposed line would have passed nearer to the centre of Thatcham.

Approaching Theale, the railway would have turned through nearly 90 degrees passing to the east of Tidmarsh and joining the GWR by a triangular junction about three-quarters of a mile to the Reading side of Pangbourne station. By means of this junction, trains from Newbury could have run west towards Didcot or east towards Reading. The Bath Road (the present A4) would have been crossed on the level and the Oxford Road at Pangbourne by a bridge. This was necessary as near Pangbourne the level of the proposed line had been raised to match that of the GWR main line. Despite the best efforts of the promoters, this proposal too was doomed to failure.

The rival companies open their new lines

Returning briefly to the London and Southampton Railway, the original Engineer of the Railway, Giles, had in 1836 projected an extension from Basingstoke through Salisbury and Honiton to Exeter, with a branch via Newbury to Oxford **(Note 2)**.

The London and Southampton Railway, as authorised in 1834, was opened from London (Nine Elms) to Basingstoke and from Winchester to Southampton (Northam Road) in June 1839 **(Note 3)**, and was opened throughout to Southampton Station (later known as Terminus) in May 1840. In the meantime, a change of name to the London and South Western Railway, more reflective of its own expansionist plans outside of the scope of this work, had been authorised by an Act of 4 June 1839.

The Great Western Railway from London to Bristol was also opened in stages, the first being Paddington (first station) to Maidenhead on 4 June 1838. The London terminus had been changed from Euston to Paddington by an Act of 1837 **(Note 4)**. Next came Maidenhead to Twyford on 1 July 1839 and thence to Reading on 30 March 1840. Further sections followed, but it was to be midway through 1841 before the last section, between Chippenham and Bath, was opened on 30 June, enabling London and Bristol to be connected by rail for the first time.

Due to the increase in cost of the main line, the Trowbridge and Bradford branches were not constructed at this time.

One of the many distinguishing features of the original Great Western Railway was to be the gauge used. In place of the more common width of 4ft 8½in between the rails then being generally adopted (although there were many variations on unconnected lines), Brunel chose a wide gauge of 7ft (in practice 7ft 0¼in) for reasons well documented elsewhere.

Brunel had the freedom to set his wider gauge as the Act for the London and Southampton Railway had singularly failed to state the gauge to be used, so creating a precedent that Brunel was able to exploit by creating his own gauge, generally known as the broad gauge.

With Newbury having missed out on being on the main line from London to Bristol, and with the first attempt to build a railway to connect the town with that main line not having come to fruition, the citizens of Newbury and district were destined to be left without a railway link for several years. It would come later.

How this link was finally achieved, and what other schemes were proposed that could have served Newbury and district are fully described in the next chapter.

NOTES

NOTE 1: KENNET AND AVON CANAL

An Act of Parliament of 1715 authorised the Kennet Navigation, by which barges would travel from the river Thames at Reading up the river Kennet as far as Newbury. After unsuccessful attempts by others, engineer John Hore of Newbury was appointed in 1718 to carry out the task. Hore was able to plan a number of artificial channels to by-pass many of the loops in the river. The result was 18½ miles of waterway, opened in 1723, with twenty locks. A towing path was added in 1724.

In 1724 John Hore was appointed by commissioners, acting under powers transferred to them by the Corporation of the City of Bath, to continue the navigation of the Avon 11 miles up river to the City of Bath. The Corporation had obtained an Act in 1712 authorising them to make "the river Avon, in the counties of Somerset and Gloucester, navigable from the city of Bath, to or near Hanham Mills". By the end of 1727, six locks had been built and barges could be brought up river to a new quay near the present Pulteney Bridge (built 1770).

In 1788, a meeting of nobility and gentry took place in Hungerford to appoint a committee to consider a "Western Canal" between Newbury and Bath. The scheme had originated as a plan to extend the navigation of the river Kennet upstream from Newbury to Hungerford. Before the summer of 1788 was over, the proposals for a canal had grown into a scheme to link Newbury and Bath. The engineer John Rennie, who specialised in docks, bridges and similar works, was in 1789 invited to survey a route for the proposed canal and made his report in 1790. The citizens of Devizes were very keen that it should pass through their town instead of taking the originally intended route via Marlborough, Calne and Chippenham. With successful lobbying of their MPs and a change of mind by John Rennie, they got their way. In 1793, he recommended that the canal should follow a more southerly route via Great Bedwyn, Devizes and Trowbridge. Marlborough would be served by a branch from Hungerford; Chippenham and Calne by a branch leaving the canal near Devizes.

John Ward, solicitor and agent to the Earl of Ailesbury and his Savernake estate, became clerk to the committee, which had to decide a route and eventually draft an Act to put before Parliament. He prepared the Act and MPs were lobbied under his direction; the Kennet and Avon Canal Act was passed and received Royal Assent in 1794. The Kennet and Avon Canal Company was established and John Ward was appointed as Principal Clerk. Construction started that year; John Rennie was appointed Principal Engineer. The Marlborough branch was not included in the Act; that to Chippenham and Calne was included but was never built.

The engineer William Jessop was consulted and in his report largely agreed with Rennie's proposals but suggested a number of route changes, recommending a summit route slightly to the north. Other changes included the length of the tunnel at Savernake, originally proposed at 4312 yards, which was reduced to just over 500 yards. The tunnel was required as the Earl of Ailesbury would not allow a cutting to disfigure his land. The raising of the summit level required six extra locks and water to be pumped to a 2½ mile summit pound; thus was created the need for the Crofton Pumping Station and the reservoir of Wilton Water.

The canal reached Kintbury in June 1797, Hungerford in October 1798 and Great Bedwyn in July 1799. It was opened throughout from Newbury to Bath on 28 December 1810.

The Kennet and Avon Canal Company acquired the Kennet Navigation for £100,000 in 1812, and by 1813 the proprietors had managed to buy up most of the shares in the Avon Navigation, from which time the whole waterway from Hanham to Reading was administered as a single enterprise. The Company was purchased by the Great Western Railway in 1852; the company having also to take over the Canal Company's liabilities and similarly maintain the canal. The maintenance requirement was further reinforced by the Regulation of Railways Act of 1873.

For further information on the canal and the navigations, the reader is directed to **Further Reading.**

NOTE 2: HISTORY OF THE LONDON AND SOUTHAMPTON/LONDON AND SOUTH WESTERN RAILWAY

For a full appreciation of the development of these railways in the area west of Basingstoke, and their relevance to the history of the area served by the railways that form the subject of this book, the reader is directed to the London and Southampton/London and South Western Railway references under **Further Reading**.

NOTE 3: OPENING OF THE LONDON AND SOUTHAMPTON/LONDON AND SOUTH WESTERN RAILWAY

The June 1839 date refers to the opening from Shapley (Winchfield) to Basingstoke; Nine Elms to Woking Common had been opened on 21 May 1838 and onwards to Shapley (Winchfield) on 24 September 1838.

NOTE 4: PADDINGTON

Before the end of 1835, a decision was made by the GWR board to abandon the intended junction with the London and Birmingham Railway and seek an independent entry into London. This was due to the difficulty of reaching agreement on several matters with that railway. Very soon after this, the directors decided on an extension to the original railway and obtained an Act on 3 July 1837 for this purpose, the terminus to be in the parish of Paddington. This was the first station; the second, larger station (which was further east than the old station and survives intact as a major part of the present station) was opened in 1854.

ACTS

London and Southampton Railway Act, 25 July 1834 (4&5 William IV, c.88)

Great Western Railway Act, 31 August 1835 (5&6 William IV, c.107)

London and South Western Railway Act, 4 June 1839 (2&3 Victoria I, c.28)

CHAPTER REFERENCES

Deposited Documents

(Q/RUm 6; A1/371/2MS): deposited plans, reference book – Berks, Wilts: GWR London to Reading and Bath to Bristol; branch from Slough to Eton (1833)

(Q/RUm 10): deposited plans, reference book - Berks: Proposed railway from Newbury to join the GWR at Pangbourne (1835)

(Q/RUm 11; A1/371/4MS): deposited plans, reference book – Berks, Wilts: GWR Bristol and Ealing; branches to Bradford and Trowbridge (1834)

(DP/C7; A1/371/3L): deposited plans, reference book – Hants, Wilts: Basing, Bath and Bristol Railway (1834)

Record Office references:

Berkshire uses Q/RUm and a number (Q for Quarter Sessions);

Hampshire uses DP(letter)(number) or H15 M52(number);

Wiltshire uses A1/371(number)MS

PUBLISHED REFERENCES

History of the Great Western Railway Volume 1 1833 – 1863

E T MacDermot Revised by C R Clinker (Ian Allan 1964).

The Great Western Railway in the 19th Century

O S Nock (Ian Allan 1972).

How the Great Western came to Berkshire – A Railway History 1833 – 1882

Daphne Phillips (Reading Libraries 1975).

2

EARLY TIMES 1840 - 1851

1840 – 1843 Newbury seeks a link with the new trunk lines

In early March 1840, even before the Great Western Railway had opened to Reading, plans were deposited for lines, on two alternative routes, to form branches from Newbury to join the soon to be opened GWR line east of Pangbourne. Railway No 1 was to follow an almost identical route to the scheme of 1835. The route of the second option, Railway No 2, was radically different all the way from its Newbury terminus to within 1½ miles of the junction with the GWR east of Pangbourne, which was retained. Commencing in Newbury facing north, rather than due east as before, on land south of the canal, the railway would have crossed the turnpike (now the A4) then headed north-eastwards, generally following the route of the present B4009, later to be followed by the Didcot, Newbury and Southampton Railway. Near Hampstead Norris, the line would have turned through a sharp curve of over 90 degrees to pass near Stanford Dingley and Bradfield and join the course of Railway No 1 near Tidmarsh. The ruling grade would have been 1:100 and earthworks heavy, comparing very unfavourably with the easy grades and modest earthworks of Railway No 1.

A similar scheme to Railway No 2 was revived in the autumn of 1843, over three years after the GWR had opened to Reading and beyond through Pangbourne. A plan for a "Newbury and Great Western Railway" line was deposited on 30 November 1843, the last date for plans to be deposited for consideration in the 1844 Parliamentary Session. Commencing in Newbury at the site of some cottages east of Northbrook Street, and initially running due east, it soon turned north east to follow a route similar to that of Railway No 2 of 1840 to a junction with the GWR at Pangbourne, a distance of just over 14¾ miles. Gradients and earthworks were equally severe, a gradient of 1:81 for over 2 miles being proposed on the climb up the Berkshire Downs.

Another scheme for a branch to Newbury was deposited within hours of the above scheme. This was not an alternative route put forward by the promoters, however, but a deadly rival promoted by the London and South Western Railway (L&SWR - née London and Southampton Railway), to connect Newbury with that railway at Basingstoke. The full title of the scheme was "THE NEWBURY RAILWAY from the South Western Railway at the BASINGSTOKE STATION TO NEWBURY", Joseph Locke Esq. FRS

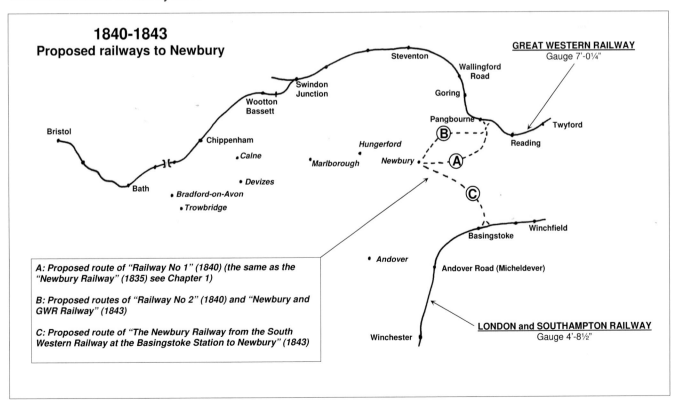

1840-1843
Proposed railways to Newbury

GREAT WESTERN RAILWAY
Gauge 7'-0¼"

Bristol · Bath · Chippenham · Calne · Devizes · Bradford-on-Avon · Trowbridge · Wootton Bassett · Swindon Junction · Marlborough · Hungerford · Newbury · Steventon · Wallingford Road · Goring · Pangbourne · Reading · Twyford · Andover · Andover Road (Micheldever) · Basingstoke · Winchfield · Winchester

LONDON and SOUTHAMPTON RAILWAY
Gauge 4'-8½"

A: Proposed route of "Railway No 1" (1840) (the same as the "Newbury Railway" (1835) see Chapter 1)

B: Proposed routes of "Railway No 2" (1840) and "Newbury and GWR Railway" (1843)

C: Proposed route of "The Newbury Railway from the South Western Railway at the Basingstoke Station to Newbury" (1843)

Engineer. Commencing in Newbury west of Stroud Green, it crossed the Green and Greenham and Crookham Commons and passed near the villages of Ashford (Ashford Hill), Baughurst and Ramsdell to form a triangular junction with the L&SWR east of Basingstoke station. Earthworks were substantial and the ruling grade would have been 1: 132; projected length 15 miles 32 chains (about 15½ miles), estimated cost £200,900.

The Basingstoke scheme had its origins in the concern of Newbury's inhabitants, whose prosperity had declined since the GWR and L&SWR had opened. Their spokesperson, the Reverend Ashworth, approached Chaplin, Chairman of the L&SWR, in the summer of 1843 for a branch from Basingstoke, which would connect Newbury with London, Winchester, Southampton and Portsmouth. At first, Chaplin did not acknowledge their intentions as sincere, suspecting that "they were coquetting with us merely to enable them to make better terms with their neighbours". On realising the sincerity of their intentions, Chaplin publicly apologised. Later in 1843, the Newbury promoters asked again, revealing that besides the Lords Carnarvon and Craven heading the landowners and commercial men interested, the Duke of Wellington of Stratfield Saye was also sympathetic.

The prospect of a Newbury branch was tempting to the L&SWR, as it could provide, by an extension through Swindon to Birmingham, a way through the broad gauge barrier represented by the GWR and thus promote trade between Southampton and the prosperous industrial north. Such a cross-country route would be 45 miles shorter than via London.

1843 - 1844 Bills are submitted for the rival schemes

Thus Bills for both the GWR Newbury - Pangbourne branch and for the privately promoted Newbury Railway to Basingstoke, which the L&SWR would rent, went forward to the session of 1844. A parliamentary committee approved the Newbury Railway and rejected the GWR Bill due to landowners' opposition. The Newbury Railway passed the House with a large majority, despite strenuous appeals from the GWR, but it was rejected by the Lords' committee. After a lengthy enquiry, they preferred the GWR plan "as the better route from London as well as forming, with the Oxford branch, a link in a much needed line of communication between the South Coast and the North of England far better than any by way of Swindon and Cheltenham". No scheme for a railway was, therefore, sanctioned in 1844.

Following the Lords' rejection of the GWR proposals, an approach was made to the L&SWR chairman in 1844, suggesting a joint line between the L&SWR at Basingstoke and the GWR at a point between Pangbourne and Reading (length 17 miles), with a branch to Newbury (11 miles), the whole being laid with a third rail to form the mixed gauge

and thus capable of taking both companies' stock. Newbury would have two routes to London, via Basingstoke or Reading, plus openings south via Basingstoke and north via Oxford. The Oxford Railway Company's broad-gauge line, opened from Didcot to Oxford in 1844, was meant eventually to reach Rugby and Worcester. With the London and Birmingham Railway seeking a narrow gauge line from Rugby to Oxford, and another planned through the Trent Valley from Rugby to Stafford to shorten routes to Ireland and Lancashire, Russell (chairman of the GWR) argued that his proposed joint line, completing a joint line to the north, would benefit the L&SWR more than its contemplated 45 mile line through Swindon. The GWR's plan was rejected by the L&SWR, who alleged that Russell's plan would encourage Newbury traffic to go to London via the GWR, besides creating such a detour between Southampton and Newbury as to kill trade between them by raising carriage charges above those to London. Both companies therefore reverted to promoting rival schemes.

The GWR proposed a line from Reading to Basingstoke and Newbury called the Berks and Hants Railway. At the same time it produced a plan for a cross-country main line to the west which, with lines already built, would link Bristol and Bath with Southampton, Portsmouth and the Isle of Wight and would be "superior in any way to any railway which could be made between Basingstoke and Swindon". It was to be called the Wilts and Somerset Railway.

1844 The Berks and Hants Railway takes shape - and a new cross-country main line is proposed

During the autumn of 1844, the Newbury branch of the Berks and Hants proposal was extended to Hungerford, whilst the Wilts and Somerset scheme was extended from Frome (which was on a branch of the proposed main line from Bath to Salisbury) via Yeovil to Weymouth. At the same time its title was altered to the Wilts, Somerset and Weymouth Railway **(Note 1)**.

The Wilts and Somerset scheme also included a branch to Devizes; such a link was sought by the citizens of that town as early as 1836 **(Note 2)**.

Rivalry continues - the Lords' Committee publishes its judgement

The L&SWR proposed a line from Basingstoke to Didcot with a junction near Thatcham to a line through Newbury, Hungerford and Marlborough to Swindon. They foresaw from the connection to Swindon a possible outlet north through Gloucester and the Birmingham and Gloucester Railway. This scheme was accompanied by a number of others to extend their empire westwards.

During September 1844, the "Five Kings", a Select Committee of the Privy Council of Trades and Plantations set up following the Regulation of Railways Act of that year,

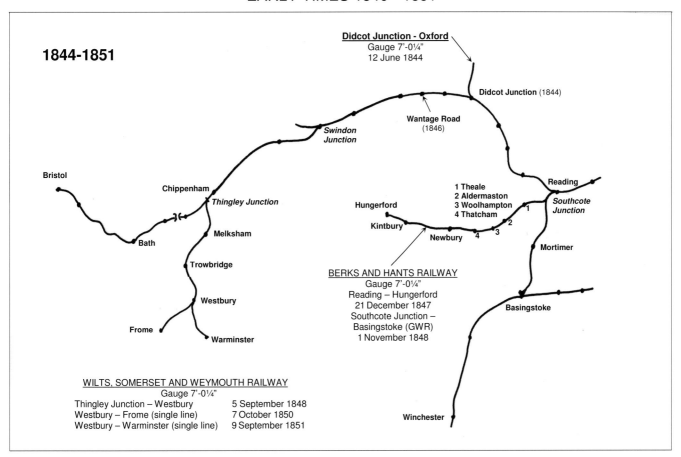

1844-1851

Didcot Junction - Oxford
Gauge 7'-0¼"
12 June 1844

Didcot Junction (1844)

Wantage Road
(1846)

Swindon
Junction

Bristol

Chippenham

Thingley Junction

Hungerford

1 Theale
2 Aldermaston
3 Woolhampton
4 Thatcham

Reading

Southcote
Junction

Kintbury

Melksham

Newbury

Bath

Mortimer

Trowbridge

BERKS AND HANTS RAILWAY
Gauge 7'-0¼"
Reading – Hungerford
21 December 1847
Southcote Junction –
Basingstoke (GWR)
1 November 1848

Westbury

Basingstoke

Frome

Warminster

Winchester

WILTS, SOMERSET AND WEYMOUTH RAILWAY
Gauge 7'-0¼"
Thingley Junction – Westbury   5 September 1848
Westbury – Frome (single line)   7 October 1850
Westbury – Warminster (single line) 9 September 1851

told the L&SWR that Newbury to London traffic belonged to the GWR, whose Berks and Hants line it approved, subject to an equal rate clause for L&SWR protection.

Immediately, the L&SWR asked the London and Birmingham Railway (L&BR) to co-operate with a scheme for a narrow gauge line from Basingstoke through Newbury, Didcot and Oxford to Rugby. The L&SWR would guarantee it south of Didcot, the L&BR to the north. The L&BR agreed, subject to Board of Trade approval. The L&SWR decided, were the line approved, that it would not extend its proposed western line beyond Marlborough; but should the Board of Trade encourage traffic by Gloucester to Birmingham, it would go to Swindon and abandon the Didcot branch.

On 31 December 1844, the Lords' committee published a judgement in the London Gazette in favour of the GWR broad-gauge schemes, which included the Berks and Hants and the Wilts, Somerset and Weymouth Railways. The rival schemes were withdrawn and the two companies came to terms; this was followed by an agreement dated 16 January 1845, which, in effect, prevented the companies from competing with each other to gain access to the same areas.

Among the other schemes deposited in 1844 was one for a

Estimate of the cost of the proposed Berks and Hants Railway, as deposited at the Parliament Office and dated the twentieth of May 1845

Berks and Hants Railway

I estimate the expense of constructing the above Railway and all proper Works and conveniences connected therewith according to the Plans and Sections thereof deposited herewith in the Parliament Office at the Sum of £400,000 Four hundred thousand pounds.

Dated this twentieth day of May 1845.

£400,000.

ANNO OCTAVO & NONO

VICTORIÆ REGINÆ.

****

Cap. xl.

An Act for making a Railway from the *Great
Western* Railway at or near *Reading* to the Towns
of *Newbury* and *Hungerford*, and also to join the
South-western Railway at or near *Basingstoke*.

[30th *June* 1845.]

WHEREAS the making of a Railway from the *Great Western*
Railway at or near the Town of *Reading* to the Towns of
Newbury and *Hungerford* in the County of *Berks*, and
also a Railway diverging from the said last-mentioned Railway to
join the *South-western* Railway at or near *Basingstoke* in the County
of *Southampton*, would be of great public Advantage, by opening an
additional, certain, and expeditious Means of Communication between
the said Places, and also by facilitating Communication between more
distant Towns and Places : And whereas the Persons hereafter named
are willing, at their own Expence, to carry such Undertaking into
execution ; but the same cannot be effected without the Authority
of Parliament : And whereas Three several Acts have been passed
during the present Session of Parliament, called " The Companies
Clauses Consolidation Act, 1845," " The Lands Clauses Consolidation
Act, 1845," and " The Railway Clauses Consolidation Act, 1845 :"
May it therefore please Your Majesty that it may be enacted ; and be
it enacted by the Queen's most Excellent Majesty, by and with the

[*Local.*]   9 Q   Advice

London, Salisbury, Exeter and Falmouth Railway. Leaving the GWR main line at Sonning, it was planned to turn south through the outskirts of Reading and then to pass near to Shinfield and Beech Hill into Hampshire before nearing Bramley and to continue on to Basing, Basingstoke, Worting, Wootton St Lawrence, Church Oakley and so to Salisbury.

1845 The Berks and Hants Railway is incorporated

The GWR had promoted the Berks and Hants through a subsidiary company, providing the necessary subscription capital in the names of some of its directors. After an initial setback when the Bill was rejected in the Commons for failure to comply with standing orders, the Bill was re-introduced. The nominally independent Berks and Hants Railway Company, capital £400,000, was authorised by the Berks and Hants Railway Act of 30 June 1845 to build two broad gauge lines from Reading:

> west via Newbury to Hungerford - 25½ miles

> south to Basingstoke Station and junction with the L&SWR - an additional 13½ miles

The GWR then took the company over and obtained an Act for its absorption (Great Western Railway Act 14 May 1846).

A network for the future is envisaged

The Wilts, Somerset and Weymouth Railway Act, also of 30 June 1845, authorised the railway of that name. In passing the preamble of the Bill, however, the Lord's committee, impressed with the need for a direct line to the west, exacted a pledge from Counsel for the promoters that the powers given should not be used thereafter to prevent such a scheme being made. In evidence before the Gauge Commission, Saunders, Secretary to the GWR, had stated that it was always intended that the Wilts, Somerset and Weymouth Railway (WS&WR) should form part of the direct line to Exeter and that the pledge asked for was willingly given.

In view of the importance attached by parliament to a direct line to the west and following the pledge to the Lords' committee, the GWR directors instructed Brunel to prepare a scheme for the session of 1846. A plan for a Berks and Hants Hungerford Extension Railway was accordingly deposited in November 1845, starting at the planned terminus of the Berks and Hants Railway at Hungerford and connecting with the WS&WR at Frome. Branches were planned to Marlborough, Devizes and Radstock, the latter intended to tap the coal traffic in that area of the Mendips.

1845 - 1846 A rash of new schemes heralds the railway mania

With the railway mania at its height, and before the final plan for the two direct routes to the west (via Newbury and via Salisbury) became clear (in 1847, see page 31), a number of rival schemes were promoted in 1845 and 1846 for new direct lines between London and the West Country. These included the Bristol and Dover Direct Junction Railway. The deposited documents show a junction with the L&SWR main line west of Weybridge station. The line would then have passed to the north of Camberley and Sandhurst and headed due west to pass north of Silchester and Tadley, south of Newtown (and of Newbury). It would then have skirted the northern escarpment of the Hampshire Downs, passing near Kintbury, Inkpen and Ham before terminating abruptly at Shalbourne, surrounded by the steep slopes of the nearby Downs. A Newbury branch would have left the main line east of Ashford Hill and joined the already authorised Berks and Hants Railway east of Newbury station. The scheme included many severe gradients and two tunnels.

Other schemes for east-west railways promoted in 1845 were: -

> the Great West of England Railway, to commence at Basingstoke and reach Falmouth;

> the London, Devizes and Bridgwater Direct Western Railway;

> the London, Newbury and Bath Direct Railway;

> the Farnborough to Crofton Railway (in connection with the above);

> the London, Bristol and South Wales Direct Railway;

> the Direct Western Railway (First Division);

> the Southern Counties Union - Bristol, Bath and Dover Railway;

> the Direct London and Exeter Railway.

At a public meeting of the Corporation and inhabitants of Devizes in October 1845, several of the above schemes were considered. The meeting decided in favour of the following three lines:

> the London, Newbury and Bath Direct Railway;

> the London, Devizes and Bridgwater Direct Railway;

> the South Midland and Southampton Railway (see page 30).

The London, Newbury and Bath Direct Railway

The London, Newbury and Bath Direct Railway (the first long-distance railway to have Newbury in its title), was promoted by the proprietors of the Kennet and Avon Canal Company. Faced with the loss of the lucrative through traffic between London, Reading, Bath and Bristol, a survey was commissioned, a favourable report made to the management committee and a Bill deposited for the 1846 Session for a line from Newbury (not connecting with the authorised Berks and Hants Railway) to Bath where it would have connected with the GWR at Bath Station.

The canal proprietors first contemplated the conversion of the canal to a railway but were recommended, in August 1845, to build alongside the waterway. From Newbury, where the line was to start near the junction of Bartholomew Street and Enborne Road, the line was to follow the canal closely, crossing it several times and avoiding the sharper turns, to Pewsey, after which the railway would have continued to run near the canal all the way to Bath except at Devizes and Trowbridge, where a separate course was found to be necessary. An alternative route was also put forward: a deviation from Free Warren, near Crofton, passing near Burbage and Milton Lilbourne and re-joining the line described above east of Pewsey; however, this deviation would not have avoided the need to raise the level of the line to a similar level (over 500ft – 153m) to that required to pass over the canal summit level at Savernake.

A link was proposed from the L&SWR at Farnborough "to or near Crofton on the line of the proposed London, Newbury and Bath Direct Railway". This route would have entered Berkshire south of Beech Hill and passed near Aldermaston, following the valley of the River Enborne to Bishop's Green and Newtown, south of Newbury, then near West Woodhay and Inkpen, passing between Ham and Shalbourne and south of Wilton to join the "canal" route near Free Warren, south-west of Crofton. Earthworks on this link would have been substantial and gradients severe; future generations can consider themselves fortunate that this Area of Outstanding Natural Beauty was not despoiled by such a railway.

The London, Newbury and Bath Direct Railway Bill passed its second reading in the House of Commons. The citizens of Bath, Bradford-on-Avon, Trowbridge, Devizes, Pewsey, Bedwyn, Marlborough and Newbury presented petitions in its favour. After these Bills were lost, it was planned that an arrangement be come to with the Berks and Hants and Wilts, Somerset and Weymouth companies. This arrangement included an agreement whereby monies invested in the Direct Railway scheme and not already spent on promoting the Bill would be exchanged for GWR shares in perpetuity on the passing of an Act of Parliament in 1847 or 1848 "with powers to make a Railway between Hungerford and Westbury, with a Branch to Devizes" (Note 3).

More rival schemes are promoted

The outcome of Brunel's plans for a direct line to the west was the Direct Western Railway, planned to link the Berks and Hants Railway at Kintbury with the Bristol and Exeter line east of Taunton, with branches to Bridgwater and Bath. However, although the GWR had previously reached agreement with the Bristol and Exeter Railway, the latter refused to endorse the scheme.

The Direct London and Exeter Railway would have run via Wokingham and Sherborne.

Despite the authorisation of the Berks and Hants Railway in June 1845, whose Basingstoke branch connected the GWR at Reading and the L&SWR at Basingstoke, that year witnessed a rash of schemes to link the midlands and the south, principally Southampton, a growing port with a great deal of potential. These included: -

> the Manchester and Southampton Railway;
>
> the Southampton, Manchester and Oxford Junction Railway;
>
> the Oxford, Southampton, Gosport and Portsmouth Railway;
>
> the South Midland and Southampton Railway;
>
> the Tring, Reading and Basingstoke Railway;
>
> the Oxford and Salisbury Direct Railway;
>
> the Midland Grand Junction Railway.

The Manchester and Southampton Railway (referred to as the "M&SR" below) was an independent scheme which was in due course promoted with L&SWR support. This proposed using existing lines from Manchester to Cheltenham, building its own line thence through Cirencester, passing under the GWR east of Swindon, then near Marlborough and Ludgershall to Andover (crossing the eventual course of the Berks and Hants Extension Railway near Wootton Rivers) and onwards via Stockbridge, Romsey and Redbridge to Southampton docks and harbour, to terminate by the Royal Pier. A branch was planned to Salisbury, Ringwood, Wimborne and Poole.

Developments in the south - and their impact on the Berks and Hants Railway

About this time, an L&SWR Bill for a 5¾ mile line linking Redbridge (a few miles west of Southampton) with Romsey was rejected by the Commons because of its purely local nature, the committee being influenced by the M&SR Bill which duplicated it between these places.

Having lost the Redbridge - Romsey Bill, the L&SWR agreed with the M&SR on 7 August 1846 to take over its proposed line from Andover to Redbridge. The M&SR would retain full user rights, use Southampton and Dorchester metals from Redbridge to Bletchynden (later called Southampton West, then Central) and be free to build independently to Southampton Pier and thence to the docks. L&SWR opposition to the M&SR was thus withdrawn. However, the M&SR Bill failed in the Lords on 22 August 1846 due to fierce GWR opposition. In an attempt to kill the narrow gauge invader, the GWR promised to mix the gauge from Oxford to Basingstoke, thus completing a north to south link between narrow gauge (4ft 8½in) railways. Much work would be needed, however, as the Basingstoke branch of the Berks and Hants Railway was under construction at this time as a purely broad gauge line, and there had been no provision for a west to south "Reading West Loop" in that railway's Act.

The rival 1845 schemes described

The Southampton, Manchester and Oxford Junction Railway would have been a 37½-mile line starting on the GWR main line just east of Swindon station and passing near to Chiseldon, Aldbourne, Chilton Foliat, Hungerford, Kintbury, West and East Woodhay, Highclere, Burghclere and Litchfield to join the L&SWR Southampton line at or near Micheldever, north of Winchester.

The Oxford, Southampton, Gosport and Portsmouth Railway was planned to start at Didcot and link with the L&SWR near Micheldever with a branch from Newbury to Swindon via Hungerford added later. It failed to pass the Standing Orders Committee of the House of Commons in May 1846.

The South Midland and Southampton Railway was planned to run from the London and North Western Railway (L&NWR – successor to the London and Birmingham Railway) at Blisworth via Reading to Basingstoke, to link there with the L&SWR. Junctions would have been made at Reading with the Great Western main line and the planned Newbury Branch.

The Tring, Reading and Basingstoke Railway would have had a similar purpose. Tring is situated north of the point where the L&NWR passes through a gap in the chalk downs. The proposed line, starting at a junction with the L&NWR near Tring Station and after passing near to Wendover and Princes Risborough, commenced climbing into the Chiltern Hills. The route would have continued through the hills via Saunderton, Bledlow, Stokenchurch and Lewknor to Henley on Thames; keeping to the west side of the Thames on somewhat easier ground, Reading was reached via Shiplake, Sonning and Caversham. Throughout the Chilterns, earthworks would have been heavy and gradients severe, with several tunnels and lengthy viaducts. After crossing the Thames, there would have been a brief flirtation with the GWR at Reading, before turning southwards and terminating at Basingstoke by a junction with the (London and) South Western Railway. The alignment south of Reading would have been similar to that followed by the authorised Berks and Hants Railway.

The Oxford and Salisbury Direct Railway was planned to join the narrow gauge railways by means of a route via Abingdon, Wantage and Hungerford. Commencing in the Parish of St Thomas, Oxford, and passing under Boars Hill by a 170 yard tunnel, the proposed route passed close to Abingdon, crossed the Great Western main line *on the level* near Steventon, thence to the south of Wantage and headed for the Berkshire Downs. A 2,420 yard tunnel would have taken the route under the 'Ridge Road' (now known as the 'Ridgeway') and the Lambourn Valley was crossed near

East Garston; heading for the Kennet Valley the Bath Road and the route of the Berks and Hants Railway were crossed, followed by Hungerford Common just east of the Port Gate. The route continued through the village of Shalbourne, under Wexford Down in a 1,540 yard tunnel and then passed near to Collingbourne Ducis, Tidworth and Cholderton before terminating in the Milford area of the 'City of New Sarum' (Salisbury) (presumably joining the branch from Bishopstoke (Eastleigh) opened in 1847).

The Midland Grand Junction Railway would have commenced at Reading and joined the London and Birmingham Railway at Blisworth, Northants, a distance of 56¼ miles. This railway, if built, would have been just as difficult to construct and operate as the Tring, Reading and Basingstoke line and befell a similar fate, being put forward at a time when the principal routes via Reading were already established if not, in the case of the Berks and Hants, yet built.

1846 The final network begins to take shape

The GWR's proposals in 1846 were: (a) to extend the Berks and Hants, authorised the previous year, from Hungerford to Westbury with branches to Marlborough and Devizes; (b) to straighten the Wilts and Somerset line, also authorised in 1845, by making the junction between the Salisbury and Weymouth lines at Westbury rather than at Upton Scudamore, about two miles to the south, and (c) to promote a company to make a railway from Yeovil to Exeter via Crewkerne, Axminster, Honiton, Ottery and Stoke Canon, with a connecting line from Axminster to Bridport and branches to Chard and Sidmouth, to be called the Exeter Great Western Railway. Paddington to Exeter trains would use the Wilts and Somerset line between Westbury and Yeovil.

For the same session, the South Western promoted: -

> a line from Basingstoke to Salisbury;
>
> the Salisbury and Yeovil Railway;
>
> the Exeter, Yeovil and Dorchester Railway;
>
> the Cornwall and Devon Central Railways.

The first, which they had a right to promote, was passed (Act of 13 August 1846). The second and third were defeated in the House of Lords by GWR opposition and the last was stopped by standing orders.

The Great Western Bills were thrown out in the Commons, opposed by the Bristol and Exeter Railway and the L&SWR. Another scheme promoted in 1846 was the Didcot and Andover Railway, from Didcot to the route of the proposed Manchester and Southampton Railway at Andover, via Newbury, East Woodhay and over/through the Hampshire Downs via Ashmansworth. A branch was planned from Compton to East Ilsley. It would be another 36 years before a railway connected Didcot and Newbury but the branch line to East Ilsley was never built, nor indeed was any railway between Newbury and Andover.

In 1846, the Gauge Commission strongly advocated a narrow gauge link on the Oxford - Reading - Basingstoke axis. In order to kill the narrow gauge invasion represented by the Manchester and Southampton Railway, the GWR through Russell (Chairman of the GWR) offered to mix the gauge from Oxford to Basingstoke, thus completing a narrow gauge north-south link. It would be another ten years before such a link would be in operation.

1847 Promotion of rival schemes continues

In 1847, the fight was renewed. The GWR again presented the Berks and Hants Extension and the Exeter Great Western (Direct Western) Railways. The former was described in full as the "Extension of the Berks and Hants Railway from Hungerford to Westbury"; the latter was altered near Exeter and branches to Charmouth and Crewkerne were added. The GWR also projected a line to connect Yeovil with Salisbury.

The Bristol and Exeter Railway again opposed the Exeter Great Western and promoted a line from Durston, on their line north of Taunton, to Castle Cary on the Wilts, Somerset and Weymouth line, which, with the Berks and Hants Extension, would form a more direct line between London and Exeter than the GWR proposals.

The London and South Western asked for powers in 1847 to make a Salisbury line themselves; they also supported the Exeter, Yeovil and Dorchester and the Cornwall and Devon Central companies.

1847 - 1848 The fates of the competing schemes are finally resolved

During 1847, the House of Commons agreed to a scheme which would, in due course, give a direct broad gauge line to Exeter by the following route beyond Hungerford: -

Berks and Hants Extension Railway to Devizes;

Wilts, Somerset and Weymouth Railway from Devizes via Westbury to Castle Cary (authorised 1845);

Bristol and Exeter Railway from Castle Cary to Durston (and thence to Taunton)

It was to be almost 60 years before such a direct route, via Westbury and Castle Cary to Taunton, would be completed, by which time all broad gauge lines would have been converted to, and all new railways built to, standard gauge of 4' 8½" (1435mm) as the narrow gauge became known. The only exceptions were the minor railways which for economic or typographical reasons adopted narrower gauges.

At the same time, the House agreed to a narrow gauge line to Exeter from Salisbury via Yeovil by authorising the

L&SWR's Salisbury to Yeovil line and the Exeter Yeovil and Dorchester's line from Yeovil to Exeter with three branches, including connections to the Wilts, Somerset and Weymouth at Yeovil. The Lords confirmed the decision of the Commons in the 1848 session. The GWR's schemes for the Exeter Great Western and Yeovil - Salisbury lines were rejected, however.

1847 - 1848 Opening of the Berks and Hants Railway to Hungerford and Basingstoke

The routes of the competing broad and narrow gauge lines from London to Exeter were thus determined in 1848, but the depression which followed the Railway Mania damped down the gauge war and many expensively won powers of both sides eventually lapsed.

The whole of the Berks and Hants Railway was let in one contract to Rowland Brotherhood of Chippenham. In August 1847, Brunel reported that the works were all but completed. His comments indicated that the works at the western end were designed to permit the line to become the main line to the West of England by means of arranging a temporary terminus at Hungerford, allowing for the projected extension to Westbury. The only major engineering works were the deep cutting between the site of Reading West Station and Southcote Junction; this was crossed by brick arch bridges carrying the Tilehurst Road and the Bath Road.

The broad gauge double line of the Berks and Hants Railway was opened for traffic in phases. The section from a junction west of Reading Station to Hungerford, about 25½ miles, was opened to passengers on 21 December 1847; accommodation for goods was not ready for another year. Intermediate stations were provided at Theale, Aldermaston, Woolhampton, Thatcham, Newbury and Kintbury. Woolhampton Station was renamed Midgham in 1873, to avoid confusion with Wolverhampton, whilst Newbury Racecourse and Reading West passenger stations opened in 1905 (for race traffic) and 1906 respectively. Newbury and Hungerford were in rail communication with the outside world at last.

The section from Southcote Junction, two miles south of Reading, to Basingstoke, about 13½ miles, was opened for all traffic on 1 November 1848. The only intermediate station was Mortimer; provision for passengers at Bramley, initially only a goods siding, was not added until 1895.

The completion of the Basingstoke line was delayed by negotiations with the hostile London and South Western Railway regarding the location of the terminus and the link between the two. As no rail connection was then possible at Basingstoke, the Berks and Hants Railway provided its own passenger and goods stations alongside the L&SWR's station; the passenger station remained in use until 1932 when one platform was amalgamated with the Southern Railway station and the remaining GWR platforms closed.

The railway from Reading to Hungerford described

Diverting southwards from the main line just west of Reading station, the new line crossed over the Oxford Road and, as mentioned above, passed through a deep cutting to reach Southcote Junction. Here the branch to Basingstoke continued southwards whereas the Hungerford line entered a long right-hand curve to take a course westwards to follow the valley of the River Kennet to its destination. Keeping initially north of the river (and the Kennet Navigation), the line passed immediately to the south of the village of Theale, where the first station was situated. Aldermaston village, some two miles southwards along the Basingstoke Road, was served by a station located where that road joined the Bath Road – in modern terms, where the A340 meets the A4. Passing close to the village of Woolhampton, the station (later re-named Midgham, as mentioned above) was conveniently situated at the crossing of the road to Brimpton and Baughurst. The line maintained its position north of canal and river to the fourth station from Reading, Thatcham, located on the crossing of the Crookham Road, about a mile from the centre of the village. This remoteness was said to be due to the opposition of a local landowner, Miss Fromont of Thatcham Farm, an old stage coach proprietor who refused to sell to the railway land nearer to the village.

The Kennet Navigation was crossed east of Newbury at a point where the river and canal are combined. After less than two miles, Newbury station was reached. Keeping south of the canal and river through Newbury, and passing immediately to the south of the town centre, several crossings of the river and canal (now the Kennet and Avon) were necessary before the line, passing north of the hill on which Kintbury village is situated, arrived at its terminus at Hungerford. Kintbury station was provided at the level crossing of the road joining the village to the Bath Road (now the A4); the station at Hungerford was located north of the canal and river and just east of the High Street.

An interesting aspect of the railway between Newbury and Hungerford is that the deposited plans for the Berks and Hants Railway included an alternative route in the Kintbury area, diverting the line south, away from the Kennet valley. This option would have commenced west of Hamstead Crossing and regained the original line at Lower Denford (about a mile east of Hungerford), a distance of over 4 miles. This may have been due to initial landowner opposition. In the event, the railway was able to follow the desired line and thus the beautiful scenery of the Irish Hill and Kintbury area was not desecrated with what would have been an expensive section of line with heavy earthworks and much disturbance of property.

The river and canal bridges were of timber initially; that crossing the canal between Newbury and Kintbury being known as Pickletimber Bridge. These bridges were

DURING THE CONSTRUCTION OF THE READING - HUNGERFORD SECTION OF THE BERKS & HANTS LINE IN 1847, THE CONTRACTOR, FINDING THAT HE WAS LOSING A NUMBER OF TOOLS AT NIGHT, ISSUED INSTRUMENTS - OF WHICH THIS IS ONE - TO HIS WATCHMEN IN ORDER TO WARD OFF UNDESIRABLE INTRUDERS. PRESENTED BY MR S. MORRIS. DIVISIONAL SUPT. GLOUCESTER. 1925.

replaced later in the century by wrought iron decks supported on brick abutments and on caisson piers where necessary, and again by modern structures in the twentieth century.

Road overbridges, where provided, were brick arches or had brick abutments with spans over the tracks which were initially of wrought iron, the latter eventually being replaced by steel spans. At certain locations, for instance at Aldermaston, side arches were provided; their purpose (and that of the openings in the abutments themselves) was to relieve the weight on the poor soils of the Kennet river valley. At a later date, the side arches of both the bridges at Aldermaston, on the south (down) side, were used for goods siding purposes.

The few road or accommodation bridges provided under the railway were either brick arches or single-span decks between brick abutments.

The main buildings were typical for the period and locality; those provided at Theale and Aldermaston were built of brick and timber in the "chalet" style with the roofs extending well over the structures beneath to form a platform awning right out to the edge of the platform, and uniformly so at each end. Shelters in a similar style were provided on the opposite platforms. These buildings, which have not survived, were very similar to those still standing at Mortimer, on the Basingstoke Branch, brought into use in 1848.

Less substantial buildings were provided at the other intermediate stations. At Hungerford, a one-sided station was provided as was the case at Reading. Thus there were both 'up' and 'down' station buildings on one platform, which was on the 'down' side. As it was believed at the time of construction (1845-7) that the line would soon after be extended to Westbury, the buildings provided at Hungerford were of a somewhat temporary nature. The 'up' station building at Hungerford and the main station building at Midgham were later destroyed by fire, in 1867 and 1888 respectively. A completely new station building was provided at Hungerford which replaced both original buildings and is believed to have been completed in 1871. A new building was also provided at Midgham. Details of these buildings are given in Chapter 3 (Hungerford) and in Chapter 4 (Midgham).

It is interesting to note that, unlike the practice on many contemporary railways, no provision was made at the stations for accommodation for the station masters. These senior staff, who bore the responsibility for all staff at each station, were accommodated in nearby houses, for instance in Station Road in Woolhampton and at Bridge House in Newbury. The latter building was located at the top of the north side station approach road and is believed to have been demolished when the station was rebuilt (Chapter 5). A "tied" house was provided for the station master adjacent to the station in Kintbury.

In addition to the usual two platforms, Newbury Station was provided with a timber overall roof covering both platforms and tracks. The 1:2500 scale map of Newbury, No XLIII.I (1880), shows two separate buildings on the up side beyond the span of the roof, one of which, the largest at the station, extended beyond the overall roof on the west side. This latter building probably contained the main booking office and waiting rooms and was situated on the north side as the main part of the town lay on that side. On the down side the plan also shows two buildings, these being outside the overall roof, one adjacent, the other to the east side. The end of the latter building can be seen in the only photograph known to be available of the east end of the station. Approach roads were provided on both sides of the station, the overall road layout being similar to that which exists today.

Short sidings were provided to loading/unloading platforms on the north-east, south-west and north-west corners of the station. That on the south-west side was probably for horses and had a short headshunt, whilst of the two on the north-west side, one was adjacent to the smaller up side building; these sidings had a long headshunt alongside the main line and extending towards Blackboys Bridge. These spurs should not be confused with the bay platforms for passenger trains provided several decades later.

The initial service consisted of five passenger trains each way calling at all stations between Reading and Hungerford; this frequency applied from Monday to Saturday. On Sundays, only two trains ran in each direction. The first services of the day originated at Hungerford and the last train of the day terminated there. At least one of the trains from Hungerford continued to Paddington, but passengers were advised to change at Reading to get to London quicker.

Journey times of these trains was about 50 minutes from Reading to Newbury and about 25 minutes onwards to Hungerford; these times would have included allowances for shunting of carriage trucks and horse boxes, also for loading and unloading miscellaneous items such as baskets and packages.

Footbridges have not been mentioned at stations and it is interesting to note that these would not then have been required, all the stations having either level crossings or adjacent bridges whilst Hungerford was a terminus. At Aldermaston, although one of the two bridges crossing the line there is adjacent to the station platforms, access was provided by vehicular approaches on each side of the line.

Goods yards were provided at each station; typically these were provided with goods sheds (which were "through" sheds, open at each end), a small number of sidings with the necessary shunting spurs and one or two short spurs of the type mentioned above. Locations relative to the passenger platforms and layouts varied; at Midgham, space was limited by the proximity to the village and at Thatcham and Kintbury stations by their proximity to the canal. The shunting spur at Thatcham crossed the road and had its own set of level crossing gates, whilst at Aldermaston the line from the west end of the goods shed passed through the side arch of the bridge. At Newbury, a wide tract of land was purchased on the up side east of the station for the double-line goods shed, cattle pens and shunting tracks and a further parcel of land for a fan of goods sidings.

1848 – 1851 The Wilts, Somerset and Weymouth Railway opens in stages

Meanwhile, to the west, progress was being made on the broad gauge line of the Wilts, Somerset and Weymouth

Railway with the opening of the section between the Great Western main line west of Chippenham (Thingley Junction), Trowbridge and Westbury on 5 September 1848. Opening to Frome took place on 7 October 1850 and the railway was vested in the GWR by an Act of 3 July 1851, S3; the transfer had in fact taken effect from 14 March 1850 (**Note 2).**

The next chapter will describe the major developments in the period up to the end of 1874. This period included the completion of the Wilts, Somerset and Weymouth railway and the abolition of the broad gauge lines in the area covered by this book.

NOTES

NOTE 1: WILTS AND SOMERSET RAILWAY - Background to the alteration of the name and objectives.

The Wilts and Somerset Railway had intended that its line should extend from Westbury only as far as Frome. However, the Bristol and Exeter Railway (B&ER), which had proposed to build a line from near Taunton through Yeovil to Weymouth, decided to curtail its scheme at Yeovil. The Wilts and Somerset Railway enlarged its proposals to include an extension from Frome through Yeovil to Weymouth. Both schemes had an easy passage through Parliament, achieving their Acts of 1845 authorising the B&ER branch to Yeovil and incorporating the Wilts, Somerset and Weymouth Railway. (Ref – Railway Magazine May 1939: 'Yeovil and its Railways')

From Westbury to Frome a single broad gauge track was provided on a double-track formation; the continuation to Weymouth was built to the same standard except that mixed gauge double track was provided between Dorchester and Weymouth.

NOTE 2: DEVIZES BRANCH

In May 1844, a public meeting in Devizes voted for the Devizes and Melksham scheme, originally proposed at a meeting in Devizes in 1836. At a meeting on 9 July 1844, Brunel presented plans for a network (Wilts and Somerset Railway), which included a Melksham - Devizes branch, and thus formulated the Wilts and Somerset Railway Company (renamed Wilts, Somerset and Weymouth Railway Company in October 1844).

In November 1845, after the WS&W Act had been passed, promoters of the branch wrote to the W&SWR and to the GWR, who were to work the nominally independent system, urging that the junction of the Devizes branch be altered to give a shorter route to Bradford and Bath. The directors prepared a Supplementary Bill altering the junction to Holt, between Staverton and Melksham; these changes were authorised by the Wilts, Somerset and Weymouth Railway Deviation Act of 1847.

NOTE 3: LONDON, NEWBURY AND BATH DIRECT RAILWAY – Report of the Select Sub-Committee, September 1846 and Petition against the Railway

Copies of the report are deposited at the Berkshire Record Office; reference D/EB/08/9. Also deposited at this Office is a petition against the proposed Railway which firstly mentions the unnecessary duplication of the authorised Berks and Hants Railway between Newbury and Hungerford; secondly the preferences of the petitioners for the extension of the railway west of Hungerford which would connect with the authorised Wilts, Somerset and Weymouth Railway and thus giving access to Bath via Trowbridge; Warminster and Salisbury; Frome (and thus the important collieries at

Radstock), Castle Cary, Yeovil and Weymouth and ultimately Exeter, Plymouth and Falmouth and several other important towns and districts in the West and South West of England (reference D/EX 1466/5/6)

NOTE 4: REACTIONS TO THE COMING OF THE RAILWAY.

The following extracts were taken from 'Newbury during the Victorian Era 1837 – 1893 Half a Century Retrospect', by Frank H Stillman.

"When the idea of a railway was first mooted, it was ridiculed in Newbury, and once when a steam coach made its appearance on the road it was not viewed with any amount of favour, as it looked likely to interfere with the trade of many who prospered by the old method. The prophets declared that a railway would never pay. There were few "probable consequences" which were not then prophesied. The boilers would habitually burst, and the travellers would be destroyed in their thousands. Trade would be ruined (railway rates were then only partially foreseen); the race of post-horses would die out; inns would be shut up. So poisonous would be the fumes vomited from the engine that vegetation would wither for miles round, and birds would fall dead in their flight.

"The project naturally created considerable excitement in Newbury, and in the snug smoking rooms of Speenhamland it was doomed to failure. The coaches still ran daily through the northern end of the borough, while the pick and the shovel of the navvy were busily employed in the southern suburbs, effecting the first signs of the revolution that was about to take place in the mode of travelling. There was a great deal of excavation to be done, and the towns-people watched the work with mixed feelings, some regarding it as opening up a new era of prosperity for the old borough, while others woefully prophesied the decrease of trade that would result upon the cessation of the coaches.

"Great was the excitement that prevailed when the first railway engine was brought down by road. It was designated 'The Jack of Newbury', a delicate compliment to the town, and it was hauled through the streets by some twenty or thirty horses. This was quite an event, and was witnessed by a crowd of people not less numerous than when some celebrated circus performer drove a team of forty horses through the town."

The following quotation is from the Appendix – the reminiscences of Mr Councillor Joseph Hopson: "An important event of course was the construction of the railway from Reading to Hungerford. I remember going to East Fields to see the commencement. The earth was loosened by ploughing layer after layer, instead of with the pickaxe, and removed in barrows; the contractors were Messrs Treadwell & Son. A railway engine and tender were expressly built for the work, and named the "Jack of Newbury". It was drawn up Northbrook-street and Bartholomew-street by 28 horses to the site of the works, where temporary rails had been laid to run the earth from Newbury to Bulls Lock".

ACTS

Berks and Hants Railway Act, 30 June 1845 (8&9 Vic I, c40)

Wilts, Somerset and Weymouth Railway Act, 30 June 1845 (8&9 Vic I, c53)

Great Western Railway Act, 14 May 1846, S4 (9&10 Vic I, c14) (B&HR amalgamated with GWR)

Wilts, Somerset and Weymouth Railway (Amendment) Act, 3 August 1846 (9&10 Vic I, c313)

Wilts, Somerset and Weymouth Railway Deviation Act, 25 June 1847 (10&11 Vic I, c60)

The Great Western Railway, Berks and Hants Extension Act, 22 July 1848 (11&12 Vic I, c.74)

Great Western Railway Act, 3 July 1851, S3 (14&15 Vic 1, c.48) (WS&WR vested in GWR)

CHAPTER REFERENCES

Deposited Documents   (see Chapter 1 for interpretation of references)

(Q/RUm 19) Newbury and Great Western Railway (No 1)   (1840)

(Q/RUm 20) Newbury and Great Western Railway (No 2)   (1840)

(Q/RUm 23) Newbury and Great Western Railway   (1843)

(Q/RUm 24) The Newbury Railway (Basingstoke – Newbury)   (1843)

(Q/RUm 26; DP/B9; A1/371/31MS) Reading, Basingstoke, Newbury and Hungerford Railway (Berks and Hants Railway)   (1844)

(A1/371/36MS) Wilts, Somerset and Weymouth Railway   (1844)

(Q/RUm 25; DP/B6; A1/371/29MS) Basingstoke and Didcot Junction Railway   (1844)

(Q/RUm 27) London, Salisbury, Exeter and Falmouth Railway   (1844)

(Q/RUm 69; A1/371/44MS) Berks and Hants Extension (Hungerford) Railway   (1845)

(Q/RUm 33; DP/B12; A1/371/39MS) Bristol and Dover Direct (Junction) Railway   (1845)

(DP/B14; A1/371/42MS) Great West of England Railway (or South Western Exeter Extension Railway)   (1845)

(A1/371/46MS) London, Devizes and Bridgwater Direct Western Railway   (1845)

(Q/RUm 43; A1/371/48MS) London, Newbury and Bath Direct Railway (original line)   (1845)

(Q/RUm 51; A1/371/49MS) London, Newbury and Bath Direct Railway (alternative line)   (1845)

(Q/RUm 56; DP/103; A1/371/50MS) Farnborough Extension (to London, Newbury and Bath)   (1845)

(Q/RUm 48; A1/371/45MS) London, Bristol and South Wales Direct Railway   (1845)

(Q/RUm 61; A1/371/41MS) Direct Western Railway (First Division)   (1845)

(Q/RUm 62A, 62B; DP/A7; A1/371/60MS) Southern Counties Union, Bristol, Bath and Dover (Direct) Railway   (1845)

(Q/RUm 64; DP/A1; A1/371/47MS) Direct London and Exeter Railway   (1845)

(DP/B16; A1/371/70MS) Manchester and Southampton Railway   (1845)

(also DP/A12; A1/371/78MS & 79MS (1846); DP/B24; A1/371/80MS)   (1847)

(Q/RUm 32; DP/A6; A1/371/61MS) Southampton, Manchester and Oxford Junction Railway   (1845)

(Q/RUm 39; DP/B18) Oxford, Southampton, Gosport and Portsmouth Railway   (1845)

(Q/RUm 50; DP/B22; A1/371/62MS) South Midland and Southampton Railway   (1845)

(Q/RUm 40; DP/A9; A1/371/64MS) Tring, Reading and Basingstoke Railway   (1845)

(Q/RUm 53; DP/B17; A1/371/53MS) Oxford and Salisbury Direct Railway   (1845)

(Q/RUm 54) Midland Grand Junction Railway   (1845)

(Q/RUm 37; DP/B20; A1/371/54MS) Richmond, Staines and Newbury Junction Railway   (1845)

(Q/RUm 65; DP/A4) Didcot and Andover Railway   (1846)

(Q/RUm 70; A1/371/71MS) GWR – Extension of the Berks and Hants Railway from Hungerford to Westbury   (1846)

PUBLISHED REFERENCES

History of the Great Western Railway Volume 1 1833 – 1863

E T MacDermot Revised by C R Clinker (Ian Allan 1964)

The Great Western Railway in the 19th Century

O S Nock   (Ian Allan 1972)

How the Great Western came to Berkshire – A Railway History 1833–1882

Daphne Phillips   (Reading Libraries 1975)

Railway Magazine May 1939: 'Yeovil and its Railways'

Reading Mercury

24.12.1847: Berks and Hants Railway - Main article and short news item

Berkshire Chronicle

25.12.1847: Opening of the Berks and Hants Railway to Hungerford

3

SLOW BUT STEADY 1852 - 1874

1852 The Great Western Railway buys up the canal and navigation companies

On the opening of the Great Western Railway throughout in 1841, traffic on the Kennet and Avon Canal was substantially reduced, and worse was to come with the opening of the Berks and Hants Railway (B&HR) to Newbury and Hungerford. The owners were happy to sell, and the GWR happy to purchase, the canal system linking Reading and Bristol in its entirety. The sale of the Kennet Navigation, Kennet and Avon Canal and Avon Navigation was authorised by the GWR Act No. 1 of 30 June 1852 and took effect from the following day.

1854 – 1856 The North-South cross-country route through Reading is established

The opening of the Berks and Hants Railway to Basingstoke had not realised the north-south cross-country route which had been intended. The L&SWR had been difficult about having a connection at Basingstoke; it may have feared that the B&H route would abstract some of its traffic. The real obstacle, however, was a break of gauge at both Basingstoke and Oxford and the reversal at Reading. By an Act of 1854 (GWR (Berks and Hants and Wilts, Somerset and Weymouth) Act 31 July 1854, S4), the GWR

was empowered to make a loop line west of Reading to connect the main line from the north and the west to the B&HR line.

The Act also required the GWR to add the third line of rails to create a mixed gauge of broad and narrow gauge lines on its existing lines between Oxford and Basingstoke at a cost of £138,000, solely for the accommodation of other railways.

In addition to this requirement, in order to obtain the Shrewsbury Amalgamation Act of 1 September 1854, the GWR agreed to be bound under penalties to complete the provision of narrow gauge rails from Oxford to Basingstoke within 18 months of the passing of the Act and afterwards to work it in association with the railways it would benefit.

The loop described above, known as the Reading West Loop, was a mixed gauge double line 45 chains (about half a mile) in length between junctions created at Reading West Junction (on the Bristol main line) and Oxford Road Junction on the B&HR line. In addition, the narrow gauge rails were provided between Oxford and Reading and between Oxford Road Junction and Basingstoke, where a connection was made to the L&SWR. Work progressed to allow the first narrow gauge goods and coal train to run on 22 December 1856; the loop was opened to passenger trains on 22 February the following year.

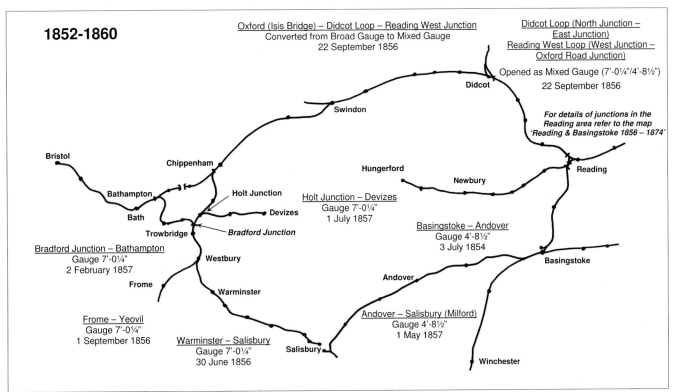

1852-1860

Oxford (Isis Bridge) – Didcot Loop – Reading West Junction
Converted from Broad Gauge to Mixed Gauge
22 September 1856

Didcot Loop (North Junction – East Junction)
Reading West Loop (West Junction – Oxford Road Junction)
Opened as Mixed Gauge (7'-0¼"/4'-8½")
22 September 1856

For details of junctions in the Reading area refer to the map 'Reading & Basingstoke 1856 – 1874'

Holt Junction – Devizes
Gauge 7'-0¼"
1 July 1857

Basingstoke – Andover
Gauge 4'-8½"
3 July 1854

Bradford Junction – Bathampton
Gauge 7'-0¼"
2 February 1857

Andover – Salisbury (Milford)
Gauge 4'-8½"
1 May 1857

Frome – Yeovil
Gauge 7'-0¼"
1 September 1856

Warminster – Salisbury
Gauge 7'-0¼"
30 June 1856

1857 The Wilts, Somerset and Weymouth network expands – and rails reach Devizes

The year 1857 was also a significant milestone further to the west. Trains reached Devizes in July that year on a branch line constructed from Holt Junction on the Chippenham - Westbury line. This year also saw the WS&WR reach Weymouth and complete the link between Bradford Junction and Bathampton, on the main line east of Bath. These lines, promoted in the original Act of 1845 (authorised on the same day as the Berks and Hants) and in a supplementary Act of 1846, which amended routes and added certain lines, were vested in the GWR by the GWR Act of 3 July 1851, from the date of the Act. Powers for the Holt Junction - Devizes and Bathampton branches had been revived by the GWR (Berks and Hants and Wilts, Somerset and Weymouth) Act of 31 July 1854, S9.

1858 Failure of the first schemes promoted to link Andover with the Great Western Railway

The broad gauge had reached Salisbury from Westbury in 1856 but the break of gauge there prevented the GWR from having direct access to Southampton from Bristol and South Wales. However, an opportunity for the GWR to reach Southampton came when the independent Andover and Redbridge Railway, which received its Act on 12 July 1858, made arrangements with the GWR to form a "direct" broad gauge line to Southampton in conjunction with a GWR-promoted line from Pewsey to Andover. (Redbridge is just outside Southampton on the Dorchester line.)

Pewsey was to be a station on the Berks and Hants Extension Railway, authorised in 1859. An alternative step to connect this railway with the Andover and Redbridge, presumably on the failure of the previous scheme, was taken when that railway sought powers in 1860 to extend northwards to Burbage, west of Savernake. The proposed Andover - Burbage line was rejected by the Commons Committee.

1859 - 1862 The Berks and Hants Extension Railway

The Berks and Hants was extended from Hungerford to Devizes by the Berks and Hants Extension Railway (B&HER), an independent railway authorised by an Act of that name on 13 August 1859. The broad gauge single line of 24 miles and 32 chains (about 24½ miles) was opened to traffic on 11 November 1862 with stations at Bedwyn, Savernake, Pewsey and Woodborough. For the first few months Savernake was the only crossing loop; in 1863 loops were added at the other stations.

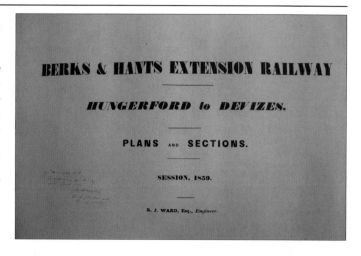

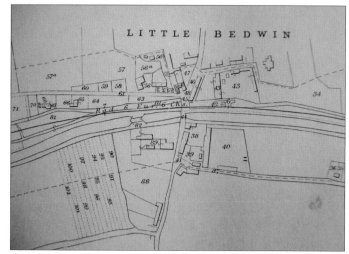

Berks and Hants Extension Railway:
upper and centre right - *cover and typical plan from the deposited documents.*
lower - *the Company's seal.*

The line was built by Messrs Smith & Knight and supervised by Michael Lane, GWR Chief Engineer, and was started in early 1861. No major engineering works were involved; the canal was followed to Pewsey and crossed west of Hungerford and again where it passes through the Bruce Tunnel at Savernake. A short tunnel (190 yards) under the castle at Devizes brought the line to a head-on junction with the already established Devizes branch. At Hungerford, the single line started at the end of the platforms and five new bridges were needed as the line threaded its way through the centre of the town, including a long span over the High Street. Many road over- and under-bridges were needed and these were built in stone or brick; in some cases arches were provided, in other cases the road or railway was carried on wrought iron spans supported by brick or stone abutments.

Bridges over the line were built for double track but underbridges were built for one broad gauge track only. An examination of the underside of these underbridges clearly shows that they were widened to accommodate double track at a later date. Level crossings on public roads were provided at a few locations; see chapter 4 for the changes made when the B&HER was upgraded and doubled at the end of the century.

Brick (and stone) buildings of a similar and very distinctive style were provided at each station; that at Pewsey has survived and remains in use. No awnings were provided to these buildings; the opposite platforms were later provided with small wooden shelters.

The new railway helped to develop the richly agricultural vale of Pewsey and was worked by the GWR for a period of 21 years under an agreement made in 1861. A direct rail service was laid on between Reading, Newbury, Devizes and Trowbridge where connections were made to Westbury, Yeovil and Weymouth, to Salisbury and to Bath and Bristol. By modern standards, the basic service of four passenger trains a day each way (one less than on the opening of the line to Hungerford in 1847) appears very sparse.

1861 – 1864 Rails reach Marlborough from Savernake

Meanwhile in 1861, the Marlborough Railway had been incorporated to run between the new Savernake station, then under construction, and Marlborough. It had originally been promoted in 1860, but was withdrawn then reintroduced in 1861 under the sponsorship of the GWR. The earliest plans for this railway had envisaged a junction with the B&HER at Burbage, in connection with the proposed Andover – Burbage line mentioned previously. Opened on 14 April 1864, the steeply graded, broad gauge, single line branch 5 miles 48 chains (about 5½ miles) long, was worked by the GWR under an agreement dated 12 April 1864.

A very poor print from the early days of photography. Savernake station looking west showing the crossing loop but only one platform

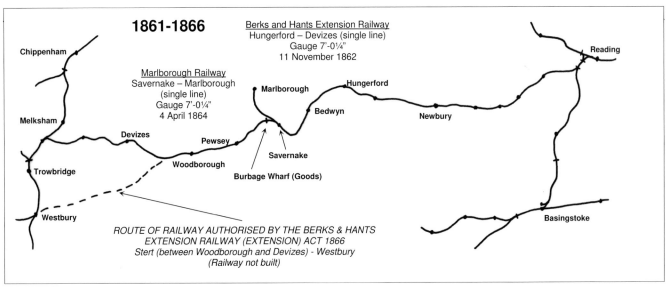

1861 – 1865 Fresh attempts made to link Andover with the Great Western Railway – and beyond

Several further attempts were made to establish a direct link between the B&H or B&HE lines and Andover and by this means to reach Southampton by the Andover and Redbridge Railway. An Andover and GWR Bill, for a line from Andover to the GWR (B&H) line at Enborne, west of Newbury, was promoted in the 1862 Session but was rejected by the Commons Committee, along with a L&SWR Bill to join these two lines. As a result of this failure, the GWR decided against financing further extensions to Southampton.

Following the costly Parliamentary battle fought over this proposed line and other contemporary schemes promoted by the GWR or L&SWR, a peace treaty was made on 23 October 1862 between the two companies. By this treaty, each company bound itself not to promote or assist any new line on the other's district, such districts being defined by a map, and agreed to offer various facilities for through traffic.

The Avon Valley Railway, deposited in 1863, was a scheme promoted to create a link between Porton and Woodborough, on the Berks and Hants Extension; Porton was a station on the London and South Western Railway, a few miles north-east of Salisbury.

An independent scheme for a narrow-gauge Andover Hungerford and Faringdon Railway was deposited in 1864 but was not successful. The proposed route is well worth describing in detail because of the impact such a line would have had on the communities it would have served, as well as on the landscape of North Hampshire and West and North Berkshire (Faringdon was then in Berkshire). Commencing at Andover Town station, on the Andover – Redbridge line, then under construction, the line would have passed through the parishes of Knights Enham, St Mary Bourne, Hurstbourne Tarrant, Faccombe, Linkenholt, Combe (1,000yd tunnel under Combe Gibbet), Inkpen (close to the church) and Hungerford.

After crossing Hungerford Common, the line would have been carried over the Berks and Hants Railway, the canal, the rivers and the Bath Road (Turnpike) on a 250yd viaduct. The line would have continued towards the Sheffords, passing close to East Garston, through the parishes of Lambourn and Letcombe Bassett, by a 1,000yd tunnel under the Ridgeway, and would then have headed for Uffington through the parishes of Childrey, Sparsholt and Kingston Lisle.

At Uffington, the line would have passed under the Great Western Railway close to the station and then run to the west of and entirely alongside the Faringdon Railway, a short branch from the GWR main line, which had been incorporated in 1860 and opened in 1864. The proposed railway would have terminated adjacent to the Faringdon Railway's station. Here it was planned to join the "authorised East Gloucestershire Railway" (Note 1).

The line described above from Andover to Faringdon was shown on the plans as Railway No. 1 and would have had a length of just over 37¼ miles. Railways Nos. 2 and 3 would have connected the proposed line to the London and South Western Railway at Andover and to the Great Western Railway (facing west) at Uffington. Railway No 4 would have been a 3-mile branch from a junction with Railway No 1 near East Garston to a terminus at Lambourn.

The impact on the Berks and Hants and the Berks and Hants Extension Railways would have been substantial. No connection was proposed with the former at Hungerford; such a link would not have been possible at that time due to the difference in gauges. The proposed railway would have attracted much traffic associated with agriculture and the racing industry away from the east-west line. However, the alternative routes for traffic would have been of benefit to the districts served; this would have applied particularly to coal, a vital commodity in the country districts as well as in the towns.

A further attempt to provide such a link was made in 1882, although no formal application has been traced.

The Andover and Redbridge Railway opened as a narrow gauge line from Michelmersh (Kimbridge Junction on the Romsey to Salisbury line) to Andover Junction on the Basingstoke to Salisbury line on 6 March 1865. The extension to the Junction at Andover, the amalgamation with the L&SWR and the change from broad to narrow gauge had been authorised in 1863.

1865 More links planned between the L&SWR, B&HER and other railways

The North and South Wiltshire Junction Railway Act, 5 July 1865, authorised a line which would have linked the B&HER at Woodborough with the southern end of a railway authorised in 1864, the Wilts and Gloucestershire; the northern end of that railway would have linked with the Midland Railway. The junction with the southern end would have been in the parish of Christian Malford; near this junction the proposed line would have passed under the GWR Swindon – Chippenham line about 4 miles north-east of the latter place and a south-facing loop would have linked the proposed line with the GWR main line.

Another railway authorised in July 1865 was The Wiltshire Railway, an extensive system of new lines which would have linked the London and South Western Railway at Porton Station, 6 miles north-east of Salisbury, with Pewsey on the B&HER, via the Avon Valley. A branch from this line would have joined Upavon with the B&HER further west, at Woodborough. Near Pewsey, the proposed line would have continued by a tortuous and hilly route to Marlborough, and then headed northwards to pass over the GWR Didcot – Swindon line east of the latter place to join the proposed East Gloucestershire Railway near Fairford. The new railway would have been 44 miles long; the short link at Pewsey and the longer link at Woodborough would have added a further 3¼ miles.

The overall plan of the railway promoters seeking a route largely independent of the GWR can thus be seen: a chain of new railways from Porton on the L&SWR, via Upavon to the B&HER at Woodborough, then northwards via Christian Malford to a link with the Midland Railway; alternatively to the B&HER at Pewsey and northwards via Marlborough and Highworth to link with the East Gloucestershire Railway **(Note 1)**. However, as presumably the capital for these new lines (very costly in the case of the Wiltshire Railway north of Pewsey) could not be found, these schemes never came to fruition.

The Upavon and Andover Railway, if authorised and built, would have linked the L&SWR at Andover with the Wiltshire Railway at Upavon and was the result of yet another attempt to link the two major narrow gauge railways.

An Act of 1866 seeks to create a direct link to Westbury avoiding Devizes

In a further attempt to create a direct line to the west, an Act was obtained in 1866 by the Berks and Hants Extension Railway (a company independent of the GWR) for a new line 13 miles in length from Stert (a point on the line between Woodborough and Devizes) to Westbury, avoiding Devizes and Trowbridge. By early 1870, a Warrant had been obtained from the Board of Trade to abandon the project. It would be another 17 years before a further Act was obtained for such a project (see Chapter 4) and the turn of the century before the scheme would come to fruition. The reason for abandonment is not known, but was probably financial.

The final years of the 1860s bring changes welcome and unwelcome

In 1867, the 'up' building of the original one-sided station at Hungerford was burned to the ground. A new station building was opened in 1871, replacing both 'up' and 'down' buildings **(Note 2)**. Also in 1867, the GWR converted its Kennet and Avon Canal Company shares to railway stock. In 1868 the block telegraph was installed on the main line but the single-line Marlborough branch continued to be worked by staff and ticket – see Glossary for explanation of these methods of controlling the movement of trains.

The first developments in what would eventually become important sources of freight traffic took place around this time. Commercial firms wishing to use the railway for transport of their output, or to receive coal, coke, raw materials or components, entered into Private Siding Agreements (PSAs) with the appropriate railway

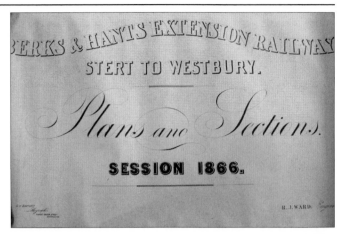

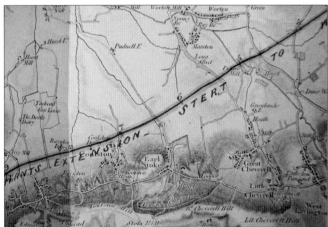

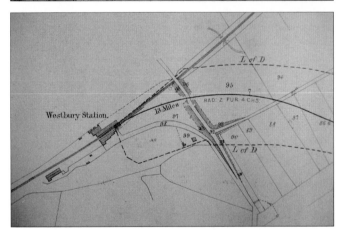

*The first scheme for a direct railway to Westbury, by-passing Devizes: **from top** - cover of deposited documents; part of map and a plan of the proposed junction at Westbury*

companies. At Newbury Goods Yard, R Skinner, maltsters, made such an agreement commencing 30 October 1868. Coal was brought in for the boiler house and malt was shipped out.

The Westbury Iron Co Ltd had commenced operations adjacent to the station in 1857. The works were sited such that they could be conveniently served by the Wilts, Somerset and Weymouth Railway. Iron ore was mined locally, but substantial supplies of coke would have been required and the finished products would have been mostly taken out by rail, no other alternative being available. The first Private Siding Agreement was dated 11 June 1870.

1869 The change-over from broad gauge to narrow gauge continues apace

In 1869, certain of the tracks in Reading Passenger Station were converted to mixed gauge and the broad gauge rails were removed between Southcote Junction and Basingstoke. To review the position with broad, mixed and narrow gauge lines in the area, the situation after the work described above was completed was as follows: -

Reading Station - Southcote Junction: mixed gauge (from Station Junction to Oxford Road Junction converted from broad gauge in 1862)

Reading (West Junction) - Oxford Road Junction (Reading West Loop): mixed gauge

Southcote Junction - Newbury – Hungerford - Devizes - Holt Junction: broad gauge

Southcote Junction - Basingstoke: narrow gauge

Thingley Junction (Chippenham) – Holt Junction – Westbury – Yeovil – Weymouth, also Westbury to Salisbury: broad gauge (except Dorchester Junction – Weymouth: mixed gauge).

A glimpse of local train operation in the early seventies

With the sparse train service on the Berks and Hants line, the double line to Hungerford must have seemed something of a luxury. The working timetable for January 1873 shows four passenger trains and one goods train in each direction between Newbury and Hungerford. It is no surprise to hear, therefore, that in May 1872 broad gauge wagons were being stored on the down line between Newbury and Hungerford, the up line being worked as a single line. The wagons had become redundant following the conversion from broad to narrow gauge of most of the main line in South Wales earlier that month. Two years later it was reported that the down line was still blocked between Newbury and Kintbury. Confirmation of this is found in the working timetable referred to above, which states that "The Single Line between Newbury and Hungerford is worked by Train Staff". The same source notes that the Single Line between Hungerford and Devizes is worked by Disc Telegraph, that between Devizes and Holt Junction by Pilotman and that between Savernake and Marlborough by Train Staff (see Glossary).

1871 A new north-west / south-east link is promoted – The South Midland Railway

Further attempts were made to set up cross-country routes on the north-west/ south-east axis, when in 1871 a South Midland Railway was promoted from Lydney (on the South

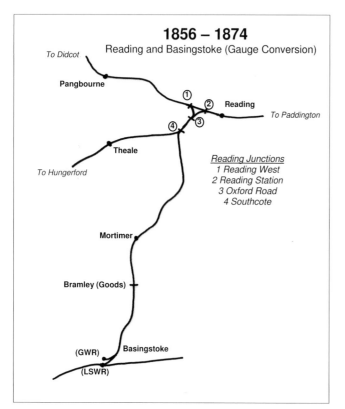

1856 – 1874
Reading and Basingstoke (Gauge Conversion)

To Didcot
Pangbourne
① ② Reading
To Paddington
④ ③
Theale
To Hungerford

Reading Junctions
1 Reading West
2 Reading Station
3 Oxford Road
4 Southcote

Mortimer

Bramley (Goods)

(GWR) Basingstoke
(LSWR)

READING and BASINGSTOKE 1856 - 1874		
Gauge Conversion Didcot/Reading - Basingstoke/Paddington		
22 December 1856	Didcot – Reading West Junction & Oxford Road Junction - Basingstoke	Broad Gauge - Mixed Gauge
22 December 1856 (opened)	Reading Loop (Reading West Junction - Oxford Road Junction)	Built new to Mixed Gauge
1 October 1861	Reading West Junction - Paddington	Broad Gauge - Mixed Gauge
March 1862	Reading Station Junction – Oxford Road Junction	Broad Gauge - Mixed Gauge
1 April 1869	Reading Station lines	Broad Gauge - Mixed Gauge
1 April 1869	Southcote Junction - Basingstoke	Mixed Gauge - Narrow Gauge
30 June - 1 July 1874	Southcote Junction - Hungerford	Broad Gauge - Narrow Gauge
30 June 1874	Reading - Southcote Junction	Mixed Gauge - Narrow Gauge
30 June 1874	Reading West Junction - Oxford Road Junction	Mixed Gauge - Narrow Gauge

Newbury: changing from broad to narrow gauge (1874)

Wales main line between Gloucester and Chepstow) via a Severn crossing, Wootton Bassett and Marlborough to Hungerford where it would fork, one branch going to Andover and the other to join the main line south of Basingstoke.

The Andover "branch" would have passed through, or near to, Shalbourne, the Collingbournes and Ludgershall, following much of the line adopted by the Swindon, Marlborough and Andover Railway, authorised the following year. The Basingstoke "branch" would have passed through, or near to, Avington (initially following the Kennet Valley and the Berks and Hants line), Gore End (Enborne Valley) and Ecchinswell, entering a tunnel under Great Knowl Hill north of Kingsclere. Emerging on Frith Common, it would then have passed through, or near to, Baughurst Street (Stoney Heath) and Monk Sherborne before entering Basingstoke Station from the west.

The scheme failed when the promoters were unable to realise the Parliamentary deposit.

1873 Success at last for the promoters of cross-country lines

Efforts to provide cross-country links from the Midlands and South Wales to Southampton eventually succeeded when, in 1873, two important cross-country lines were authorised which would connect with, and have a profound effect upon, the B&HR, the B&HER and the Marlborough Railway.

The Swindon, Marlborough and Andover Railway

The first of these railways to be incorporated, by just two weeks, was the Swindon, Marlborough and Andover Railway (SM&AR), by an Act of that name dated 21 July 1873. Railway No 1 was authorised to run from a junction with the GWR west of Swindon to connect with the Marlborough Railway at Marlborough station. Railway No 2 was to run from a junction with the Berks and Hants Extension Railway at Wolfhall Junction, three-quarters of a mile east of Savernake station, to a junction with the L&SWR Basingstoke - Salisbury line 1½ miles west of Andover at Red Post(s) Junction.

All the lines described above were to be single lines, as indeed was the section of B&HER to be used between Savernake and Wolfhall Junction. Running powers were granted over the Marlborough Railway and the B&HER between the points mentioned. The SM&AR was permitted to use the GWR station at Swindon and the L&SWR station at Andover Junction. The latter station was opened in 1854 and connected to Redbridge, on what later became the Southampton – Bournemouth line, by the Andover and Redbridge Railway in 1865. The Act did not require any changes to the alignment or gradients on the Marlborough Railway; nor were there were any plans to improve facilities at Savernake station, which consisted of one platform, a passing loop and a few sidings.

The Didcot, Newbury and Southampton Junction Railway

The second of these railways to be incorporated, on 5 August 1873, was the Didcot, Newbury and Southampton Junction Railway by an Act of that name. The railway was to commence at the GWR station at Didcot Junction and join the main Basingstoke-Winchester line about 2½ miles north of Micheldever, a station on the main Basingstoke – Winchester line; it would have passed over the Berks and Hants line at Newbury and under Greenham Common in a tunnel. There was to be a branch about 2¼ miles long from Compton to East Ilsley and a loop about 1½ miles long to connect with the L&SWR at Whitchurch. No running powers were included in the Act and no connection was planned with the existing line at Newbury, although that railway was shortly to be converted to the narrow gauge.

1874 The end of the broad gauge on the Berks and Hants lines and their branches

In February 1874, the GWR directors addressed the situation caused by the existence of a group of broad gauge lines located between extensive networks of narrow gauge lines. They reported that ". . . the Directors have had to consider the best mode of dealing with the question of the gauge on the Wilts, Somerset and Weymouth, and the Berks and Hants Railways, and they are of the opinion that the convenience of the public will be best met, and the interest of the Proprietors best secured, by the alteration from Broad to Narrow Gauge of all the Lines in the district which these Railways accommodate". Parliamentary sanction to alter the gauge of GWR lines had been obtained in 1866.

The time had come to convert the B&H, B&HE lines and adjacent lines to the narrow gauge. Work to convert the entire Wilts, Somerset and Weymouth group of lines had been carried out in June 1874. Between 26 June and 3 July 1874, the lines between Reading (junction with the main line), Southcote Junction, Newbury, Devizes and Holt Junction; Reading West Junction and Oxford Road Junction; and the Marlborough branch, totalling about 64 miles, were converted to narrow gauge from broad or mixed gauge. All these lines remained as built, that is double line from Reading to Hungerford and on the Reading West loop, single line from Hungerford to Holt Junction via Devizes and on the Marlborough branch.

The last broad gauge train ran on 30 June 1874. The following day through narrow gauge trains began running between Reading and Trowbridge, using the down line only between Southcote Junction and Hungerford. By 4 July, all lines had been converted and the ordinary train service resumed. Local response to this engineering achievement was, however, muted when it was discovered that not only had no changes of any substance (i.e. *no improvements*)

been made to the train service that was in place before the change of gauge, but third class fares had been increased.

With the encumbrance of the broad gauge dispensed with on the local lines, and the shape of the network determined for the next two decades, Chapter 4 traces developments which would lead to the creation of the main line railway that we are familiar with today.

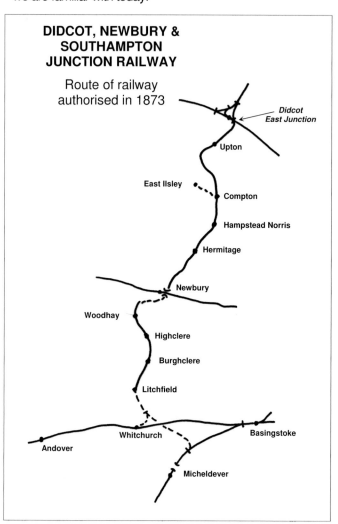

DIDCOT, NEWBURY & SOUTHAMPTON JUNCTION RAILWAY

Route of railway authorised in 1873

NOTES

NOTE 1: EAST GLOUCESTERSHIRE RAILWAY

This was the name given to a scheme for a number of new lines including a link between Faringdon and Cheltenham which together with the Andover and Faringdon Railway would have made a direct connection between the L&SW and Midland Railways. The ultimate goal was to link the Midlands and Southampton, avoiding the GWR completely.

An Act of 1862 was obtained for this scheme, first proposed in 1861. However, the only railway built under the Act was a branch line from the terminus of the Witney Railway to Fairford, in East Gloucestershire, opened in 1873. The scheme was submitted again in 1864 with a line from Cheltenham to Faringdon and Witney, the same year as the Andover, Hungerford and Faringdon project was proposed. No part of this new scheme ever came to fruition.

NOTE 2: HUNGERFORD STATION

Hungerford Station was the terminus of the B&HR when it opened in 1847 and it appears that only temporary station buildings were provided, as at that time substantial efforts were being made to continue the line to Westbury, as noted in Chapter 2. In 1862, when the B&HER was opened to Devizes, efforts to reach Westbury were again being made, as noted in the previous paragraph. The fire in 1867 destroyed one of these buildings, the so-called 'up' station; it seems clear that despite the abandonment of the scheme for a direct line to Westbury the GWR finally decided to provide a permanent and substantial station building appropriate to the needs of the district.

ACTS

Great Western Railway Act No. 1, 30 June 1852 (15&16 Vic I, c140) (purchase of Kennet and Avon Canal)

Great Western Railway (Berks and Hants and Wilts, Somerset and Weymouth) Act, 31 July 1854, (17&18 Vic I, c202)
S4 (authorisation of Reading West Loop)
S9 (Holt Junction - Devizes and Bradford-Bathampton branches)

Berks and Hants Extension Railway Act, 13 August 1859 (22&23 Vic I, c105)

Marlborough Railway Act, 22 July 1861 (24&25 Vic I, c167)

Berks and Hants Extension Railway Act, 4 May 1863 (26&27 Vic I, c3) (Marlborough Railway)

Wiltshire Railway Act, 5 July 1865 (28&29 Vic I, c.318)

North and South Wiltshire Junction Railway Act, 5 July 1865 (28&29 Vic I, c.338)

Berks and Hants Extension Railway (Extension) Act, 28 June 1866 (29&30 Vic I, c154) (Stert to Westbury)

Swindon, Marlborough and Andover Railway Act, 21 July 1873 (36&37 Vic I, c194)

Didcot, Newbury and Southampton Junction Railway Act, 5 August 1873 (36&37 Vic I, c229)

CHAPTER REFERENCES

Deposited Documents (see Chapter 1 for interpretation of references)

(Q/RUm 97) GWR – Branch to connect Berks and Hants Railway with GWR etc (Reading West Curve) (1854)

(Q/RUm 105; A1/371/95MS) Berks and Hants: Hungerford and Devizes Extension (1858)

(A1/371/98MS) Marlborough Branch Railway (1859)

(A1/371/99MS) Marlborough Railway (1860)

(Q/RUm 110; DP/191) Andover and GW Railway (1861 - rejected 1862)

(A1/371/102MS) Avon Valley Railway (1863)

(Q/RUm 119; DP/241) Andover, Hungerford and Faringdon Railway (1864)

(A1/371/108MS) North and South Wiltshire Junction Railway (1864)

(A1/371/111MS) Wiltshire Railway (1864)

(DP/273; A1/371/118MS) Upavon and Andover Railway (1865)

(A1/371/113MS) Berks and Hants: Stert to Westbury Extension (1865)

(Q/RUm 136; DP/B30; A1/371/121MS) South Midland Railway (1871)

(DP/317; A1/371/122MS) Swindon, Marlborough and Andover Railway (1872)

(Q/RUm 140; DP/313) Didcot, Newbury and Southampton Junction Railway (1872)

Hungerford Common with baulk road on both lines (believed to be 'narrow gauge' but still relevant to 1874)

PUBLISHED REFERENCES

History of the Great Western Railway Volume 1 1833 – 1863

E T MacDermot Revised by C R Clinker (Ian Allan 1964)

History of the Great Western Railway Volume 2 1863 – 1921

E T MacDermot Revised by C R Clinker (Ian Allan 1964)

The Illustrated Guide to the Great Western Railway 1852

George Meason (Berkshire County Library in conjunction with Countryside Books 1983)

How the Great Western came to Berkshire – A Railway History 1833 – 1882

Daphne Phillips (Reading Libraries 1975)

The Great Western Railway in the 19th Century

O S Nock (Ian Allan 1972)

For references to the London and South Western Railway: Marlborough Branch (GWR); Swindon, Marlborough and Andover Railway; Didcot, Newbury and Southampton Junction Railway: see **Further Reading**

Reading Mercury

8.11.1862 (Private Opening of the Berks and Hants Extension Railway)

Ibid: 15.11.1862 (Berks and Hants Extension (public opening))

Ibid: 22.11.1862 (Berks and Hants Extension Line)

Ibid: 29.11.1862 (Berks and Hants Railway (memorial laid before the directors) and Berks and Hants Extension Railway (reference to Bill to extend the powers of the company))

Berkshire Chronicle

15.11.1862 (Meeting of the proprietors of the Great Western Railway who dissent from the policy pursued by the board)

Newbury Weekly News

21.11.1867 (Hungerford – Destruction of the Great Western Railway Station by fire)

Reading Mercury

23.11.1867 (Hungerford – The Destruction of the Railway Station by Fire)

Newbury Weekly News

25.6.1874 (Great Western Railway - Alteration of Gauge (Notice) and Editorial – lengthy review of the history of the broad gauge)

Ibid: 2.7.1874 (Great Western Railway - Alteration of Gauge: Editorial – satisfaction with abolition of broad gauge, review of the changes to timetable)

Ibid: 9.7.1874 (Great Western Railway - Alteration of Gauge: Editorial – dissatisfaction with the increase in third class fares)

4

LINES IN ALL DIRECTIONS 1875 - 1900

A Railway to Lambourn - First Attempt

In 1875, the Newbury and Lambourn Tramway Co Act was obtained, to construct a tramway from Newbury station through the town centre (and Donnington) to Lambourn. The scheme had first been mooted in 1873. After a ceremonial start of work and about a mile of track had been laid, the scheme was abandoned due to financial difficulties.

Slow Progress on the Didcot - Southampton Line

By 1876, no progress had been made towards construction of the Didcot, Newbury and Southampton Junction Railway (DN&SJR) incorporated in 1873. In the summer of 1876, an Act dated 24 July was obtained granting an extension of time and giving powers to make a working agreement with the GWR. Such an agreement had already been made, on 26 June.

Nearly three years later, progress had still not been made and a Bill to abandon the undertaking had got as far as its Third Reading before being withdrawn as the company had been taken over. The new owners, solicitors acting on behalf of the Earl of Carnarvon and other landowners in the Newbury area, hastily arranged a ceremonial first turning of the sod at Newbury on 26 August 1879.

A new Act was obtained in 1880. The Didcot, Newbury and Southampton Junction Railway (DN&SJR) Act of 9 July 1880 substituted new railways for those authorised in 1873. At Newbury, connections were to be made with the Berks and Hants Railway east and west of the station, at locations later to be called Newbury East Junction and Enborne Junction. However the DN&SJR retained powers to build an independent line between these points, the power not to be exercised without the consent of the GWR.

The route originally authorised south of Newbury was regained at Burghclere. There were to be north- and south-facing links with the L&SWR Basingstoke to Salisbury line at Whitchurch and a deviation to the original route at the south end would have created a junction with the L&SWR Basingstoke to Southampton line north of Popham Tunnels, about 10 miles north of Winchester. The latter proposal was strongly objected to by the L&SWR.

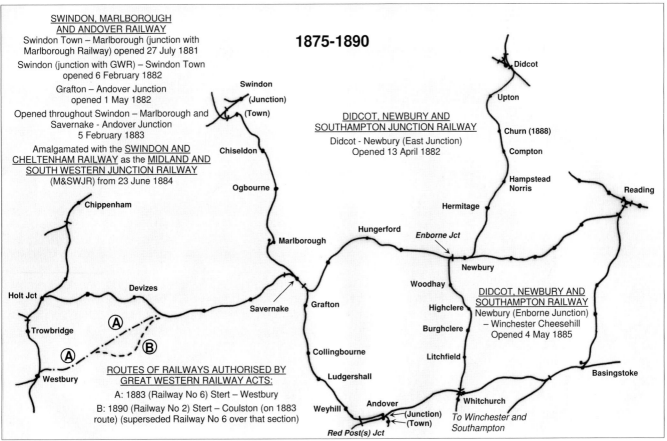

The railway authorised was divided into two sections. The Newbury Section comprised the route between Didcot and the junction at Newbury, whilst the Southern Section comprised all other authorised lines. The East Ilsley branch was therefore incorrectly included in the Southern section!

Construction was confined at first to the Didcot - Newbury section of 17¼ miles, and by July 1881, the works had progressed sufficiently for the Directors to take a trip over the first part of the railway. However a period of bad weather then followed and the line was not ready for formal opening until the following year.

A Railway to Lambourn - Second Attempt

In 1881, the basic scheme for a railway from Newbury to Lambourn was revived as a light railway. The proposal was to use the DN&SJR, then under construction, for about one mile northwards from Newbury and then proceed to Lambourn by Shaw (and, presumably, Donnington and Speen). The inhabitants of Shaw raised objections and although passed by the House of Commons, the House of Lords rejected the Bill.

Swindon to Marlborough opens

On 27 July 1881 the first section of the Swindon, Marlborough and Andover Railway (SM&AR) was opened between Swindon Town station and Marlborough, Railway No 1 of those authorised in 1873. As it was not at that time possible to link with the GWR at their Swindon station, then known as Swindon Junction, services started from the new Town station. Intermediate stations with single platforms were provided on the 11½ miles of single-track line at Chiseldon and Ogbourne. The new station at Marlborough was adjacent to the terminus of the branch from Savernake, opened in 1864. Although this new line may seem remote from the Berks and Hants line, within 18 months trains from Swindon would be authorised to continue from Marlborough on the GWR branch to Savernake; then to continue on the B&HER for the short distance to Wolfhall Junction en route to Andover and Southampton.

Opening to Didcot

A succession of significant events took place in 1882. On 13 April, following a formal opening the previous day, the Newbury to Didcot line was opened to the public. A single line 17¼ miles long, it was the first line in the district to be built on the narrow gauge, by then known as the standard gauge, with the exception of the short length of the Lambourn Tramway laid in 1875. All the works were built for double track, including bridges over and under the line. The line was worked by the GWR under an agreement dated 4 May 1882.

Stations were provided at Upton, Compton, Hampstead Norris, and Hermitage, all of which except Hampstead Norris were also passing places. A platform at Churn was initially provided in 1888 to serve the rifle ranges located there. In 1894 the platform was extended and a goods siding added, mainly for military purposes – summer training camps were held in the area; it was not publicly advertised as a stop until 1905. Upton was renamed Upton and Blewbury in 1911 and a halt added at Pinewood, north of Hermitage, in 1933.

At Newbury station, substantial alterations were made to accommodate the Didcot trains and the planned train service to Winchester; the necessary improvements having been agreed, as well as the apportionment of the cost, between the GWR and the DN&SJR. The up platform was lengthened towards Reading and a bay provided for the Didcot trains. On the south-west corner, the down platform was lengthened and a bay provided for the Winchester trains, plus another siding, at the end of which were both side-loading and end-loading platforms. The former would have been used for horses (cattle would have been dealt with in the goods yard) and the latter for carriages on flat trucks. This siding was provided with a headshunt, at the end of which was a small turntable. On the north-west corner, the only change was the alteration of one of the sidings to run alongside the small building mentioned in Chapter 2.

First steps towards a through line from Swindon to Andover

On the 1 May 1882, the line constructed by the Swindon, Marlborough and Andover Railway between Grafton (near Savernake) and Andover was opened to traffic. The railway had obtained Acts of 1878, 1879 and 1880 which included provisions for extensions of time and powers to construct new or deviation lines. A temporary connection with the L&SWR main line west of Andover, at Red Post(s) Junction, was used until 19 November when a separate third line to Andover was brought into use. The newly opened section was single line throughout with double platform stations and crossing loops at Grafton, Collingbourne, Ludgershall and Weyhill. The line was not to be isolated for long, however, the link between Grafton and the Berks and Hants Extension line at Wolfhall Junction, east of Savernake, being made early in the following year. This was possible as an Act of 1882 included powers to compel the GWR to put Savernake Station in order and to install block telegraph on the Marlborough Branch. A further Act, of 1883, was obtained authorising the SM&AR to use the Marlborough Branch. The completion of the railway between Swindon and Andover is fully described on page 50 and shown on the Railway Clearing House map (page 70).

The area around Ludgershall and the adjacent army garrison town of Tidworth were, within 20 years, to be of considerable significance to the Railway; however, that is for Chapter 5.

The Great Western Railway looks west from Hungerford

The Berks and Hants Extension Railway was absorbed by the GWR as from 1 July 1882. B&HER shares of £100 were exchanged for GWR shares of £87.10s.0d in value. This was done as part of a long-term strategy by the GWR to improve the railway between Hungerford and Westbury to form a direct route to the west. The applications of 1845, 1846 and 1847 (see Chapter 2) had sought to join these two places, but the application of 1859 had resulted in a railway to Devizes, as supported by the residents of that town.

An Act of 1866 had sought a Stert to Westbury extension (see previous chapter), but that scheme was abandoned in 1870. A new Act was obtained in 1883 for a direct line to Westbury from the B&HER; commencing in the parish of Urchfont, the new line would be just over 13 miles in length. The village of Stert is in the parish of Urchfont. This Act also authorised a new line between Castle Cary, on the Westbury - Yeovil line, and Langport, on the Yeovil - Taunton line, which was intended to form the principal link in providing a cut-off between Castle Cary and Taunton. No work was started, however, on either scheme; seven years elapsed before the Stert and Westbury scheme (as it was later known) was revived again (page 52) and 15 years before the Castle Cary - Langport scheme was revived (Chapter 5).

The Didcot, Newbury and Southampton (Junction) Railway looks to Southampton

A further DN&SJR Bill received royal assent on 10 August 1882. The powers given included the authority to build a new railway nearly 33½ miles long, commencing at a junction with the new line already authorised at Burghclere, and terminating at the waterfront at Southampton. The 1880 route was to be deviated for several miles south of Burghclere to give a better line and level and the remainder of the Micheldever line route south of Litchfield (authorised in 1873) was abandoned, as were the north and south loops originally proposed at Whitchurch.

The new connection proposed at Whitchurch was to be formed by a south-facing loop joining the L&SWR line east of the station, facing west. This would have given through running between Newbury and Salisbury. It would also have given, via the proposed Hurstbourne and Fullerton line, for which the L&SWR obtained powers in 1882, an alternative route from Newbury to Southampton.

In addition, powers were granted to build a line 10½ miles long from Burghclere to the GWR at Aldermaston, to provide a competitive route from London to Southampton, 88½ miles long compared with the 79-mile length of the existing line from Waterloo. Stations would have been provided at Kingsclere and Brimpton. The L&SWR, which had opposed the Bill, secured the insertion of a clause

Above - GWR 2-4-0 No 1361 'Pembroke' was one of several locomotives purchased from the Pembroke and Tenby Railway, before it was absorbed by the GWR in 1897. Built by Sharp Stewart in 1866, it was rebuilt at Tenby in 1897 and worked on the Didcot line until withdrawal in 1902. It is seen in the 'Didcot' bay at the old Newbury station (John Allen collection)

Right - An Agreement between the Great Western Railway Company and the Didcot Newbury and Southampton Junction Railway Company dated 23rd January 1885 – (Enborne Junction) (original document – Kevin Robertson collection)

whereby it could require the DN&SJR to make a connection to the L&SWR main line north of Winchester, near the junction with the branch to Alton.

By this time, deputations from Portsmouth and Bournemouth, inspired by the example of Southampton, the residents of which had long sought a direct connection with the Midlands and North of England, were urging the DN&SJR board to extend the line to their towns. The efforts of the deputation from Bournemouth, which had grown from a population of 700 in 1851 to 17,000 and was poorly served by existing railways, appeared to have been successful when a DN&SJR (Bournemouth and Poole) Extension Bill was deposited for the 1883 Session of Parliament.

The Bill was withdrawn at an early stage, having achieved its purpose; the L&SWR being moved to seek powers for the present direct line to Bournemouth from Brockenhurst via Sway. All that the DN&SJR achieved from the 1883 session was permission to drop the word Junction from its title and an Act of 16 July consolidating the authorised capital.

In the meantime, construction was well advanced over a length of 10½ miles from Enborne Junction to a point beyond Litchfield where the abandoned line to Micheldever would have diverged. On 22 March 1883, work began on the next stage of 15½ miles to Bar End, Winchester. A start was made on the Whitchurch Loop and in Southampton where land had been bought and fenced off.

However, the cash for the planned works at Southampton was not forthcoming. Shortly after the appointment of James Staats Forbes, initially as Director, then as Chairman, in September 1883, work on the Southampton extension was suspended and never resumed. The shareholders of the renamed Didcot, Newbury and Southampton Railway, however, backed by local opinion, were determined to press on as far towards Southampton as possible. The whole of the company's resources were directed in a drive towards Winchester; work on the Whitchurch loop was stopped and the L&SWR was advised that there was no money to complete this loop or the connection to their railway north of Winchester, which that company had served notice requesting that it should be built.

The London and South Western Railway tries again for Bristol

A new attempt by the London and South Western Railway Company to reach Bristol had been made in 1882 when it supported and agreed to work the Bristol and London and South Western Junction Railway. This line would have started at Grateley, between Andover and Salisbury, and traversed Salisbury Plain to Westbury, reaching Bristol by means of the North Somerset line from near Radstock and thence to a new terminus in Bristol. Before reaching the

Parliamentary Committee, the proposal was altered at its western end to use the Somerset and Dorset line to Bath and the Midland Railway's line onward to the existing station in Bristol. The amended Bill was decisively defeated in April 1883.

A railway is planned to link Pewsey and Salisbury – but is never started

An Act was obtained in 1883 for a Pewsey and Salisbury Railway, to be built between Pewsey, on the Berks and Hants Extension Railway, and the GWR line at Salisbury. It would be worked by the GWR with running powers to Southampton. Although it has been stated that the scheme was abandoned after the 1884 agreement with the L&SWR, an extension of time was granted by an Act of 1886 and the scheme was not finally abandoned until 1891 by an Act of that year.

Opening from Swindon throughout to Andover

Meanwhile, the Swindon, Marlborough and Andover Railway was opened throughout on 5 February 1883. The two Swindon stations having been connected when the link was opened on 6 February 1882, trains used the new line from the GWR station at Swindon to Marlborough, which had opened from Swindon Town in 1881. Trains then continued, by means of a junction between the two adjacent lines, on to the Marlborough Railway to reach Savernake where they joined the Berks and Hants Extension Railway for three-quarters of a mile towards Crofton. At the newly-created Wolfhall Junction, named after the nearby manor house, they branched off to cross the Kennet and Avon Canal and shortly reached Grafton, from which isolated location services to Andover had started in May 1882. Improvements to Savernake Station, including provision of a second platform and a better standard of signalling, were necessary before the service could start, and were completed in January 1883. All of the lines built and brought into use were single track, with the exception of the link line between the Swindon stations and the connection at Marlborough, which were double track.

The Swindon, Marlborough and Andover Railway Company merged with the Swindon and Cheltenham Extension Railway Company in 1884 to form the Midland and South Western Junction Railway Company (M&SWJR). During the ensuing five years the company obtained further Acts giving it further powers and for other purposes.

Promoters try again for Lambourn - Act obtained and construction started

Back in Berkshire, the Lambourn Valley Railway had obtained an Act in August 1883 for a railway to run direct from Newbury station up the valley, not utilising the Didcot and Newbury line as had been proposed in the 1881 scheme. The Newbury Weekly News reported the first signs of construction in April 1885. However, another 13 years was to elapse before the railway would be completed and open to the public.

Newbury linked with Winchester

On 4 May 1885, just over three years after the opening of the line to Didcot, the line from Newbury to Winchester was opened by the Didcot, Newbury and Southampton Railway. The new line, single track throughout, left the Newbury - Hungerford line at Enborne Junction, just over a mile from Newbury and terminated at Cheesehill Station in Winchester, a distance of 25¼ miles from Enborne Junction. A further six years was to elapse before the line was extended to join the London and South Western Railway south of Winchester and thus provide, at last, a through route to Southampton.

Stations, all passing places, were provided at Woodhay, Highclere, Burghclere, Litchfield, Whitchurch and Sutton Scotney. Prior to the opening of the Didcot line, in 1882, alterations had been made at each end of Newbury station to provide bay platforms for the Didcot and Winchester trains. Stations were later provided at Kings Worthy (1909) and Worthy Down (open for public use in 1918). The line featured many long deep chalk cuttings through the Hampshire Downs and the 440 yard long Winchester Tunnel, immediately north of the platforms at Cheesehill Station. As with the Didcot – Newbury section, the line from Newbury to Winchester was built as double track, but only a single line was laid.

The line was worked by the GWR under an agreement with the DN&SR dated 14 August 1884 on the same terms as applied to the Didcot - Newbury section.

Newbury becomes a hub, another station succumbs to fire, the Great Western looks to improve the service to Weymouth

By 1885, then, Newbury had lines radiating north, east, south and west and had expectations of a branch line up the Lambourn Valley in the foreseeable future. Admittedly, the Winchester line was of little use for through freight, but for passengers London, and Reading with its connections, could easily be reached from the area south of Newbury. Passengers for Southampton and points beyond were faced with a walk between the two stations at Winchester, as quoted in timetables, of "about one mile".

Back on the Berks and Hants line, The Newbury Weekly News and Berkshire Chronicle reported in February 1888 that Midgham station, booking office and waiting room burnt down on 31 January **(Note 1)**.

In August 1889, the GWR took over the steamer service between Weymouth and the Channel Islands. As early as 1857, the GWR had worked with another company to provide services to Jersey and Guernsey from Weymouth.

Plans were laid to improve the train service from Paddington to Weymouth, but these took over 10 years to materialise, as we will shortly see.

Southampton at last - courtesy of a link with the London and South Western Railway

Newbury got its direct link to Southampton when, on 1 October 1891, the line between Winchester Cheesehill and Shawford Junction, on the L&SWR main line south of Winchester, was opened by the Didcot, Newbury and Southampton Railway. The line was built as a single line 2¼ miles long, with a 670 yard long viaduct across the Itchen Valley. South of Winchester, the route had been approved by the Act of August 1882, being part of the Southampton Extension; the link between this route and Shawford Junction, and the connection to the main line of the L&SWR at the junction, were approved by an Act of 7 August 1888. Total cost of the 44¾ miles of new lines from Didcot to Shawford Junction was £1¼ Million.

Under an Act of 26 July 1889, all un-constructed lines and works authorised by the DN&SR's 1882 act were abandoned, except the Aldermaston Branch, in which the GWR was said to still be interested. The branch was never built, however, and abandonment was authorised by an Act of 1891.

By an agreement of 10 October 1889, to which all three companies (DN&SR, GWR, L&SWR) were party, the L&SWR was bound to work the Shawford Junction Line; the agreement also included provisions for proper station accommodation at Southampton Docks station (later known as Southampton Terminus), the destination for trains from Newbury, to carry and accommodate at that station, and at all intermediate stations south of Winchester, DN&S traffic of all kinds to from or over the Shawford Junction line with all places on the DN&S and lines beyond north of Winchester. In November 1892, the L&SWR resolved to purchase the Southampton Docks Company.

Developments on the main line and Marlborough Branch

A direct link between the B&HER east of Devizes and Westbury was revived again in 1890 when a Great Western Railway Act of that year included an amended alignment of a part of the new link, again commencing in the parish of Urchfont, joining the line proposed in 1883 in the parish of East Coulston, a distance of 6¾ miles. A further four years would elapse before the route of the line would be finalised.

Major changes were planned for the Berks and Hants line when, in 1892, plans were announced for a reservoir in the Kennet Valley below Newbury, stretching to Aldermaston. The scheme would have involved a diversion of the railway for 10½ miles, including the stations at Thatcham, Midgham and Aldermaston, but was abandoned after opposition from all quarters.

Better times for Thatcham Station were to follow, however, when new station buildings were opened on 24 August 1893.

In 1894, the GWR obtained a further Act for the Stert and Westbury Railway; the Act was GWR (No 1) of 1894, S4. The GWR Act of 1883 had included an alignment for this route, part of which was later amended by the GWR Act of 1890. By connecting the line between Newbury and Devizes at a point west of Woodborough, near the village of Stert, directly with Westbury, the detour via Devizes and Trowbridge could be avoided. In addition, a more easily graded line could be provided and over 14 miles saved on the journey from Paddington via Newbury to Westbury, Yeovil and Weymouth. In due course, as had always been intended, the new "cut-off" line would form part of a direct route to the west.

Two openings took place in 1895. When the Basingstoke branch of the Berks and Hants Railway was opened in 1848, only one passenger station was provided, at Mortimer. Bramley had only been provided with a goods siding, but a passenger station was opened in April 1895. A few weeks earlier, on 10 March, a new curve just over a quarter of a mile in length was opened connecting the Trowbridge - Bath line with the Trowbridge - Chippenham line, to be known as the Bradford-on-Avon Loop. By this route, trains could travel directly from the Berks and Hants Extension line at Devizes to Bristol. Equally usefully from the operating point of view, trains between Chippenham and Bath could be diverted over the loop when their route was closed, for instance for work on Box Tunnel.

Thirty-five years of independent existence for the Marlborough Railway Company ended in 1896, when it was amalgamated with the GWR (which had run the trains on the line since its opening in 1864) as from 1 July 1896. The independent company was acquired by the offer of 120 GWR shares for each 100 of their stock. This was authorised by the GWR (Additional Powers) Act of 7 August 1896, S40 (Note 2).

New private sidings bring extra traffic to the line

A number of new private sidings were connected to the line between Reading and Holt Junction in the period covered by this chapter. As noted in the previous chapter, these were usually covered by Private Siding Agreements (PSAs); however the commencement dates of these are not necessarily the opening dates of such sidings, or dates of the first traffic. See Appendix 3 for full details of these Agreements.

There were a number of watermills on the River Kennet and its tributaries, many of which have survived as private houses and one as a very well-known theatre. Calcot Mill, on the outskirts of Reading, was served by a siding connected to the up line between Theale and Southcote Junction; the first PSA was in 1890, followed by a new one in 1898, reflecting a change of ownership.

Tile (or Tyle) Mill, west of Theale and south of the line, was served by a loop off the down line, from which, via a wagon turntable, a siding at right-angles to the main line served the mill. The loop and siding are believed to date from 1876; the first PSA is dated 1895. As at Calcot Mill, these sidings would have enabled corn to be delivered to the mill and flour to be shipped out.

There were two developments at Newbury. With demand increasing in the town, a new Gas Works was built by Newbury Corporation adjacent to the line, east of the goods yard. The construction of private sidings, followed by the PSA made in 1883, enabled coal to be imported and coke and other by-products to be dispatched. Adjacent to the goods yard, a second siding was established in 1894; the name on that PSA was William Skinner. As at the first siding, the main import was coal and the output malt.

There were no private sidings between Newbury and Devizes. West of the latter place, the seam of iron ore which gave rise to the Westbury Iron Works was also present in the area around Seend station, 4¼ miles west of Devizes. A siding established here was the subject of a PSA in 1887; the ownership changed in 1889 and in 1894 it was noted that the siding had not been used for some time.

Reading Station rebuilt for the Twentieth Century

Between 1895, when preparation work started, and 1899, Reading station was completely rebuilt, in the process converting it from a broad gauge-era single sided station to a station befitting its existing traffic and anticipated additional traffic from the new route to be provided to Westbury, to be described later in this chapter. The Berks and Hants line was accessible from all through lines and from the three bay platforms provided on the south side at the west end. Goods facilities were also improved during this period (Note 3).

Opening to Lambourn – and a tragedy

The independent Lambourn Valley Railway Company opened its line from Newbury to Lambourn, nearly 12½ miles, on 4 April 1898 (Note 4). Stations were provided at Speen, Stockcross & Bagnor, Boxford, Welford Park, West Shefford, East Garston, Eastbury and Lambourn. Initially, there were no crossing places. Basic goods facilities were provided at Boxford, Welford Park, West Shefford, East Garston and Lambourn. West Shefford was renamed Great Shefford in 1900.

The sharpest curve on the line was 20 chains radius and the steepest gradient was 1:60. The only major earthworks were at Speen, where the line passed under the roads now known as Speen Lane and Bath Road (A4).

The old Reading one-sided station, from which many journeys on the Berks and Hants line to Devizes or Trowbridge would have started. Seen after removal of the broad gauge rails (1892) and before work on the new station started in 1897 (GWR)

The new railway had its own line into Newbury station, running parallel with the main line from near West Fields into its own platform. These works, involving widening the cutting west of Newbury station, reconstruction of Bartholomew Street bridge and the provision of a new bay platform and other facilities at the old Newbury station, were built by the GWR and charged to the Lambourn company.

Regrettably, the opening week was marred by the death of two boys playing on the line at the bridge over the canal. The line had been unused for so long it had become a playground and a popular country walk **(Note 5)**.

The Marlborough and Grafton Railway opens - Cross-country trains avoid the Berks and Hants line and Savernake Station

Another railway adjacent to the Berks and Hants was opened in 1898, on 26 June. Trains on the Midland and South Western Junction Railway (M&SWJR) had suffered from having to use the Great Western Railway between

Savernake and Wolfhall Junction. In the course of time, the GWR's charges, methods of operation and general attitude had become unacceptable. The M&SWJR decided to build a deviation line to run directly from Marlborough to Grafton, and powers were sought by a company set up for the purpose. The appropriately named Marlborough and Grafton Railway Act of 7 August 1896 authorised a double line to connect these stations, passing over the Great Western Railway and the canal just east of Wolfhall Junction.

Gradients on the new line were easier than on the Marlborough Branch; to achieve this, a 647-yard tunnel was needed near Marlborough. The line then descended the hillside above the B&HER, coming close to the Branch at one point. After crossing the B&HER and the canal, a junction was made with the existing single line between Wolfhall Junction and Grafton; from this junction to Grafton the line was doubled. The adjacent railway and canal bridges were both on a substantial skew, as can be seen today in the case of the canal bridge. These bridges, of about 78ft and 68ft span respectively, consisted of steel plate girders, steel trough flooring and concrete abutments faced with brick.

Just over a year after opening, on 1 August 1899, the Marlborough and Grafton Railway was vested in the M&SWJR, which had worked the line from opening day. In its seven mile length was one station, known at the time as Savernake (M&SWJR) and located at a distance quoted in timetables of "about 250 yards" from the GWR station. The M&SWJR was so determined to be independent of the GWR in the area, that the link between Wolfhall Junction and Grafton had been closed on the day that the new railway opened. Business needs prevailed, however, and the link was re-opened for wagon transfers on 1 November 1900 and to all traffic on 2 July 1902.

A map of the entire southern section of the Midland and South-Western Junction Railway, from Swindon to Andover, as published by the Railway Clearing House in 1906, is given on page 70.

The Pewsey and Salisbury scheme revived – as a Light Railway

The GWR obtained a Light Railway Order for the Pewsey and Salisbury Railway on 6 August 1898, followed on 31 August by a Devizes Branch Order for a junction facing Devizes. The scheme was a revival of a scheme for which, as an ordinary railway, authorisation had been obtained in 1883 (see page 50). Whilst the intention was clearly to connect Pewsey and Salisbury and provide transport for the requirements for the War Department on Salisbury Plain, the opposition of that body meant that the Order was restricted to portions of the proposed line either side of the War Department's property. An extension of time, to seven years from 6 August 1898, was granted by the Pewsey and Salisbury Light Railway (Extension of Time) Order 1901 **(Note 6)**.

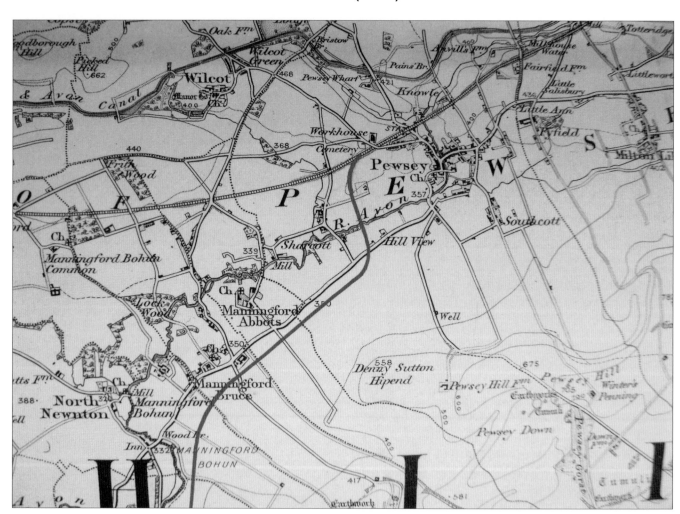

Route plan of the proposed Pewsey and Salisbury Light Railway at Pewsey, as authorised by the Light Railway Order (LRO) on 6 August 1898. Shortly afterwards, an LRO was obtained for a junction facing Devizes, known as the Devizes Branch Order (the plan on page 60 also refers) (Wiltshire and Swindon History Centre)

Improvements to the Berks and Hants Extension Railway – and a brand new railway

For the remainder of this chapter, the efforts of the GWR to provide a better link between the end of the double track Berks and Hants line at Hungerford and the Wilts, Somerset and Weymouth line at Westbury will be described. Work on the construction of the Stert and Westbury Railway started in 1897; a description of the project follows on page 58.

At the same time, a scheme for the improvement of the winding single-line Berks and Hants Extension line from Hungerford to the junction of the new line, 20 miles, was put in hand **(Note 7).** The GWR (Additional Powers) Act of 1897 authorised the purchase of lands at Hungerford and on the Extension line; included in the Act was authority to remove certain level crossings and replace by them by bridges as described below.

Below - Pauling & Co Ltd's locomotive 'Stanley' on a works train during the project to double the track beyond Hungerford, as described in the text. The work appears to be aimed at improving the drainage. The nearest track appears to be the original, being 'baulk road' converted from broad to standard gauge in 1874, whilst the other track is of the cross-sleeper type as was standard at the time. The location is probably between Pewsey and Patney & Chirton and the date 1899 or 1900 (Kevin Robertson collection)

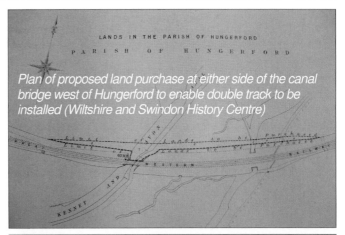

Plan of proposed land purchase at either side of the canal bridge west of Hungerford to enable double track to be installed (Wiltshire and Swindon History Centre)

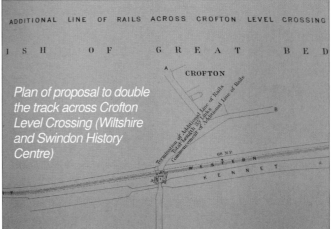

Plan of proposal to double the track across Crofton Level Crossing (Wiltshire and Swindon History Centre)

The old line was doubled throughout and the gradients improved by raising, lowering or diverting the line. The doubling was carried out in the following stages (dates of opening to traffic):

Hungerford to Bedwyn: 2 October 1898

Bedwyn to Wolfhall Junction: 8 January 1899

Wolfhall Junction to Savernake (GWR): 19 November 1899

Savernake (GWR) to Pewsey: 15 October 1899

Pewsey to Woodborough: 31 December 1899

Woodborough to Patney & Chirton (see below): 29 July 1900

At the point where the double line to Westbury commenced, a junction was created with the single line to Devizes, which thenceforth became a branch. At this location, known at the time as Stert, a station was built. Initially referred to as Patney Bridge, the station was named Patney & Chirton by the start of the passenger service.

At Hungerford, the platforms were realigned in 1897-8 and a new layout provided, with two new signal boxes. The existing main station building and the goods shed, both on the down side, were retained; a small wooden shelter was provided on the new up platform. Platforms at Bedwyn, Savernake and Pewsey were lengthened substantially. At Woodborough, there was insufficient room to lengthen the platforms due to the adjacent road bridge; although powers were sought to lengthen the bridge, the work was never carried out.

The old broad gauge road, converted to narrow gauge in 1874 and consisting of bridge rails bolted to longitudinal timbers, was relaid with new steel rail and cross sleepers. The radius of the sharpest curve was increased to 70 chains (about 1,500 yards) and the steepest grades were reduced. The most severe grades given in the 1950 Working Time Table are 1: 114 rising Hungerford - Bedwyn, 1:103 rising Wolfhall Junction - Savernake and 1:132 falling Savernake - Burbage. The level of the railway at Savernake, the summit between London and Westbury, had been dictated by the need to cross the summit level of the Kennet and Avon Canal, which was in tunnel at that point.

Bridges carrying the track were widened to take the second line. In Hungerford, two new spans were provided across the High Street; the bridge crossing the canal to the west of the town was rebuilt. Road bridges over the line had been built for double track. The remaining level crossings on public roads were replaced by bridges; the only exception

On the new line between Stert and Westbury, work is in progress excavating a new cutting by purely manual means, the muck being removed in small tip wagons on a narrow gauge track laid for the purpose and moved as the work progressed – a 'temporary way' (Kevin Robertson collection)

In these two photographs, a steam shovel is being used to excavate the bulk of the material in the cuttings, the material being moved out in two different types of wagon. Manual labour was apparently used to create stable cutting slopes according to the type of soil encountered. The track appears to be standard gauge and there is a 'temporary way' at ground level in the lower photograph, with second-hand rails (from the old broad gauge rails removed in 1874) spiked to the sleepers (Kevin Robertson collection)

being the public right of way on the Roman Road at Crofton. At Little Bedwyn the road was stopped up and diverted over a new bridge, with a footbridge being provided at the site of the crossing. The bridge south of Great Bedwyn (Mill Bridge) was also built at this time to replace a level crossing as indicated by the plates attached to the parapets of the steel span indicating the maker and year of manufacture. The requirement to replace these crossings was included in the Great Western Railway (Additional Powers) Act 1897. Extensive alterations were carried out at all stations, including as previously mentioned lengthening of platforms to cater for the expected increase in traffic. Estimated cost of these works was £30,000.

The contractor for both the Berks and Hants Extension doubling and the new line from Stert to Westbury was Pauling and Co Ltd of 26 Victoria Street, Westminster.

The new line - Stert and Westbury

The new line was 13¾ miles long from the point at which it diverged from the old line between Woodborough and Devizes close to the 81¾ milepost from Paddington, near the village of Stert. As the new double track line effectively started at the new station Patney & Chirton at 81 miles from Paddington, actual length of new construction was 14½

miles. It shortened the distance from Paddington to Westbury, Yeovil and Weymouth by 14¼ miles. At Westbury, it joined the Wilts, Somerset and Weymouth line just to the north of the station (Note 8).

The steepest gradient on the new line was 1:222 and the sharpest curve 60 chains radius (about 1,300 yards); 39 bridges were built. The depth of cuttings and height of embankments were considerable in order to achieve the standard laid down at the time. As the line ran through Greensand and Clay, on the edge of Salisbury Plain, there was some trouble with slips (Note 8).

Beyond the new station Patney & Chirton, the line to Devizes became a separate single line, the station being a junction although not so named.

Initially the line ran alongside the Devizes line for about a mile, then passed through a deep cutting, 1¾ miles in length, beyond which a passenger and goods station was provided at Lavington for the villages of Market Lavington and West Lavington, each over a mile by road to the south. Between a point about a mile from the junction and Lavington, the line is on the ruling grade of 1:222, falling towards Westbury. Between Lavington and Edington, the other station provided on the new line, a 120-yard long brick

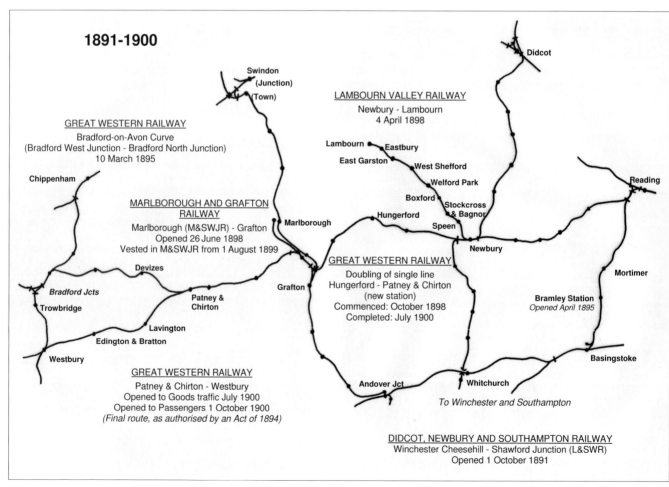

viaduct of 8 spans was built. Edington, called Edington & Bratton by the start of passenger services, was also provided with passenger and goods accommodation. Between just west of Lavington and Westbury station, the line is level except for about 1¾ miles between Edington and Westbury, falling at 1:500 towards Westbury.

Westbury station, now only 95½ miles from Paddington, previously 109¾ miles, was entirely rebuilt and remodelled. Two island platforms, each 600ft long and 40ft wide, were constructed, reached by a subway from the approach road at the lower level; large waiting and refreshment rooms were provided at platform level. Westbury was already served by a fast cross-country service twice a day from Portsmouth and Southampton via the Severn Tunnel to Newport and Cardiff. In addition local trains ran to Bristol, Swindon,

Devizes and the Berks and Hants line, Salisbury and Weymouth.

Ample goods accommodation and exchange sidings were also provided. Blast furnaces had been established in 1857 for smelting the iron ore found in the vicinity; although within a year of the arrival of the new line, the Westbury Iron Works was closed down, the New Westbury Iron Company was formed in 1903 and breathed new life into the iron industry in the town.

The new line, the Stert and Westbury Railway, was opened to goods traffic on 29 July 1900 and to passenger traffic on 1 October 1900. Facilities at the three new stations were available from the opening of the line. However, at Patney & Chirton, although no goods facilities were provided at opening, a small goods yard was added later, open to traffic

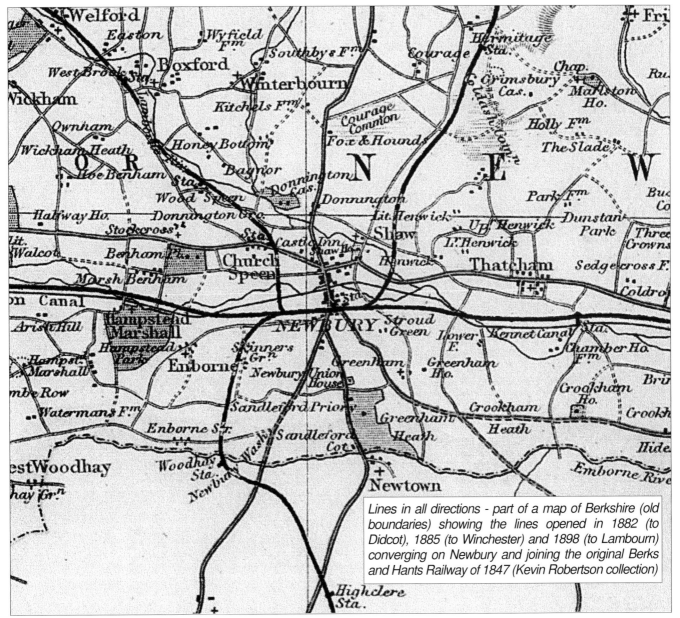

Lines in all directions - part of a map of Berkshire (old boundaries) showing the lines opened in 1882 (to Didcot), 1885 (to Winchester) and 1898 (to Lambourn) converging on Newbury and joining the original Berks and Hants Railway of 1847 (Kevin Robertson collection)

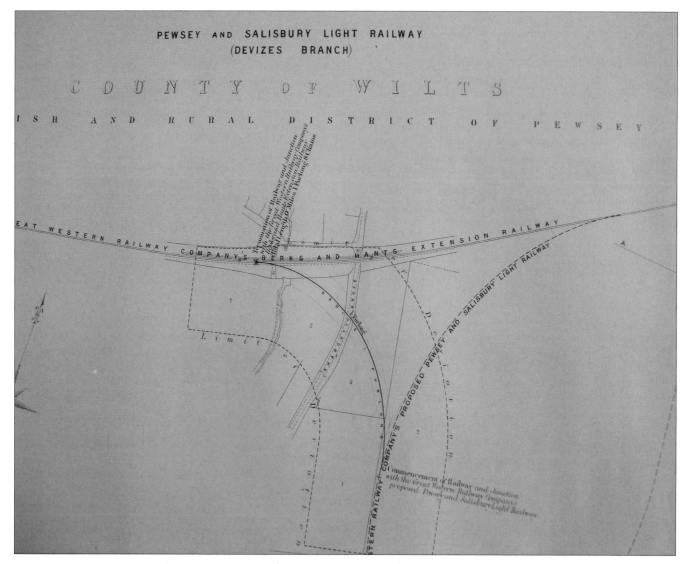

Plan of the proposed junction between the authorised Pewsey and Salisbury Light Railway and the erstwhile Berks and Hants Extension Railway at Pewsey, as authorised by the Devizes Branch Order of 31 August 1898 (Wiltshire and Swindon History Centre)

from 1 October 1904. Here, also, a military platform on its own siding was added in July 1909. The platforms at Lavington were lengthened in 1903, making them more suitable for military traffic and for serving long-distance trains.

As previously stated, the new line formed a "cut-off" for trains from Paddington via Newbury to Westbury, Yeovil and Weymouth, saving over 14 miles compared with the route via Devizes and Trowbridge. In addition, the new line

was double track and more easily graded than the old route.

The next decade, the Edwardian era, would bring further significant changes to the lines described in these first four chapters. For convenience, and following the custom of the time, the railway from Reading to Devizes will be described as 'the Berks & Hants line' whereas the new line from Patney & Chirton to Westbury will be described as 'the Stert and Westbury line'.

Opposite page - *A horse-drawn tram, driver, conductor and passengers, together with some local boys, pose for the photographer in Oxford Road, Reading. The tram has just passed under the Berks and Hants Railway bridge. Dated 1893, this view pre-dates Reading West station, later to be built on the embankment to the right of the bridge, by 13 years. See Chapter 6 for a description of the rebuilding of the bridge in 1938 (Reading Libraries)*

NOTES

NOTE 1: MIDGHAM STATION

Newbury Weekly News 2 February 1888, Berkshire Chronicle 4 February 1888 reported that Midgham station, booking office and waiting room burnt down on 31 January.

A Pictorial Record of Great Western Architecture A Vaughan 1977, plates 48 and 514 illustrate a handsome station building which was clearly a replacement for the wooden original, although the caption states that this was the original station.

NOTE 2: MARLBOROUGH RAILWAY COMPANY

GWR Magazine August 1896 - (Half-yearly Report of Directors)

NOTE 3: READING NEW STATION

GWR Magazine August 1896 - "tenders will be invited shortly for the construction of the new passenger station"; December 1896 - "contract for the new station at Reading has at last been signed!"; August 1897 - "the erection of new stations at ...... Reading ...... have made good progress"; August 1899 – "the reconstruction of the station at .... Reading .... is well advanced".

Railway Magazine September 1897 – "Erection of new stations (including Reading) making good progress"; January 1898 – "Meanwhile, the new Reading Station is being built and others remodelled"; June 1899 - Reading New Station GWR – plans of old and new and train services.

NOTE 4: LAMBOURN VALLEY RAILWAY

Railway Magazine May 1898: "The Lambourn Valley Light Railway was opened on April 2. It branches from the GWR at Newbury, and there are six intermediate stations ...... The sharpest curve on the line is 20 chains radius and the steepest gradient 1: 60."

"The Lambourn Valley Railway" (see **Further Reading**): "The private opening was fixed for Saturday, April 2 1898, the full public opening taking place on the following Monday, April 4."

NOTE 5: DEATHS ON THE LAMBOURN VALLEY RAILWAY

A very serious accident occurred on Good Friday, April 8, 1898, during the first week of the train service. The line had been without trains for so long that the section between West Fields and Speen had become a playground for children and a favourite walk for adults. Two boys, aged 11 and 13, were playing on the bridge over the canal and were crossing the track to follow the progress of a boat when the 2.15pm from Lambourn came upon them. It was said that the driver and fireman were both distracted by the sight of three women walking on the line some distance beyond the canal bridge. One boy was killed almost instantly and the other, severely injured, died later that day. A full account of the accident, the subsequent inquest and the burial services for the two boys is given in the Newbury Weekly News for Thursday 14 April, 1898. The boys were buried in Newtown Cemetery.

NOTE 6: PEWSEY AND SALISBURY LIGHT RAILWAY

GWR Magazine August 1897: "Order authorising the construction of a Light Railway between Pewsey and Salisbury in the County of Wilts", Paddington Station 26 July 1897.

Ibid: July 1898: Notice of Special General Meeting ...... following Order will be submitted ..... "Order authorising the construction of a Light Railway in the Parish of Pewsey in the County of Wilts", Paddington Station 25 July 1898.

Ibid: August 1898 (Half-yearly Report): Includes reference to "the order for the construction of a light railway ...... has, in consequence of the opposition of

Theale station taken from the road bridge, looking towards Reading. Theale was one of two stations (the other was Aldermaston) built in the so-called 'chalet' style. As part of the general improvements to the line in the 1897 – 1900 period, the tracks through the station have been re-aligned to the normal standard-gauge spacing; this has necessitated widening the platforms. The photograph is believed to date from the turn of the century or soon after (John Allen collection)

the War Department, been restricted, unless with their consent, to the portions of the proposed line between Pewsey and the northern boundary of their property on one hand and Salisbury and the southern boundary of their property on the other. At the present the War Office will not allow us to pass absolutely through their territory, but we may hope for further developments within a reasonable time". At a later stage of the Meeting ..... "Then the votes of the proprietors are asked for ...... Pewsey and Salisbury Light Railway £50,000".

Ibid: January 1899: Notice of Half-Yearly General Meeting - "... a resolution will be submitted to the proprietors to sanction the creation and issue of the capital authorised by "The Great Western Railway (Pewsey and Salisbury) Light Railway Order 1898" and the exercise of borrowing powers and the creation and issue of debenture stock."

Ibid: February 1901: At a Special General meeting, which followed the Half-Yearly General Meeting on 14 February 1901, it was agreed that the following Light Railway (Draft) Order be submitted: "Order for extending the respective times limited for the Compulsory Purchase of Lands and for the Construction of Light Railways authorised by the GWR (Pewsey and Salisbury) Light Railway Order 1898 and the Pewsey and Salisbury (Devizes Branch) Light Railway Order 1898.".

Railway Magazine April 1901 p313: under "The "Greater" Western Railway": "... In Wiltshire, two short branches are to be constructed: One from Pewsey, on the Berks and Hants main line, south to Upavon; and another north from near Salisbury to Durrington, near to Amesbury and the famous Stonehenge. It seems as though these two lines might be continued to meet each other, and so provide a much shorter way to Salisbury." A table following states the length of these two lines as 6 and 10 miles respectively and their object as "local".

Ibid: September 1901 p287: under "What the Railways are Doing" – "The Great Western Railway has at the present time the following lines under construction: ...... (inter alia) Pewsey and Salisbury Light Railway ......"

Ibid: March 1902 p276: under "What the Railways are Doing" – "In addition to (expenditure quoted) the Great Western Railway estimates to expend £200,000 during the same period (six months) on the following new lines, etc., now under construction : ...... (inter alia) Pewsey and Salisbury Light Railway ......"

NOTE 7: DOUBLING OF LINE, Hungerford to Stert

GWR Magazine January 1897 – "Considerable progress has been made with the works in connection with the doubling between Hungerford and Stert and to the uninitiated eye little appears to be wanting towards its completion but the removal of earthworks in places and the laying of the permanent way."

Ibid: August 1905 p143: "The commencement, in 1897, of the widening and improvement of the Berks and Hants line between Hungerford and Stert; previous to 1897 a double line existed from Reading to Hungerford only, the line from the latter point to Devizes being single, and in many places both steep and tortuous. The length of line to be doubled was 19½ miles, and the work was divided into two contracts – the first from Hungerford to Savernake, and the second from Savernake to Stert. Both contracts were carried out by Messrs. Pauling and Co., of Westminster, and were completed in sections, the last length being opened for traffic on July 29 1900."

Railway Magazine March 1898: ".... the Company proposes to spend in the near future on improvements ...... the following works: Doubling between Hungerford and Stert: £30,000"; May 1899 – noted good progress with construction of the Stert and Westbury Railway and the doubling of the Berks and Hants line.

NOTE 8: THE STERT AND WESTBURY LINE

GWR Magazine January 1897: "Reference is made in another column to the loop line from the Berks and Hants line to the Weymouth line which will form part of the new route to the West of England. We are now able to give some further particulars concerning the new line, the construction of which will, we understand, be commenced almost immediately. The line will be double line throughout and will leave the present Berks and Hants line at a point near the 81½ mp and about four miles and a half the London side of Devizes. From the junction, which will be known as Stert Junction, it will pursue a fairly direct course to Westbury, skirting the Salisbury Plain on the way. There will be two stations, the first at West Lavington, four miles and a half from Stert Junction and the other at Edington, nine miles from the junction.

"The stations will be very similar in arrangement. There will be the usual up and down platforms connected by a footbridge, a goods shed with connections to up and down lines and a crossover road and refuge sidings.

*Three views of Aldermaston station. Unlike the situation at Theale, the tracks have retained the spacing inherited from the broad-gauge era and the roofs of the buildings extend to the platform edges. In the **upper** picture, the water-softening plant (see Chapter 5) may be seen above the roof of the main building. In the **lower right** picture, it can be seen that both sidings consist of old broad-gauge 'baulk road', altered to standard gauge in 1874. The upper photograph was taken after the installation of the water softening plant in 1904, probably during the ensuing decade; the other photographs were probably taken at the same time (John Allen collection)*

"Near West Lavington it is proposed to provide water troughs, similar to those on the main line near Goring and Bristol. From Stert Junction the new line will fall towards Westbury with a uniform gradient of 1:225 for 5 miles; beyond that distance the gradients, although still falling in the same direction, will be slight or level. The total length of the loop will be rather over 13 miles, and the distance from Westbury to Paddington by the new route will be about 94¾ miles as against 101 miles 15 chains (about 101¼ miles) by way of Devizes and 109 miles 61 chains (about 109¾ miles) by the main line and Chippenham.

"As far as we can ascertain, there will, in the ordinary course, be no place at which it will be necessary to cause speed to be reduced between Southcote Junction (two miles beyond Reading) and Westbury, as the present single line from Hungerford to Stert will be doubled and the junction at Stert will be arranged in favour of the new line."

As noted in the text on page 58, published gradient diagrams give a gradient of 1:222 from Stert, with two short sections of 1:264.

<u>Railway Magazine</u> Volume 1 December 1897: "Actively engaged on Stert and Westbury line (13m 67c)"; April and May 1899 – noted good progress with construction of the Stert and Westbury Railway and the doubling of the Berks and Hants line.

<u>GWR Magazine</u> August 1898 (Half-yearly Report): Then the votes of the proprietors are asked for ...... Westbury Station £30,000

Ibid: September 1899: "The new link between Stert and Westbury is nearly completed, and will be opened for goods traffic soon after Christmas."

Ibid: August 1905 P143: The construction of the connecting link between Stert (or Patney and Chirton) on the Berks and Hants line and Westbury station on the Wilts, Somerset and Weymouth line: The construction of this line was started in 1897, and it was opened for goods traffic on July 29 1900 and for passenger traffic on October 1 of that year. It is 14½ miles in length and whilst the country through which it passes is not a difficult one from an engineering point of view, some extensive slips both in the cuttings and on the embankments gave trouble, and delayed the completion of the line some months. Messrs. Pauling and Co. was the contractor.

The apparent discrepancy in length of the new line as described in the GWR Magazines from 1897 to 1905 will be noted. Both the length of 13 miles of new line and the mileage to Westbury are stated incorrectly in January 1897. These figures should be 14½ and 95½ miles (to the nearest quarter-mile) respectively. As the mileages via the old routes are stated correctly, it is possible that incorrect or out-of-date figures for the new line were given to the magazine at the earlier date.

Three views of Midgham Station. The earliest, **right**, shows the laying of cross-sleeper track on the up line, replacing the old baulk road – the down line is yet to be done. The signal box was new in 1897; it is likely that the photograph was taken soon after as it is believed that the entire baulk road was replaced before the Stert and Westbury line was opened and the Berks and Hants became the main route to Weymouth. The main, **lower**, photograph, taken after the track works were completed, shows the unique style of station building which replaced that burnt down in 1888. The

higher roof is that of the goods shed. The improved edge of the platform will also be noted. In the **middle left** photograph, quiet is resumed after the departure of an up train (Upper and lower – Kevin Robertson collection; middle – West Berkshire Museum)

LINES IN ALL DIRECTIONS 1875 - 1900

Thatcham Station, rebuilt in 1893, looking towards Reading. The photograph was probably taken between the turn of the Century and the first development at Colthrop in 1912 (West Berkshire Museum)

ACTS AND LIGHT RAILWAY ORDERS

Didcot, Newbury and Southampton Junction Railway Act, 24 July 1876 (39 & 40 Vic I, c.184) (extension of time for purchasing the land and completing the railway)

Swindon, Marlborough and Andover Railway Act, 16 July 1878 (41 & 42 Vic I, c.13) (extension of time)

Swindon, Marlborough and Andover Railway Act, 3 July 1879 (42 & 43 Vic I, c.91) (new or deviation lines)

Swindon, Marlborough and Andover Railway Act, 29 June 1880 (43 & 44 Vic I, c.18) (further powers)

Didcot, Newbury and Southampton Junction Railway Act, 9 July 1880 (43 & 44 Vic I, c.47) (further powers)

Swindon, Marlborough and Andover Railway Act, 10 August 1882 (45 & 46 Vic I, c.195) (further powers, including those to compel the GWR to put Savernake Station in order and to install block telegraph on the Marlborough Branch)

Didcot, Newbury and Southampton Junction Railway Act, 10 August 1882 (45 & 46 Vic I, c.197) (conferring further powers and enabling the railway to be extended to Southampton and Aldermaston)

Great Western Railway (Additional Powers) Act, 19 August 1882, S46 (45 & 46 Vic I, c.214) (Berks and Hants Extension Railway vested in Great Western Railway)

Pewsey and Salisbury Railway Act, 16 July 1883 (46 & 47 Vic I, c.113) (authorisation for the railway)

Swindon, Marlborough and Andover Railway Act, 16 July 1883 (46 & 47 Vic I, c.121) (further powers, including those relating to Marlborough to Savernake)

Didcot, Newbury and Southampton Railway Act, 16 July 1883 (46 & 47 Vic I, c.129) (consolidation of capital and change of name of company)

Lambourn Valley Railway Act, 2 August 1883 (46 & 47 Vic I, c.176) (Act of Incorporation)

Great Western Railway Act, 20 August 1883 (46 & 47 Vic I, c.193) (authority to make and maintain certain ways and works, etc) *(no work started)*

Swindon, Marlborough and Andover and Swindon and Cheltenham Extension Railway Companies (Amalgamation) Act, 23 June 1884, S4 (47 & 48 Vic I, c.64) (amalgamation from date of Act)

Didcot, Newbury and Southampton Railway (Extension of Time) Act, 16 July 1885 (48 & 49 Vic I, c.131)

Didcot, Newbury and Southampton Railway (Money) Act, 6 August 1885 (48 & 49 Vic I, c.176)

Pewsey and Salisbury Railway (Extension of Time) Act, 4 June 1886 (49 & 50 Vic I, c.28)

Midland and South Western Junction Railway Act, 25 September 1886 (50 Vic I, c.46) (further powers)

Midland and South Western Junction Railway Act, 23 May 1887 (50 & 51 Vic I, c.42) (further powers)

Didcot, Newbury and Southampton Railway Act (Extension of Time) Act, 23 August 1887 (50 & 51 Vic I, c.181) (further powers (extension of time))

Tramway Orders Confirmation (No. 1) Act 28 June 1888 (51 & 52 Vic I, c.64) – Newbury and Lamborne Tramway (Release of Deposit) Order 1888

Lambourn Valley Railway Act, 24 July 1888 (51 & 52 Vic I, c.139) (further powers)

Didcot, Newbury and Southampton Railway Act, 7 August 1888 (51 & 52 Vic I, c.147) (further powers including link between Southampton Extension and Shawford Junction)

Didcot, Newbury and Southampton Railway Act, 26 July 1889 (52 & 53 Vic I, c.102) (abandonment of all un-constructed lines and works authorised by the 1882 Act, except the Aldermaston Branch)

Midland and South Western Junction Railway Act, 12 August 1889 (52 & 53 Vic I, c.163) (abandon certain portions of the railway and other purposes)

Great Western Railway Act, 4 August 1890 (53 & 54 Vic I, c. 159) (S2: changes to new line to Westbury authorised by GWR 1883 Act)

Pewsey and Salisbury Railway (Abandonment) Act, 11 May 1891 (54 & 55 Vic I, c.10) (abandonment of railway)

Didcot, Newbury and Southampton Railway Act, 11 June 1891 (54 & 55 Vic I, c.42) (abandonment of Aldermaston Branch)

Lambourn Valley Railway Act, 27 June 1892 (55 & 56 Vic I, c.164) (to revive and extend the time for completing the railway)

Lambourn Valley Railway Act, 20 July 1894 (57 & 58 Vic I, c.138) (extension of time)

Great Western Railway (No 1) Act, 31 July 1894, (57 & 58 Vic I, c.143) (S4: Authorisation of final scheme for the Stert and Westbury Railway)

Great Western Railway Act, 6 July 1895 (58 & 59 Vic I, c.118) (maintenance, management and use of Lambourn Valley Railway)

Marlborough and Grafton Railway Act, 7 August 1896 (59 & 60 Vic I c.230) (authorisation for the railway)

GWR (Additional Powers) Act, 7 August 1896, S40 (59 & 60 Vic I, c.232) (amalgamation of Marlborough Railway with the Great Western Railway)

Midland and South Western Junction Railway Act, 15 July 1897 (60 & 61 Vic I, c.128) (abandon a certain railway and other purposes)

CHAPTER REFERENCES

Deposited Documents (see Chapter 1 for interpretation of references)

(DP/375; A1/371/127MS) Swindon, Marlborough and Andover Railway (deviations) (1879)

(Q/RUm 161; DP/371) Didcot, Newbury and Southampton Junction Railway (1879)

(Q/RUm 165; DP/384) Didcot, Newbury and Southampton Junction Railway (New Railways and other works) (1881)

(Q/RUm 166) Newbury and Lambourn (Light Railway to connect with D&NSR north of Newbury and run via Shaw to continue up the Lambourn Valley) (1881)

(DP/398; A1/371/131MS) Bristol and London and South Western Junction (1882)

Didcot, Newbury and Southampton Railway Act, 6 August 1897 (60 & 61 Vic I, c.213) (further powers (including doubling of line Didcot – Winchester))

Great Western Railway (Additional Powers) Act, 6 August 1897 (60 & 61 Vic I, c.248) (reference Lambourn Valley Railway)

Great Western Railway (Pewsey and Salisbury) Light Railway Order, 6 August 1898

Pewsey and Salisbury (Devizes Branch) Light Railway Order, 31 August 1898

Great Western Railway (New Works) Act, 12 August 1898 (61 & 62 Vic I, c.254) (S4: Castle Cary and Langport Railway (see Chapter 5))

Midland and South Western Junction Railway Act, 1 August 1899, (62 & 63 Vic I, c.178) (S6: Amalgamation of Marlborough and Grafton Railway with the Midland and South Western Junction Railway, from date of Act)

Above - *Kintbury station from the level crossing. Probably early Twentieth Century - track has been relaid but the platforms, while clearly lengthened since the station was opened in 1847, have not yet received their new edge copings (see later photograph in Chapter 5) (John Allen collection)*

Opposite page - *The classic photograph of an up train at Newbury old station, and the new running-in board. This much-published photograph is included not only because of its extreme relevance but because it is based on a much better original version of the postcard. The train, buildings and surroundings are all clearer. The locomotive is a '3232' class 2-4-0, built 1892-3 (H J Patterson Rutherford, West Berkshire Museum collection)*

Below - *Hungerford station c. 1892 before the tracks were re-aligned and the platforms altered as described in the text. The buildings replaced the originals of 1847, including those burnt down in 1867. The new station is believed to have been opened in 1871 - the style is similar to other GWR stations opened around that time. Baulk road track has yet to be replaced (Hungerford Virtual Museum)*

(Q/RUm 175) Lambourn Valley Rly (via Speen - similar to final route) (1882)

(A1/371/132MS) Great Western Railway: Stert to Westbury (1882)

(DP/403; A1/371/133MS) Pewsey Salisbury and Southampton Rly (1882)

(A1/371/136MS) Bristol and London and South Western Junction Railway (1883)

(DP/406; A1/371/139MS) Swindon, Marlborough and Andover Railway: Marlborough to Savernake (1883)

(Hants 4M92/Q/2/6; A1/371/141MS) Collingbourne and Avon Valley (1887)

(A1/371/142MS) Midland and South Western Junction Railway (1888)

(A1/371/144MS) Great Western Railway No 2 (Stert and Westbury) (1889)

(Q/RUm 190) Lambourn Valley Railway (deviations) (1889)

(A1/371/145MS) Great Western Railway No 1 (Stert and Westbury) (1893)

(Q/RUm 219) Lambourn Valley Railway (alterations) (1894)

(A1/371/150MS) Marlborough and Grafton Railway (1895)

(A1/371/154MS) Pewsey and Salisbury Light Railway (1897)

(A1/371/156MS) Pewsey and Salisbury Light Railway (deviation & Devizes Section) (1898)

(DP/546; A1/371/158MS) Midland and South Western Junction Railway: Ludgershall and Military Camps Light Railway (1898)

(A1/371/159MS) Great Western Railway (relevant parts - Diversion of footpath at Urchfont; Additional land at Beechingstoke for track doubling work) (1899)

(Hants 10M57/TR14; 23M72/TR13) Highclere, Kingsclere and Basingstoke Light Railway (1899-1901)

(A1/371/161MS) Great Western Railway (relevant part - Woodborough (lengthening of bridge)) (1900)

PUBLISHED REFERENCES

History of the Great Western Railway Volume 2 1863 – 1921

E T MacDermot Revised by C R Clinker (Ian Allan 1964)

How the Great Western came to Berkshire – A Railway History 1833 – 1882

Daphne Phillips (Reading Libraries 1975)

The Golden Age of the Great Western Railway 1895-1914

Tim Bryan (Patrick Stephens Ltd 1991)

The Great Western Railway in the 19th Century

O S Nock (Ian Allan 1972)

Time Tables of the Great Western Railway 1902 – January, February, March and April (reprint)

Newbury Weekly News

4.8.1881 Didcot, Newbury and Southampton Junction Railway – Important Meeting (General Meeting of Shareholders 28.7.1881); A Trip with the Directors on the New Line (Special train on railway under construction)

Ibid: 11.8.1881 The Swindon, Marlborough and Andover Railway (From a Correspondent – a trip over the new line from Marlborough to Swindon)

Ibid: 6.4.1882 The New Railway – Opening on Wednesday next; The Didcot and Newbury Railway – Official Inspection; The Didcot, Newbury and Southampton (Extension) Bill (progress report)

Ibid: 6.4.1882: The Lambourn Valley Railway Bill (progress report)

Ibid: 6.4.1882 Berks and Hants Extension Railway (report of Half-Yearly Meeting)

Ibid: 13.4.1882 The Newbury and Didcot Railway - Editorial; Ditto - Opening Ceremony

Ibid: 4.12.1884 Serious Railway Accident – Six Men Injured

Ibid: 30.4.1885 Newbury, Didcot and Southampton Railway – Opening from Newbury to Winchester (to take place the following day)

Ibid: 7.5.1885 Didcot, Newbury and Southampton Railway – Opening to Winchester (Editorial)

Ibid: 2.2.1888: Fire at Midgham Station – The Booking Office Destroyed (January 31)

Berkshire Chronicle

4.2.1888: Serious Fire at Midgham Station

Newbury Weekly News

23.2.1888 – A Train Blocked at Pewsey (Snowstorm); Lambourn – Bill passed by the Examiner

Ibid 6.3.1890 (extract only): Report of meeting (Inadequate railway station accommodation and necessity of certain improvements to the train service)

Ibid: 24.3.1898 Accident on the Lambourn Railway – A Boy Killed

Ibid: 31.3.1898 Official Inspection of the Lambourn Valley Railway

Ibid: 7.4.1898 Lambourn Valley Railway – Inspection by Board of Trade – The Inaugural Train – Opening Ceremony at Lambourn

Ibid: 14.4.1898 – Shocking Accident on the Lambourn Valley Railway – Two Boys Killed on Good Friday

Ibid: 7.7.1898 – Covering-in of the Lambourn Platform at Newbury Station

Opposite page, above - *The Berks and Hants Extension Railway station at Bedwyn, situated in the village of Great Bedwyn. Track and platform improvements indicate an earliest date of around 1900. The number of railway employees is impressive for a station with only one siding and no goods shed (John Allen collection)*

Below - *The attractive small station at Bedwyn, seen from the adjacent overbridge. This view may pre-date the one above, as the track does not look in such good condition. Maximum use is being made of the minimal siding storage available; no goods shed was ever provided here (John Gale collection)*

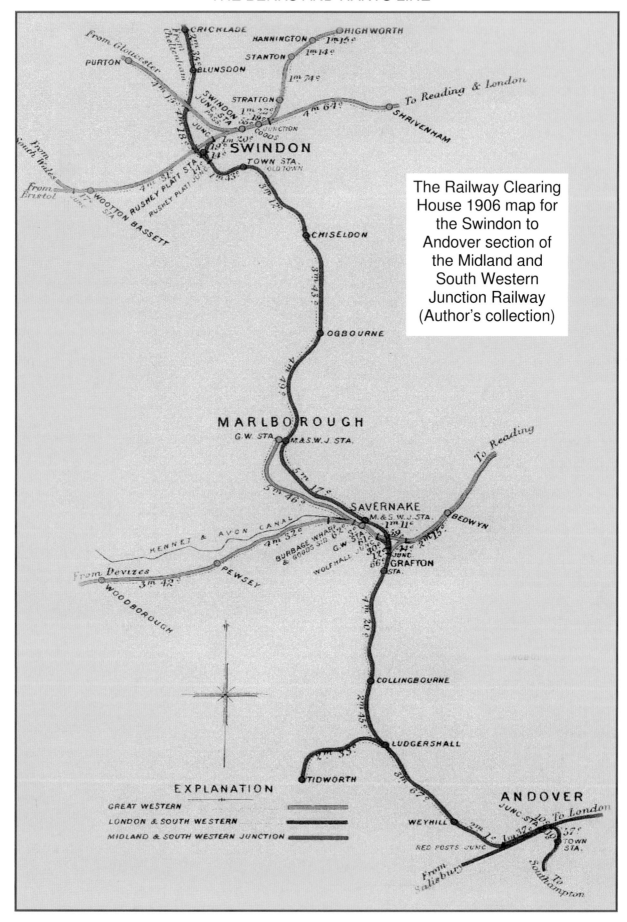

The Railway Clearing House 1906 map for the Swindon to Andover section of the Midland and South Western Junction Railway (Author's collection)

A much larger version of Bedwyn's station at Savernake, which included a refreshment room. The station at this time was known as Savernake (GWR); a separate station served the Midland and South Western Junction Railway's line from Marlborough to Andover Junction. In the 1897-1900 period, the track and platforms were improved and a footbridge and a small building with waiting rooms and toilets on the down (left side) platform were provided.

Pewsey station, with the main station building of an intermediate size between those at Bedwyn and Savernake. In this view westwards, the stone-built platform walls have been raised and new edge copings provided. It is believed that the lamps are lit by gas - Pewsey had its own gasworks. The photograph can be dated to the turn of the Century, shortly after the completion of the platform works.
(both, John Allen collection)

Above - *Woodborough station seen from the adjacent road bridge, with all the staff on duty scattered about the station. As the tracks have not yet been relaid with new rail and cross sleepers, the photograph may be dated around the time of the track doubling (1899-1900), or even before. The station building is smaller than those at Savernake and Pewsey but slightly larger than that at Bedwyn.*

Below - *The original station at Devizes, with its all-over roof similar to that at Newbury, as it would have appeared after the abolition of the broad gauge in 1874, with the tracks through the platforms retaining the old baulk road. In a reversal of the situation at Aldermaston, the nearby siding has subsequently been relaid. The saddle tank is on a local train. Photograph can be dated before the station was rebuilt in 1909-1910. (Both - John Allen collection)*

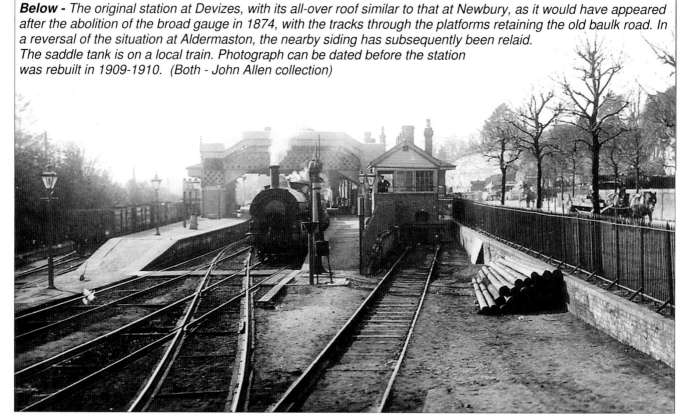

5
PROGRESS AND CONSOLIDATION
1901-1922

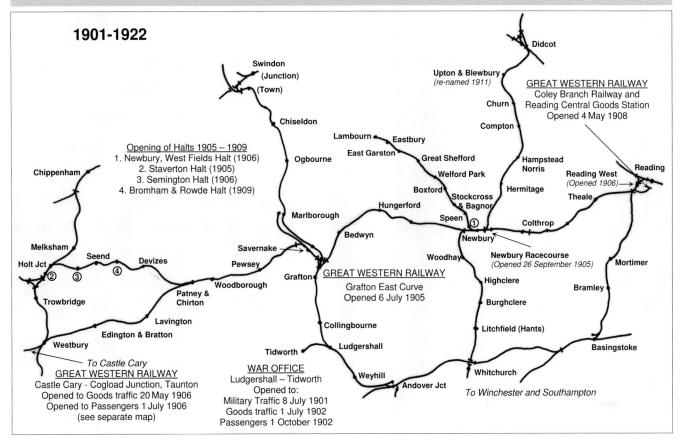

1901-1922

Opening of Halts 1905 – 1909
1. Newbury, West Fields Halt (1906)
2. Staverton Halt (1905)
3. Semington Halt (1906)
4. Bromham & Rowde Halt (1909)

GREAT WESTERN RAILWAY
Coley Branch Railway and
Reading Central Goods Station
Opened 4 May 1908

Upton & Blewbury
(re-named 1911)

Reading West
(Opened 1906)

GREAT WESTERN RAILWAY
Grafton East Curve
Opened 6 July 1905

Newbury Racecourse
(Opened 26 September 1905)

To Castle Cary
GREAT WESTERN RAILWAY
Castle Cary - Cogload Junction, Taunton
Opened to Goods traffic 20 May 1906
Opened to Passengers 1 July 1906
(see separate map)

WAR OFFICE
Ludgershall – Tidworth
Opened to:
Military Traffic 8 July 1901
Goods traffic 1 July 1902
Passengers 1 October 1902

To Winchester and Southampton

Newbury benefits from the improved services to Weymouth

With the opening of the new Stert - Westbury cut-off to passenger trains in October 1900, as described in the previous chapter, London - Weymouth expresses were first diverted to run via Newbury and the cut-off for the summer service of 1901. Initially, Newbury was served by two Paddington - Weymouth trains slipping coaches there; in the other direction the first Weymouth – Paddington train called. By 1910, the situation had improved; the morning train from Paddington called at Newbury and two later trains slipped coaches there, whilst three trains from Weymouth called at Newbury. ('Slip coaches' - see **Glossary**.)

The distance from London to Weymouth by the new line was reduced to 154½ miles, a saving of 14¼ miles over the old route, and only 11¾ miles longer than the L&SWR route via Southampton. The three daily express trains were timed to do the journey in less than four hours in each direction **(Note 1)**.

The importance of Weymouth from a railway traffic point of view dates from 1889, when the GWR took over the service of the Weymouth and Channel Islands Steam Packet Company. Sea journeys were considerably accelerated and twin-screw (twin-propeller) electrically lit steamers were provided. The train service, which at that time ran *via* Swindon, was amended to suit the daily boat sailings. In the same year, the tramway laid along the quaysides to Weymouth Quay, which had been opened for goods traffic in 1865, was opened for passenger trains. Competition between the GWR and L&SWR for traffic to the Channel Islands ceased when the traffic was pooled (shared) following an agreement made in 1899.

Commencing in May 1900, daily services to Guernsey and Jersey were introduced, in daylight hours in each direction; on the opening of the Stert – Westbury cut-off line to passenger services as noted above, the train services run in connection with the boat services were accelerated.

Following the introduction of the new service, substantial works were undertaken at Weymouth to provide a new harbour and jetties and to improve the rail connection; these works were completed in 1904. Passengers to and from the Channel Islands were an important source of income; later in the decade it was reported that other significant traffic included potatoes from Jersey and daffodils and narcissi from Guernsey.

The DN&SR tries again for Southampton

A final attempt to establish an independent link between the DN&SR at Winchester and the docks at Southampton was made when a group of Southampton people obtained the Southampton and Winchester Great Western Junction Railway Act, which received Royal Assent in 1901. The promoters were no more successful than their predecessors in raising capital and the scheme was abandoned in 1905. The arrangements for handling traffic would remain basically the same for the life of the DN&SR route; the one exception being the provision of a connection between the two lines north of Winchester provided for freight traffic between 1943 and 1951 (see Chapters 6 & 7).

At a half-yearly meeting of the DN&SR in 1903, the Chairman was quoted as saying: "There was no shutting their eyes to the fact that the Didcot line would never be what it was intended to be until it could be by hook or crook carried into Southampton".

The final attempt to provide a new link to Bristol

Despite the existence of two through routes to Bristol since 1895, with the opening of the Bradford-on-Avon Loop in that

year, another attempt to add to the railway infrastructure was made in Autumn 1902, when a Bristol, London and Southern Counties Railway was promoted by some inhabitants of Bristol. Commencing at Avonmouth Docks and serving Bristol and Bath, the route continued via the Avon Valley and Trowbridge to join the L&SWR at Overton, a few miles west of Basingstoke. The L&SWR rejected the proposal and the Bill was rejected by the Commons Committee on 11 June 1903 due to lack of financial support (see L&SWR References in **Further Reading**).

Water troughs for the new express trains

Water troughs were established on a level section of the Berks & Hants line just west of Aldermaston Station, between Mileposts 45 and 46. Opened in June 1904 and generally known as Aldermaston Troughs, they were provided on both lines and were 560 yards long. The treatment plant, situated on the down side near the station and having its own siding, used a new system of water softening developed in the USA and had a capacity of 10,000 gallons per hour. A further set of troughs was installed at about the same time between Westbury and Frome and opened in the same month. Provision of water troughs at 45 and 97 miles from Paddington permitted the newly re-routed Paddington - Weymouth expresses to run throughout without needing to take water from a lineside source. Even more significantly, on opening of the new through route to the West in 1906 (see later in this chapter) and with the contemporary opening of troughs near Exeter, express trains to the West could run through to Plymouth without a stop **(Note 2)**.

Aldermaston troughs, looking towards Reading (John Allen collection)

New military traffic for the Berks & Hants line

Several developments took place at this time due to the increasing military activity on Salisbury Plain. A branch from Ludgershall, on the M&SWJR between Wolfhall Junction and Andover, was built to Tidworth for the War Office and arrangements made for it to be operated by the that railway. Application for a Ludgershall and Military Camps Light Railway had been made in 1898 by the M&SWJR and authorisation given by an Agreement dated 19 November 1900 between HM Principal Secretary of State for the War Department and the company. The branch came into military use in July 1901; opening for public use followed in 1902 (goods in July and passengers in October) **(Note 3)**. The military activity brought a considerable increase in rail traffic, both passengers and freight, and the line from Grafton (at the end of the double track railway from Marlborough) to Weyhill through Ludgershall was doubled in stages during 1900 - 1902. To enable through traffic to be worked by the GWR, running powers between Wolfhall Junction and Ludgershall were granted to that company by the M&SWJR.

To facilitate the movement of through traffic to and from the Tidworth/Ludgershall area via Newbury, particularly via the Didcot line, a double track link was opened on 6 July 1905 between the Bedwyn - Savernake (GWR) line and the Marlborough - Andover (M&SWJR) line near Grafton, to be known as the Grafton Curve. The junction with the Berks & Hants line was called Grafton Curve Junction (later renamed Grafton East Junction) and the other Wolfhall Junction (MSWJ). The link was authorised by the Great Western Railway Act, 15 August 1904, S5 **(Note 4)** and built under an agreement of 1903, whereby the GWR secured running powers over the M&SWJR line from Wolfhall Junction to Ludgershall, as noted above.

Although not connected with the Berks & Hants line, it is of interest to note here that bricks for Tidworth Camp were made at Dodsdown Brickworks, near the village of Wilton, and from 1902 onwards were conveyed to sidings on the M&SWJR just north of Grafton Station by the privately owned Dodsdown Brickworks Railway. Both brickworks and railway closed in 1910.

Innovations for local traffic

In the meantime, an event with considerable significance for the future took place in October 1904. The GWR successfully inaugurated a road motor car service between Marlborough and Calne stations, via Fyfield and Avebury.

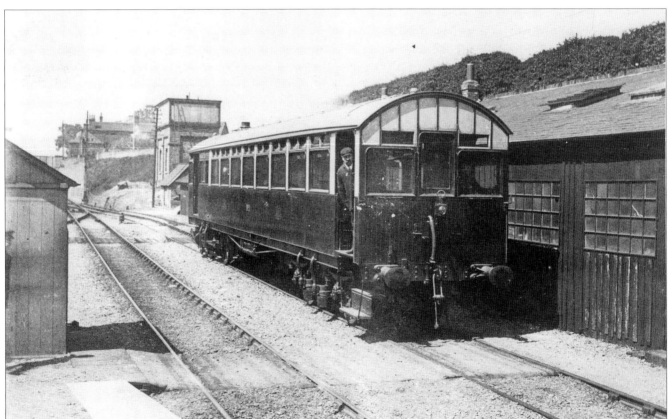

Steam Railmotor for the Lambourn branch line, seen at Newbury (see page 74 'Changes on the Lambourn Valley line'). This is believed to be No 1, which, with its sister No 2, operated on the branch in 1904 and again in 1905 (West Berkshire Museum)

At this time, steam rail motor cars were being introduced on branch lines and on stopping services on main lines throughout the British Isles; the replacement of local passenger trains by rail motor cars in the Trowbridge and Westbury districts took place during 1905 and included the entire local service on the new line between Westbury and Patney & Chirton.

Changes on the Lambourn Valley line

Economies were made on the line in 1903. A Light Railway Order, under the Light Railway Act of 1896, was applied for in 1903, but the application was refused. In many respects the railway at that time was a typical light railway, with its lightly-laid track and low platforms.

On 1 July 1905, the Lambourn Valley Railway (LVR) was vested in the GWR by the GWR (Additional Powers) Act of 1905. The new owner undertook a number of improvements, which were carried out in the 1908-9 period (see later in this chapter); meanwhile, on 1 October 1906, a new halt was opened at West Fields on the outskirts of Newbury. Improvements to rolling stock had already been made in May 1904, when the whole of the LVR's rolling stock was withdrawn and replaced by two of the new rail motor cars loaned by the GWR; it is of interest that the horse-box traffic was worked by these cars.

Opening of Newbury Racecourse and Station – more new traffic

Back on the main line, a significant source of additional traffic was offered when, following the incorporation of the

Newbury Racecourse Company Limited in April 1904, a decision was made to build a top-class racecourse alongside the line east of Newbury. "The Story of Newbury Race Course" by Frank Osgood gives valuable information on events relating to the railway's connection with the racecourse. At a board meeting of the company in November 1904, an agreement with the GWR for conveyance of land and provision of railway accommodation was produced and agreed. In addition, at least one excursion train was to be provided from Paddington each raceday.

Newbury Racecourse Station was opened on 26 September 1905, the first day of the inaugural two-day meeting. It was provided with four platforms, two on the main line and two for terminating trains. A single line connection was made with the main line at the Newbury end. Two signal boxes were provided, that at the Newbury end having a short life, being replaced by the new Newbury East Junction Signal Box in 1910. At that time, the box at the London end, initially known as Newbury Racecourse East Signal Box, dropped the "East" from its name. The station was intended to be used only for race traffic and on non-race days no trains called or terminated at any of the four platforms.

The Berks & Hants line becomes a part of the main line from London to the West Country

In 1906, the last important link needed to complete the direct main line from Paddington to the West Country via Newbury was opened. This link connected Castle Cary, on the Weymouth line between Westbury and Yeovil, to the Bristol

Newbury Racecourse Station from Racecourse Road Bridge (West Berkshire Museum)

and Exeter (B&E) line east of Taunton. Between the two lay the B&E's branch from Taunton to Yeovil, a single line, opened in 1853 as a broad gauge line and altered to standard gauge in 1879 **(Note 5)**.

The first section of the new link, working westwards, was a new double track railway, 15½ miles long, from Castle Cary via Somerton, to a junction with the old B&E branch at a new junction, Curry Rivell Junction. This section, known as the Castle Cary and Langport line, was authorised by the Great Western Railway (New Works) Act, 12 August 1898, S4. A 1053-yard long tunnel and 116-yard long viaduct were needed at Somerton.

this book, the above description of the completion of the final link is given both to illustrate the piece-meal way in which the direct route to the West of England via Newbury developed and to provide at least some explanation as to why it took almost 60 years from the opening of the first section between Reading and Hungerford to complete the link to Taunton.

The new link between Castle Cary and Cogload Junction was opened throughout to goods trains on 20 May 1906 and to passenger trains on 1 July 1906. The latter event was a day earlier than planned, as on the 1 July, a portion of Box Tunnel on the route via Swindon had caved in, so the

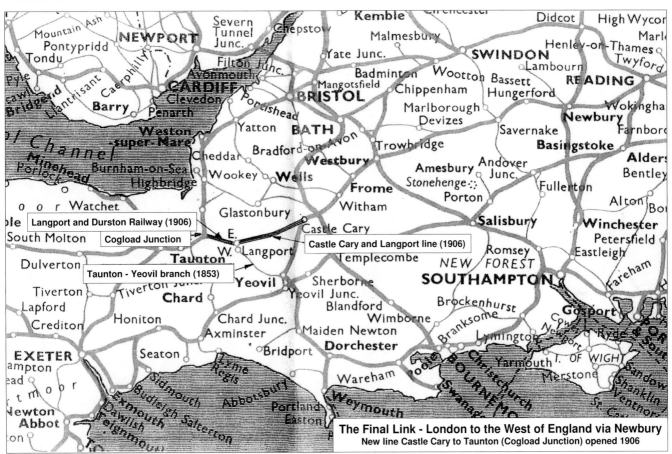

The Final Link - London to the West of England via Newbury
New line Castle Cary to Taunton (Cogload Junction) opened 1906

The next section of about 4 miles used the old Taunton - Yeovil branch which was doubled and very much improved from Curry Rivell Junction to near Athelney, where another new junction was created, Athelney Junction. A new viaduct, 211 yards long, was provided at Langport. From Athelney Junction, the third section, a new double track main line nearly 3 miles in length, was built directly towards Taunton, joining the Bristol - Taunton line at a new junction called Cogload Junction. These works, known collectively as the Langport and Durston Railway, were authorised by the Great Western Railway Act of 15 August 1904, S5.

Whilst being well outside the geographical area covered by

new route was the only one to and from the West of England available that day. The saving in distance between Reading and Taunton, compared with the route via Bristol Temple Meads station, was 20¼ miles; the distance from Paddington to the main station at Plymouth (North Road) was 225¾ miles compared with 230¾ miles from Waterloo by the L&SWR route.

The "Cornish Riviera Limited" express was diverted to the new line as from 21 July 1906 **(Note 6)**. It then became a daily train leaving Paddington at 10 30 am, was accelerated, and altered to run throughout the year. Slip coaches were carried for Weymouth, slipped at Westbury, and for the

Paignton line, slipped at Exeter. At the same time, the bulk of other West of England traffic was diverted to the new route.

From Hungerford to the junction with the Bristol – Exeter line east of Taunton, the scheme to provide an alternative, and more direct, route to the West, had involved the doubling and reconstruction of 23½ miles of line and the building of 33 miles of entirely new railway. The total cost was estimated to be around £1,100,000 and the aim to provide a first-class route without restriction either in regard to speed or load. For the newly-opened line, the sharpest curve was quoted as being 60 chains radius and the ruling gradient 1:264; the permanent way was of the Company's heaviest type and due consideration was given to likely requirements of the future including matters such as clearances, etc.

used by expresses to Weymouth (from 1901) and to the West Country from July 1906, as already described.

A few months earlier, the April 1906 edition of the Great Western Railway Magazine had announced, under The Engineering Department – New Stations: "Ensuing on the development of the historic town of Newbury, the Directors have authorised the present station being replaced by one of a thoroughly up-to-date character. The platforms are to be set back to permit the laying down of two extra lines with a view to the centre roads being clear for the accelerated services to the west when the Castle Cary and Langport line is open for passenger traffic. A new goods shed and extensive siding accommodation are included in the proposals and needless to add – the township being located in an important horse breeding centre – ample horse

View of the old Newbury Station from the west end, looking towards Reading. The photograph is dated 1908, ten years after the Lambourn Bay, with its canopy, was added and immediately before work started on the new station (Kevin Robertson collection)

Newbury Station to be rebuilt for the future

The station at Newbury, built for the opening of the Berks and Hants Railway from Reading to Hungerford in 1847, had been subject to many changes since its opening. Bay platforms had been provided for the trains to Didcot and Winchester and for the opening of the Lambourn Valley Railway in 1898. However, the main portion of the station remained as built, its narrow platforms adjacent to the two tracks which served all stopping trains and which were also

loading accommodation is a special feature." In the same month, in a brief report in the Railway Magazine, it was stated that the cost of the necessary work "is fixed at £80,000".

However, in the following year, no progress had been made, and a report appeared in the Newbury Weekly News (6 June) which stated: "The Notice Paper of the House of Commons contained the following, with regard to Newbury Station, placed there by Mr Mackarness, MP:

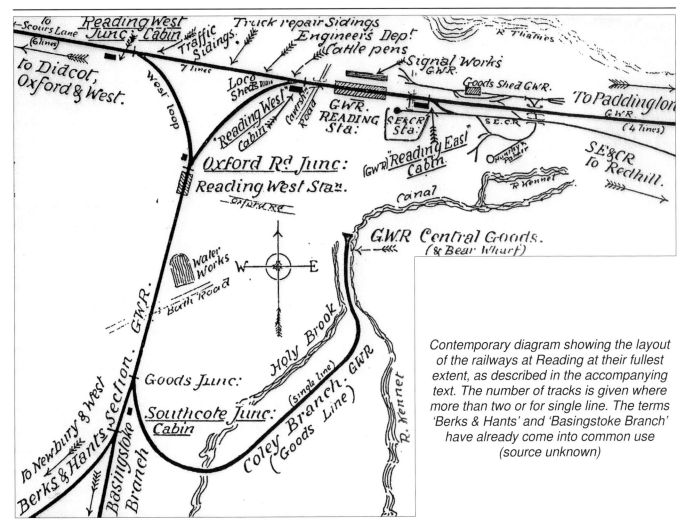

Contemporary diagram showing the layout of the railways at Reading at their fullest extent, as described in the accompanying text. The number of tracks is given where more than two or for single line. The terms 'Berks & Hants' and 'Basingstoke Branch' have already come into common use (source unknown)

"To ask the President of the Board of Trade, whether he is aware that the Great Western Railway Station at Newbury is on the down side in some places not more than six feet wide and nowhere more than 14ft wide, and that express trains pass through it every day at from 60 to 67 miles an hour; whether the station was built upwards of 50 years ago and is quite unfitted for the traffic and trains which now pass through it, and that its continuance in its present condition is attended with danger to life and property; and whether he will inquire (sic) why the decision come to by the board of the company more than two years ago to build a new station has never been carried out."

New passenger and goods facilities in the Reading area

On the section between Oxford Road Junction, Reading, and Southcote Junction, two events took place during this period. On 1 July 1906, a new passenger station, Reading West, was opened, principally to serve the cross-country trains between such places as Birkenhead and Bournemouth, which by taking the Reading West Loop had not previously called at Reading. The station also performed

a useful function in serving a large area of West Reading otherwise somewhat remote from other stations. Situated beside the Oxford Road bridge, it was also connected by footpath to the Tilehurst Road. The platforms were constructed of timber and the station building was given an attractive appearance conforming to the rural character of the immediate neighbourhood **(Note 7)**.

In 1908 a goods-only branch was opened from a new Coley Branch Junction (just north of Southcote Junction) through the grounds of Coley Park and turning northwards to a new goods station called Reading Central Goods. Known then as the Coley Branch Railway (Reading), this 1¾ mile long line, which opened on 4 May 1908, was authorised by the GWR (Additional Powers) Act of 4 August 1905, S5. Single track throughout, it was built to main line standards with a speed limit of 15mph; all types of locomotive were permitted except the 'King' class, introduced in 1927 **(Note 8)**. According to the Reading Mercury (9 May 1908) the Goods Depot would deal with "coal, coke, timber, bricks, stone, hay, straw, grain and other descriptions of mineral and merchandise traffic". A full description of the depot is given in 'Rail Centres: Reading' by Laurence Waters.

Reading West Station, north view from the down platform. The lengthy platforms were provided to serve the long-distance trains to the South Coast that did not call at Reading's main station; the station also served the rapidly-developing area along the Oxford and the Tilehurst Roads (Kevin Robertson collection)

Increased traffic leads to improvements in signalling

Another development resulting from the increased traffic on the main line was the changes to signalling arrangements west of Newbury in 1907. The signal cabin at Enborne Junction, opened in 1885 upon the opening of the line to Winchester, was closed and a new cabin provided in the fork between the two lines. Intermediate block posts were established at Hampstead Crossing (sic), between Enborne Junction and Kintbury, and at Fairfield Crossing, between Hungerford and Bedwyn, each block section previously being 4 to 5 miles long.

The Lambourn line in the news again

Further work to bring the Lambourn Valley Branch up to GWR standards took place during the 1908-1910 period. These works included raising platforms to standard height, general improvements at Lambourn (including a new station), extension of the loop and provision of waiting shed

and horse loading accommodation at Great Shefford, lengthening the goods loop at Boxford, conversion of Welford Park into a crossing place and the introduction of electric train staff working (see **Glossary**).

Following their successful application on certain main lines of the GWR and on the single track Fairford branch, "Audible Signal Ramps" replaced all semaphore distant signals on the Lambourn branch in September 1909. As the train's locomotive passed over a ramp, the driver was given an indication in the cab of the stop signal ahead being set at danger (steam whistle) or at clear (bell). Due to the removal of the lineside distant signals, all locomotives running on the branch had to be fitted with the equipment. The warning system was in use on the branch for almost twenty years, being taken out of use in March 1929.

Newbury station rebuilt at last

In July 1908, it was announced in the Great Western Railway Magazine that a contract had been let to A.N. Coles, Plymouth for new station buildings and verandahs

__Opposite__ and __following page__. Three wonderful views showing the new Fairfield Crossing Signal Box of 1907, an intermediate block post between Hungerford and Bedwyn. The signalman also controlled the level crossing, rendering the crossing keeper's cottage redundant for its original purpose. The already extended cottage survives today. Inside the signal box, all the levers, the block section apparatus and the diagram (high on the front wall) may clearly be seen, together with the tool cupboard and the single gas ceiling lamp (GWR)

(canopies) and a new footbridge; the same source stated (in 1910) that work started in May 1908.

During the above period the station was completely rebuilt under traffic, with two through tracks, two through platforms on loops outside the through tracks and new bay platforms for the local trains. A comprehensive report in the Great Western Railway Magazine for August 1910 (p209) describes the scheme in detail and where relevant is quoted at length in the following text:

"The general features of the scheme were the construction of entirely new "up" and "down" platforms, station buildings and approach roads and the reconstruction of three overbridges to the requisite increased span for the additional lines. The buildings on both platforms are of red brick with Bath stone dressings, roofed with dark brindled tiles, and present an effective and pleasing appearance. On the "up" side, to which a broad approach leads from the town, the platform is 1,065ft long and 22ft wide, 330ft being covered in, a bay 360ft long being provided at the west end for Lambourn trains and another 440ft long at the east end for Didcot trains. The main buildings are on this platform and

have a length of 206ft. They comprise a booking hall, waiting room, refreshment and tea rooms, postal telegraph office, parcels office, cloak room and the usual rooms for station staff. The refreshment and tea rooms are panelled in fumed oak and have Roman marble mosaic floors and cathedral glass windows. The "down" platform 950ft long and 20ft wide (covering being provided over 330ft of its length) contains at the west end a bay 460ft long for Winchester trains. The usual waiting room accommodation is also provided. A covered footbridge of a single span of 95ft connects the platforms and a loading bank 310ft long is provided on the "down" side for horse-boxes etc. The station is lighted by incandescent gas lamps."

In addition to the track alterations mentioned above, on the down side a pair of tracks, known as No 1 and No 2 loops, was provided extending from the Racecourse station to connect with the down platform loop at Newbury station. Their principal purpose was to facilitate movement of freight trains between these places clear of the main line. On the up side a direct connection from the Didcot bay platform to the Didcot line was not possible due to the position of the old goods shed alongside the main line, so Didcot-bound trains

Two views of the reconstruction of Newbury station in 1908-1910. The upper, much-published, photograph shows work in its early stages; the inadequacy of the old station as an important junction on a main line can clearly be seen. In the lower, rather poor image, taken in the same direction but from a higher viewpoint, the complex nature of the rebuilding of the station under traffic can be appreciated (Upper: Kevin Robertson collection; Lower: West Berkshire Museum)

had to join the main line for a short distance. At the west end of the station, the original three-track layout was retained, the Lambourn branch forming the third line and passing under Bartholomew Street and running parallel to the main line for about 650 yards before turning away to the north.

The goods shed, believed to date from the opening of the line to goods in 1848, was retained and not replaced as originally planned. A new cart weighbridge, cattle pens and horse-landing accommodation were provided together with a new entrance into the goods yard from Cheap Street with an improved gradient compared with the old approach. Various additional sidings were provided throughout the layout, one of which served the new horse landing accommodation alongside the Winchester Bay.

Bridges, retaining walls, signal boxes – and a turntable

The Racecourse, Greenham Road and Cheap Street bridges were all replaced, but Bartholomew Street Bridge was retained, having been reconstructed to accommodate the Lambourn Valley Railway and brought into use in 1898.

"Race-course Bridge is formed of two plate girders, each 61ft 5ins long, with cross-girders at 5ft intervals (centres), brick jack arches and concrete filling supporting the roadway, which is 13ft wide.

"Greenham Road Bridge comprises two spans, each formed with a pair of plate main girders, one span being carried by a girder 55ft 4in long, matched by one 50ft 8in long, due to the abutment being on a skew; and the remaining span by girders, each 57ft long; the inner ends of all the girders being supported on a pair of steel columns braced together. Cross girders at 5ft intervals (centres) and jack arches, with concrete filling, support the roadway, which has a width of 18ft in the clear.

"Cheap Street Bridge consists of a single skew span 87ft on the square, with 4 girders, the length of each being 96ft 9in. The curved main girders, between which runs the roadway 25ft in width, are 10ft deep and 27ft apart (centres); between these girders and the outside girders on each side are the footways, each some 7ft 6ins wide. Above the footways curved bracing connects the main and outside girders on each side. The cross girders under the road are at 10ft intervals, with rolled steel joists longitudinally at 4ft intervals.

Under the paths rolled steel joists are placed at 5ft intervals. The flooring is of buckled plates and the roadway consists of tar asphalte (sic)."

New signal boxes known as Newbury West Box, Newbury Middle Box and Newbury East Junction Box were provided. The latter box replaced two others, one box of the same name that had been provided when the Didcot line was opened in 1882, and Newbury Racecourse West Box, only five years old.

The drawings and contracts for the works were prepared in the office of the Engineer Mr W W Grierson and the work carried out under the supervision of the Divisional Engineer Mr J N Taylor, the contractors being: station buildings Mr A N Coles, Plymouth, with sub-contractors for the steelwork - Messrs Hill & Smith, Brierley Hill; three road bridges Messrs Finch & Co, Chepstow. The earthworks, retaining walls etc were carried out by the Company's own men. The formal opening of the new station took place on 29 May 1910. Track alterations, mainly in the goods yards, continued to 1911-12.

At Newbury Racecourse Station, in addition to the improvements at the west end resulting from the Newbury Station works, a turntable and four carriage sidings were added at the east end for the servicing and stabling of the racecourse specials.

Private sidings boost goods traffic

Mention has already been made of the Central Goods Depot at Reading, served from the Berks & Hants line and opened in 1908. By 1914, companies with private sidings in the depot were Baynes (timber), Cooperative Wholesale Society (preserves factory) and H & G Simonds (brewers).

In the case of the timber company, bulk timber would have been brought in and finished products (such as pit props) taken out; coal would have been required if a steam engine was used to supply power to the sawmill. Coal would also have been required for the boilers in the factories. Traffic for the preserves factory inward would have included fruit and onions and outward the preserves for distribution worldwide. The brewers would have required a constant supply of raw materials; while a substantial proportion of their products would have been sold locally and in adjacent counties, bottled beer would have had wider distribution by rail.

The massive two-road goods shed at Newbury, dating from 1848, seen from outside and inside. The upper view appears to have been taken from a goods train standing on the down goods lines, provided during the station reconstruction. The building is adjacent to the up main line; it was not rebuilt as originally planned as part of the works and therefore Didcot trains had to join the main line for a short distance before turning north. The locomotive is GWR Armstrong outside-framed '360' class 0-6-0 No 369 built at Swindon 1866, the lower view of the interior is included to show the diversity of goods dealt with at Newbury; also featured is the crane which (in its rebuilt form) now stands at Newbury Wharf. Whilst the upper photograph is dated sometime after 1910, when the main works were completed, the interior view is dated 1904 (GWR)

The first private siding agreement (PSA) at Colthrop, in 1912, resulted in access being provided from both up and down lines to the down (south) side of the line west of Colthrop Crossing, to serve J Henry & Co Ltd's four sidings. From 1918, the agreement was with the Colthrop Board & Paper Mills Ltd. Under an agreement of 1922, two west-facing sidings were provided on the down side at Colthrop for Cropper and Co Ltd.

In Newbury Goods Yard, a siding was provided under agreement for Plenty & Son Ltd in 1903; this was done by providing a spur off William Skinner's siding. Plenty's were marine engineers, principally manufacturers of steam and diesel engines and, later, pumps. A new PSA for Skinner's siding was held by W Skinner & Co (Newbury) Ltd from July 1913; in November 1913 this was transferred to H Baird & Sons Ltd.

At the Calcot Mill siding, the PSA changed hands twice in the period covered by this chapter, to J T Dewe from Dewe Bros in 1905 and to Holland Bros in 1922.

Changes also took place at the Tile (Tyle) Mill siding, when F L Smith took over the Agreement in 1901 and the loop off the down main line was changed to a siding, accessible only by westbound (down) goods trains. The spur from this siding to the mill was retained; access being by a wagon turntable (see **Glossary**). The PSA changed hands twice in the next decade; during that period the sidings fell out of use, but a revival took place in 1918 when Messrs Baines (Reading) Ltd took over the Agreement following their purchase of the mill and its conversion to a sawmill. The siding next to the main line was restored and a new one added; however, the spur to the mill was not retained.

The presence of iron ore in the Westbury area, as mentioned in Chapter 2, led to increased traffic. At Seend, west of Devizes, siding facilities were covered by a PSA of 1906 (Seend Iron Mines Co, terminated in 1911) and later by the Avon Valley Iron Co (siding served by aerial ropeway, PSA dated 1919). At Westbury, the PSA was transferred to

the New Westbury Iron Co Ltd in 1904 and additional facilities including a new crusher required a new PSA in 1917.

Improvements down the line 1906 - 1914

The importance of military traffic to the stations on the fringe of Salisbury Plain, Patney & Chirton and Lavington, was emphasised when works to improve the accommodation for this traffic were carried out at the former station in 1909. These mainly consisted of provision of a carriage siding and other sidings on the down side, of a timber platform and carriage siding on the up side, conversion of a siding into an up passenger loop and extension of the down platform. A military siding was brought into use at Lavington in 1914.

Patney and Chirton – staff group on down platform (Kevin Robertson collection)

As part of the general upgrading to stations already described, at Devizes in 1909-1910, verandah coverings (canopies) were provided in place of the overall roof, the waiting accommodation was improved and the footbridge was replaced.

A five-road engine shed, with many other sidings and a turntable was provided at Westbury and opened in April 1915. The decision to construct this shed was first reported in 1908, when it was stated that about 30 engines, also rail motors, were stationed at Trowbridge and about 20 other engines working in the area were divided between Salisbury and Frome sheds.

Other works carried out to facilitate the working of traffic in the foregoing period included: Marsh Signal Box (between Midgham and Colthrop) opened 1906 to deal with additional trains to the West Country; Colthrop Crossing Signal Box opened 1912 replacing Colthrop Siding Signal Box opened 1899; Enborne Junction Signal Box opened 1907 replacing

The bucolic surroundings of Patney & Chirton, looking west and seen after the improvements of 1909. Trains to and from the Devizes line could use the outer face of the island platform without entering the main line (Kevin Robertson collection)

the signal box provided for opening of the Winchester line in 1885 (previously mentioned); Fairfield Crossing Signal Box opened 1907 replacing previous box (also previously mentioned); Grafton East Junction: Bank Engine Siding added 1913, to enable a banking locomotive to assist down freight trains going from the GWR main line to the M&SWJR line with military traffic; Woodborough: Up Refuge Siding added May 1910.

The impact of the First World War 1914 - 1919

With the outbreak of war in 1914, government control of the railways was placed in the hands of the Railway Executive Committee.

In common with all other railways, the main line and the cross-country lines carried substantial amounts of extra traffic. In passenger terms this included troop transport and ambulance trains; in respect of goods, additional trains carried munitions and other supplies to the south coast ports for shipment to the Channel ports on the Continent.

Racing ceased at Newbury Racecourse in 1914 after possession by the War Office for military purposes, but subsequently some meetings were held in 1915 and 1916. In April 1916, the War Office ceased occupation but the Ministry of Munitions took over certain areas. After the August 1916 race meeting, the Ministry took over the whole of the racecourse and used it as an inspection depot, tank

repair park and shell dump. From the siding nearest to the racecourse, a spur gave access to a 6-road inspection shed, and another, crossing the race track itself, led to the shell dump with up to seven parallel tracks. There were two west-facing head-shunts for these facilities. Release of the land and buildings was not made until 1919, racing being resumed in April of that year. It is believed that the sidings were not removed until 1923 - presumably the section of line crossing the race track was removed in 1919!

Post-war improvements to the line's signalling

During 1920 and 1921, what would be referred to today as upgrading works were carried out at several sites, as follows: Theale (c 1920), Aldermaston (May 1920), Thatcham (1921) and Hamstead Crossing (March 1921): Signal Boxes replaced; Kintbury: extra siding added by 1920; Crofton Crossing Signal Box: replaced by ground frame by 1920.

The Great Western Railway becomes one of the "Big Four" railways

Government control of the railways ended in August 1921. In the same month, the Railways Act 1921 laid the foundations of the 'Big Four', the Great Western, London Midland and Scottish, London and North Eastern and Southern Railways. Practically all the lines described in this book either remained as part of the 'new' Great Western Railway (GWR) or were absorbed into it. The new railways formally came into being on 1 January 1923.

The Didcot, Newbury and Southampton Railway and the Midland and South Western Junction Railway become part of the GWR

Although its trains were worked by the GWR, the Didcot, Newbury and Southampton Railway had remained an independent concern. Following the Railways Act, the DN&SR was absorbed into the GWR from 1 January 1923 by the Great Western Railway (Western Group) Preliminary Absorption Scheme (No 4), 1922 dated 27 March 1923. The entire railway was transferred, a total route length of almost 42¾ miles from Didcot to Newbury East Junction and from Enborne Junction to the boundary with the L&SWR south of Winchester Chesil station. The line south of this point to Shawford Junction, a length of just over 2

miles built by the L&SWR, was transferred to become part of the Southern Railway.

The Midland and South Western Junction Railway had not only remained an independent concern but worked its own trains between Cheltenham and Southampton and intermediate points. Its ownership stretched from Andoversford on the Cheltenham - Kingham line to Red Post Junction on the Andover – Salisbury line. Running powers (see **Glossary**) enabled its trains to reach Cheltenham Spa Lansdown (Passenger) and High Street (Goods) and Southampton Town and Docks via Redbridge. It also owned the spur from Rushey Platt Junction (Swindon) to the GWR main line and operated the government-owned Tidworth branch. The total route length was almost 62¾ miles. It was absorbed into the Great Western Railway from 1 July 1923 by the GWR (Midland and South Western Junction Railway) Absorption Scheme dated 28 September 1923.

Possibly the entire staff under the command of Mr G K North, Stationmaster at Newbury in 1909, assembled on one of the platforms of the old station. Mr North, seated centre stage, would have been responsible for all passenger and goods station staff, signalling staff, maintenance staff including permanent way and possibly engine crew and guards as well. The timing of the group photo may have been related to the imminent demise of the old station (John Allen collection)

STATISTICS OF SUBSIDIARY COMPANIES at 31 December 1921:		
Item	DN&SR	M&SWJR
Issued capital (£ million)	1.31	1.65
Net Income for 1921 (£)	15674	24947
Annual dividend on Ordinary Shares (%)	Nil	Nil
Route Length (miles)	42¾	62¾
Locomotives	-	29
Carriages	-	58
Wagons and Service Vehicles	-	379
Employees	-	700
Source: History of the Great Western Railway Volume 1: Consolidation 1923 – 1929.		

NOTES

NOTE 1: WEYMOUTH REFERENCES

Great Western Railway Magazine August 1889 p111, September 1889 p126, July 1897 p106, August 1897 p125-6, January 1904 p3;

Railway Magazine July 1897 p4, May 1903 p410-4, June 1903 p471-7 Steamboats & Steamboat Services of the GWR; March 1908 p230-8 & May 1908 p396-403 Weymouth as Railway Centre; July 1908 p66-7 Train Services; May 1912 p380 Weymouth as Holiday Centre & Seaport; October 1912 December p340 Control of station and line south of Dorchester by GWR.

'The Bath to Weymouth Line' Colin Maggs

NOTE 2: WATER TROUGHS

Great Western Railway Magazine

December 1905: Aldermaston – 2 troughs – MP 45¼ - 45¾, length 1680ft, opened 29.06.04 (Westbury 28.06.04, Exminster 25.06.04)

NOTE 3: TIDWORTH BRANCH

The Midland and South Western Junction Railway (see **Further Reading**) and RM July 1950 p501 and October 1950 p719

NOTE 4: GRAFTON CURVE

Great Western Railway Magazine August 1904 p125 – contract let; October p166 – work started by Messrs Jackaman & Son

NOTE 5: CASTLE CARY – LANGPORT – ATHELNEY – COGLOAD JUNCTION

Great Western Railway Magazine August 1905 and May 1906; comparison with LSWR route to Plymouth RM May/June 1949 p142 'The LSWR at Plymouth'; early opening to passenger traffic 'Rail Centres Swindon' p11; Reading Mercury 3.07.06; Newbury Weekly News 5.07.06

NOTE 6: DIVERSION OF CORNISH RIVIERA

Railway Magazine September 1928 p205

Our second trip down the line, visiting many of the stations in the era covered by this chapter, starts with the station garden at Theale. Station Garden Competitions were common in the first half of the twentieth century and with a little pruning, the up platform at Theale looks to be in the running for a prize. Dated before 1920, when the signal box was replaced (John Allen collection)

NOTE 7: READING WEST STATION

Great Western Railway Magazine April 1906 states that the new station will be erected to accommodate and foster the increasing residential requirements of the locality; Opening date from 'Rail Centres: Reading' – no original source yet found

NOTE 8: READING CENTRAL GOODS

Traffic - see Railway Magazine February 1986, also 'Rail Centres: Reading'.

ACTS AND LIGHT RAILWAY ORDERS

Pewsey and Salisbury Light Railway (Extension of Time) Order, 5 July 1901

Great Western Railway Act, 26 July 1901 (1 Edward VII, c.123)

Southampton and Winchester Great Western Junction Railway Act, 17 August 1901 (1 Edward VII, c.274)

Didcot, Newbury and Southampton Railway Act, 11 August 1903, (3 Edward VII, c.159)

Great Western Railway Act, 15 August 1904, (4 Edward VII, c.197) (S5: Grafton Curve)

Southampton and Winchester Great Western Junction Railway (Abandonment) Act, 30 June 1905, (5 Edward VII, c.4)

Great Western Railway (Additional Powers) Act, 4 August 1905, (5 Edward VII, c.139)

Didcot, Newbury and Southampton Railway Act, 8 July 1914, (4 & 5 Geo V, c15)

Railways Act, 19 August 1921, (11 & 12 Geo V, c.55)

CHAPTER REFERENCES

Deposited Documents   (see Chapter 1 for interpretation of references)

(DP/B41 & B42; A1/371/163MS): Bristol, London and Southern Counties Railway (1902)

(Q/RUm 245): Lambourn Valley Light Railway (1902)

(A1/371/165A/MS): Great Western Railway: Minor Alterations (ref: Grafton Curve) (1903)

(Q/RUm 246; A1/371/165B/MS): Central Wilts Light Railway: Hungerford to Chippenham (1903)

(A1/371/169/MS): Great Western Railway: (relevant part) Marlborough (additional land) (1911)

(A1/371/170/MS): Great Western Railway: (relevant part) Grafton (additional land for engine siding and vehicle access at Grafton Junction) (1913)

Above - *Staff group at Theale, gathered at the Reading end of the down platform shelter (Kevin Robertson collection)*

Opposite page *A sunnier location is chosen at Aldermaston, where presumably the staff all had confidence in their knowledge of the timetable! (Kevin Robertson collection)*

PUBLISHED REFERENCES

History of the Great Western Railway Volume II 1863 – 1921

E T MacDermot Revised by C R Clinker (Ian Allan 1964)

History of the Great Western Railway Volume I Consolidation 1923 – 1929

P Semmens (Guild Publishing/George Allen & Unwin 1985)

The Golden Age of the Great Western Railway 1895-1914

Tim Bryan (Patrick Stephens Ltd 1991)

The Great Western Railway in the 20th Century

O S Nock (Ian Allan 1971)

The Bath to Weymouth Line

Colin Maggs (The Oakwood Press 1982)

An Illustrated History of the Didcot, Newbury and Southampton Railway

P Karau, M Parsons & K Robertson (Wild Swan 1984)

Rail Centres: Reading

Laurence Waters (Ian Allan 1980)

Rail Centres: Swindon

Colin Maggs (Ian Allan / Booklaw Publications 2007)

The Midland and South Western Junction Railway

Colin G Maggs (David & Charles 1980)

The Story of Newbury Race Course

Frank Osgood (Kingsclere Publications Ltd 1993)

GWR Timetable 1902 (Reprint)

(Ian Allan   - no date)

Bradshaw April 1910 (Reprint)

(David & Charles - 1968)

Newbury Weekly News 21.09.05 & 28.09.05: Newbury Races (Programme for, and report of, Inaugural Meeting)

Berkshire Chronicle 3.07.06: "GWR Enterprise – Shortened Route to the West – Remarkable Times"

Newbury Weekly News 5.07.06: "Westward Ho! By Great Western Railway *via* Newbury – Remarkable Run from London to Plymouth – Splendid Service to the West"

Ibid: 6.06.07: Newbury Station – Notice Paper of the House of Commons

Reading Mercury 9.05.08: The New Central Goods Station at Coley, Reading – opening on Monday 4 May 1908

Newbury Weekly News 4.03.09: Newbury Railway Station – progress on demolition of old and building of new station

Ibid: 2.06.10 (a) Newbury Station – "Practically Completed – A Wonderful Transformation"; (b) Newbury to the North *via* Didcot and the Great Central Railway; (c) GWR and LSWR Agreement described and refers to result that "as from the 28 (sic) all passengers from ocean liners will be landed at Millbay Docks Plymouth and proceed to London over the GWR route"

Ibid: 24.10.12 The King's visit to Hungerford (Monday 21)

Ibid: 2.10.19 First Day of the Railway Strike – Newbury Race Meeting hit by the strike on the second day, Saturday

Up side buildings of the new Newbury station, probably taken soon after completion in 1910. The photographer is standing on the bank which can be seen in the photograph below (West Berkshire Museum)

The track layout at the new Newbury station soon after completion, with work in progress to lower the level of the area opposite the up side buildings. The signal box seen is Newbury West. This layout, with the exception of the tracks in the Lambourn Bay area, survived intact until the entire track layout was simplified and replaced for the Multiple Aspect Signalling Scheme of 1977-1978 (Kevin Robertson collection)

Two views of Newbury station looking westwards, thought to be both from the same period as evidenced by the livery and type of vehicles in the 'Didcot' Bay. The fresh appearance of the platforms and the footbridge would suggest the photographs were taken within a few years of the station's completion. The signal in the upper photograph, taken from Cheap Street Bridge, is of considerable interest; known as a 'backing signal', it permitted a shunting move to be made from the down platform to one of a number of lines, including those in the goods shed. This signal survived until the replacement of the bridge for the Newbury Inner Ring Road in 1964 (both: John Allen collection)

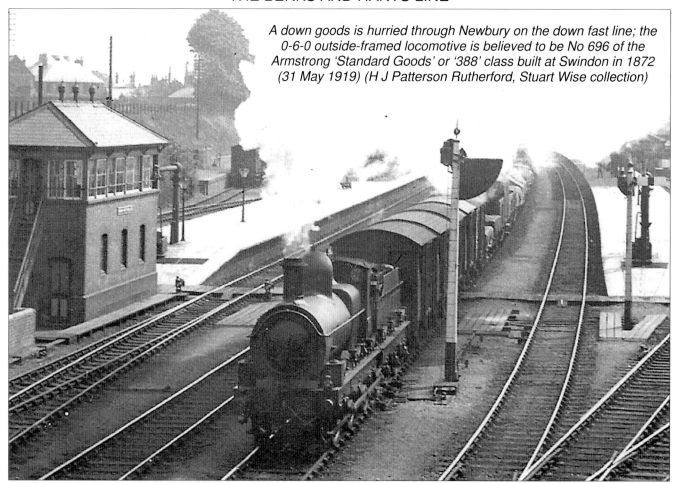

A down goods is hurried through Newbury on the down fast line; the 0-6-0 outside-framed locomotive is believed to be No 696 of the Armstrong 'Standard Goods' or '388' class built at Swindon in 1872 (31 May 1919) (H J Patterson Rutherford, Stuart Wise collection)

Cosburn's Advertising Station at the top of Station Approach. Not only have the buildings survived to this day, despite the changes wrought by the Ring Road, but the site is still used for advertising. If anyone knows when 'Judith' was staged at the Corn Exchange, the date can be established; there may of course be other clues (Kevin Robertson collection)

Two views of Kintbury. In the upper photograph, changes to the infrastructure may be detected compared with that on page 67 (chapter 4), including upgrading of the platforms and the replacement of the shunting signal in the foreground. The lower photograph almost defies explanation. Possibly, an excursion train, too long for the platform, is just arriving – none of the carriage doors are open. The starting signal is set at 'Danger'. Not everybody is crowded on the platform; some are on the platform ramp or on the road by the gates (both, John Allen collection)

View looking west of Hungerford station after the platforms were realigned in 1897-8, leaving the down side buildings somewhat offset from the edge of the platform. An up local train is ready for departure (John Allen collection)

A closer view of the buildings erected circa 1871 to replace that burnt down in 1868 and the adjacent buildings. The footbridge and up side platform shelter were also provided when the station was rebuilt as described in the photograph above (John Allen collection)

Above - Steam Railmotor No 74 is the star of this posed photograph dated 1912 at Hungerford, together with the driver, fireman, guard (with bugle), the stationmaster, other staff and passengers. (John Allen collection)

Below - local dignitaries shelter from the rain as they await the arrival of the King on a private visit to Chilton House on 21 October 1912. The stationmaster, on the right, is in his smartest attire in honour of the occasion (John Allen collection)

Above - *Hungerford Level Crossing is closed awaiting a train and the signalman is at the window of his box keeping an eye on the young girl using the pedestrian wicket gate. Such gates were a common feature of crossings, allowing pedestrians to cross the line when the main gates were closed and only being locked on the imminent approach of a train. The signal box pre-dates the doubling of the line, was enlarged in 1939 and demolished by a derailed freight train in 1971 (Author's collection)*

Below - *A final look at Hungerford station as it appeared soon after its reconstruction in 1897-98. The new up side waiting room and awning can clearly be seen, also the long siding on the left, the purpose of which is not known (John Allen collection)*

Bedwyn station looking towards Newbury from the road bridge. Apart from being taken after track doubling, there are no clues as to the date. However, a comparison with the photograph on page 68 shows that a much larger waiting shelter has been provided on the down platform (John Allen collection)

This view of Savernake GWR station is full of interest. Members of the local hunt are on the up platform presumably preparing to depart with their mounts on their special train to an unknown destination. There appear to be more horseboxes in the adjacent siding, behind which the Berks and Hants Extension Railway station building stands out. The building on the down platform, provided at the time of the track doubling, can clearly be seen; on the roadside behind is the Savernake Hotel, built at the same time as the Marlborough Branch in 1863-64 (Kevin Robertson collection)

Above - *Burbage Wharf goods shed and sidings looking west from the adjacent overbridge. This facility was provided in 1899 as there was a lack of space for a goods yard at Savernake station and interchange of traffic with the GWR-owned canal (running behind and close to the railway fence) was anticipated, hence the name. Although well equipped with crane and cattle pens, there seems little traffic in evidence.*

Below - *A view of Pewsey station looking west which is believed to be later than that shown on page 71, based mainly on the addition of a footbridge; however, the replacement of gas lighting by oil lends an air of mystery to this scene. The photograph pre-dates the replacement of the signal box in 1923 (both, John Allen collection)*

Above - *This classic view of Woodborough is probably contemporary with the Pewsey view opposite. Passengers await a westbound train whilst the porter stands by to assist with the loading and unloading of baskets, packages and parcels.*

Below, left - *The frontage of the signal box is the chosen location for this diverse group of men standing behind their Stationmaster at Woodborough. The function of each man may be a subject of debate, but there is no doubt which one is the permanent way ganger!*

Below, right - *This staff group at Lavington appears to be contemporary with that at Woodborough above and was probably taken soon after the opening of the station. As described at Newbury, the Stationmaster (back row, right) was responsible for all the staff in his section which may have included those at Edington & Bratton as well (all, John Allen collection)*

Above - *A posed view of Lavington station looking east. Comparison of the uniforms with the Woodborough group (above) suggests that this photograph was taken a generation later. This station was one of two on the Stert and Westbury Railway, opened in 1900.*

Below - *Edington and Bratton station looking west. Opened in 1900; although provided with similar facilities to Lavington, the station's catchment area was very small and it was destined to be the first passenger station on the Berks and Hants line to close (both, John Allen collection)*

6
GROUPING TO NATIONALISATION
1923 - 1947

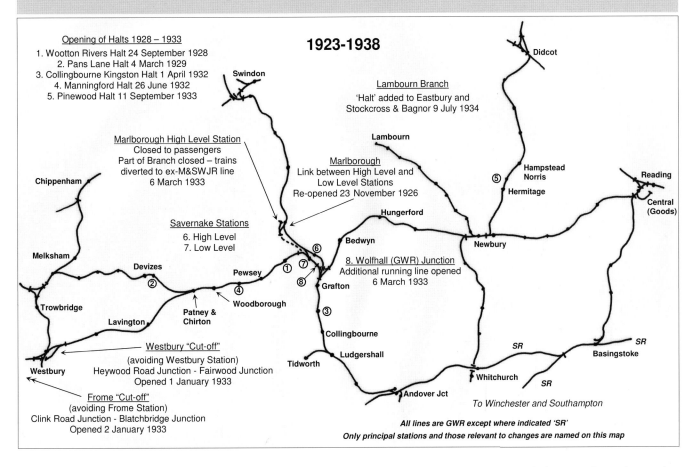

1923-1938

Opening of Halts 1928 – 1933
1. Wootton Rivers Halt 24 September 1928
2. Pans Lane Halt 4 March 1929
3. Collingbourne Kingston Halt 1 April 1932
4. Manningford Halt 26 June 1932
5. Pinewood Halt 11 September 1933

Lambourn Branch
'Halt' added to Eastbury and
Stockcross & Bagnor 9 July 1934

Marlborough High Level Station
Closed to passengers
Part of Branch closed – trains
diverted to ex-M&SWJR line
6 March 1933

Marlborough
Link between High Level and
Low Level Stations
Re-opened 23 November 1926

Savernake Stations
6. High Level
7. Low Level

8. Wolfhall (GWR) Junction
Additional running line opened
6 March 1933

Westbury "Cut-off"
(avoiding Westbury Station)
Heywood Road Junction - Fairwood Junction
Opened 1 January 1933

Frome "Cut-off"
(avoiding Frome Station)
Clink Road Junction - Blatchbridge Junction
Opened 2 January 1933

To Winchester and Southampton

All lines are GWR except where indicated 'SR'
Only principal stations and those relevant to changes are named on this map

Rationalisation and Improvement 1923 – 1932

The grouping of the railways into the "Big Four" brought new opportunities to rationalise duplicated facilities and avoid confusion to passengers. A modest start was made on 1 July 1924 with the renaming of the Savernake and Marlborough stations. The one at Savernake on the Marlborough and Grafton line, originally Savernake (M&SWJR), became High Level, whilst the GWR station on the Berks and Hants Extension Railway was renamed Low Level. At Marlborough, the ex-M&SWJR station was renamed Marlborough Low Level, the original GWR station becoming High Level. Also from this date, Whitchurch station on the DN&S section was renamed Whitchurch (Hants) to avoid confusion with similarly-named stations in Glamorgan and Shropshire that were served by the GWR following the grouping.

In October 1926 the GWR made a proposal to apply to the

Ministry of Transport for permission to close the entire Kennet and Avon Canal system. An application for abandonment of the proposal was made in April 1928.

In the same year, the link between the High Level and Low Level stations at Marlborough was restored for the transfer of goods; in due course this link would become the only means of access to the High Level station.

As private sidings were being developed elsewhere to take advantage of new freight opportunities, the earlier closure of the Calcot Mill led to the removal of the siding in January 1928. Meanwhile, at Colthrop a new layout was brought into use in October 1927 under a private siding agreement to serve Colthrop Board & Paper Mills Ltd. At Theale (West) a private siding for Wraysbury Sand & Gravel was available for use in February 1929. This siding was to be the precursor of a substantial range of private owner facilities to be developed at this site.

At Newbury, alterations to the goods yard to create four pairs of sidings, rather than the fan that existed previously, proceeded in stages from 1923 to 1933. At the east end of the goods yard, a private siding agreement (PSA) was made in 1923 for a new siding for B.P. Co. Ltd. In 1934, access was provided by means of a new PSA to an industrial development at Colthrop to the east of the board mills on the down side, the new line crossing the road adjacent to the existing level crossing. Later in the decade, in 1937, a private siding agreement was made with Newbury Corporation to give access to Newbury Gas Works and the works headshunt was lengthened. In the same year the private siding agreement for the sidings at Theale was transferred to the Theale and Great Western Sand & Gravel Co Ltd.

While the need for rationalisation and economy was leading to the closure of little-used stations and lines elsewhere in the country, one new halt was opened in 1928, another in 1929 and two in 1932. The first to be opened was Wootton Rivers Halt on the main line between Savernake and Pewsey, on 24 September 1928 (shown as Wootton Rivers in the 1932 timetable). This was soon followed by Pans Lane Halt, between Patney & Chirton and Devizes, just under three-quarters of a mile from the last named, on 4 March 1929. Collingbourne Kingston Halt, on the ex-M&SWJR line between Grafton & Burbage (generally referred to as Grafton) and Collingbourne, was opened on 1 April 1932, and Manningford Halt, on the main line between Pewsey and Woodborough, on 26 June of that year. However, a proposal in 1929 to provide a halt to be called Froxfield, between Hungerford and Bedwyn, was not proceeded with. The halt would have been sited where the line passes close to the Bath Road at the east end of the village.

The Great Western Railway had been one of the forerunners in developing a system for warning train drivers of signals set at caution ahead. As we have already seen, such a system was installed on the Lambourn branch in 1909 and this remained in use until 1929. The system was later developed to operate the brakes automatically on the train if the warning to the driver was not acknowledged and was known as Automatic Train Control (ATC). In 1930 ATC was extended from Reading through Newbury and Westbury to Taunton; it was completed to Plymouth in 1931.

The Development (Loan Guarantees and Grants) Act of 1929 enabled the Government to guarantee investment in new works by the railways, primarily to alleviate employment. The GWR was able to take advantage of the Act to carry out substantial improvements to its main lines in the 1930s. The extension of Automatic Train Control noted above was also carried out using money available under the Act.

New Works and Developments in 1933

Two new building schemes of significance were the Westbury and Frome cut-offs, also known as avoiding lines, which enabled West of England and Weymouth expresses and through freights not calling at these places to avoid these stations and their associated 30mph speed restrictions. These new lines were authorised by the Great Western Railway Act, 1930 and are described as Railway No 2 (Westbury) and Railway No 3 (Frome). The former is of particular relevance and is described in the Act as follows: "A railway (No 2) 2 miles 2 furlongs and 4 chains in length wholly in the county of Wilts commencing in the parish of Dilton Marsh in the rural district of Westbury and Whorwellsdown by a junction with the Company's Wilts Somerset and Weymouth Railway and terminating in the parish and urban district of Westbury by a junction with the Company's Stert and Westbury Railway." The junctions referred to are at the west and east ends of the new line respectively. It is interesting to note the use of the names of the railways as originally authorised.

Work started in 1930 and the contractor for both sections was the railway contracting firm of Logan and Hemingway. These new sections of main line were opened for traffic at the start of 1933 (Westbury 1 January, Frome 2 January) and were brought into use for freight at the end of March 1933 and for passenger trains at the beginning of the summer timetable on 17 July 1933; together they involved the construction of 4½ miles of new line at a total initial contract cost of £220,000. The new junctions on the Westbury cut-off were Heywood Road and Fairwood; the new line was almost 2½ miles long and was slightly *longer* than the original line. The Frome cut-off was slightly over 2 miles long and saved a distance of somewhat less than a quarter of a mile. No speed limits were stipulated on these lines; in later years speed restrictions were necessary due to problems with the stability of the earthworks. In fact, in 1939, the GWR is on record as stating: "exceptional settlement trouble has been experienced over both these lines, and it is for this reason that even yet, after five years, it is not deemed wise to permit maximum speed running on either" **(Note 1)**.

In 1935, a short siding was added at Heywood Road Junction to accommodate the locomotive required for taking the slip portions of trains avoiding Westbury into the station; from 8 April the Weymouth slip portion of the Cornish Riviera was slipped at the Junction (see **Glossary**). Prior to the provision of this siding, such trains had to pass through the station, where the slip portion would be detached.

Opposite - Ex-M&SWJR 2-4-0 no.1335 on a down local passing over Aldermaston Troughs (Maurice Earley)

104

The area around Savernake also witnessed changes in 1933; these took place in order to rationalise the duplication of facilities in the area which had existed since 1898 (Chapter 4). No alterations were made to the main line through Grafton Junction, Wolfhall Junction and Savernake, or to Savernake Low Level station. The branch line from that station to Marlborough was diverted to serve the Low Level (ex-M&SWJR) station in Marlborough; the High Level (ex-GWR) station was closed to passengers and the redundant section of the original Marlborough Branch was closed completely. The separate line from Marlborough, which enabled trains on the ex-M&SWJR route to avoid the Berks & Hants line altogether, crossing over the latter line between Savernake Low Level and Wolfhall Junction, was retained but reduced in status and capacity to a single line. Savernake High Level station on this line was also retained; however, its status was also reduced, one platform only being used, the other line through the station becoming a goods refuge siding only.

The changes came into effect on 6 March 1933; from this date the only passenger trains to continue to use Savernake High level were one through train each way between Southampton and Cheltenham and one Saturdays only train each way between Tidworth and Swindon Junction (as the GWR station in Swindon was then known) **(Note 2)**.

Once again, for the first time since 1898, regular passenger trains used the curve between Wolfhall Junction (GWR), on the main line, and Wolfhall Junction (M&SWJR); the curve had been re-opened for passenger traffic early in 1932. In order to ease working of trains over this curve, an additional running line was provided between Wolfhall Junction (GWR) and the bridge over the canal.

The signal boxes at each end of the Grafton Curve, which remained open as a double track connection to enable through running between Newbury and Ludgershall, were renamed as follows: on the main line - Grafton East Junction (was Grafton Curve); on the MSWJ line - Grafton South Junction (was Wolfhall Junction (M&SWJR)).

Full details of the changes to the railways in the Savernake and Marlborough areas can be found in the numerous books and articles published on the M&SWJR.

Another new halt was opened in 1933, on 11 September - this time on the Didcot and Newbury line. Pinewood Halt was located by an overbridge about three-quarters of a mile north of Hermitage and served a part of the village that was some distance from the station.

Another substantial improvement made in 1933 was to the pier and harbour at Weymouth. The need for improved accommodation at the port for the Channel Island and French traffic had been apparent for a number of years. There were heavy seasonal imports of flowers, new potatoes and tomatoes from Jersey and Guernsey, and broccoli and other vegetables from France. The nature of this traffic called for speed in discharge from vessels and dispatch by rail. Following negotiations between the GWR and Weymouth Corporation, a scheme for improvements, costing over £120,000, was agreed: the main harbour works to be financed by the Corporation backed by the GWR; permanent way, cranes, capstans paid for by the GWR; and widening the quay road, pier extensions, dredging and public amenities paid for by the Corporation. There were also improved arrangements for dealing with the increasingly heavy summer passenger traffic; the capacity of the platforms was increased from 4 to 36

coaches whilst facilities for handling baggage, customs examination etc were also improved. All passenger and freight traffic from Weymouth was under the control of the GWR; that destined for the London area passed over the Berks & Hants line.

Developments and Changes 1934 to 1939

Numerous additional trains were introduced on the main line during the nineteen-thirties: many of them intended to help cope with the summer holiday crowds. In 1934, 900 new services were brought into operation by the GWR, many running on Saturdays only. In order to create further block sections (see **Glossary**) and thus increase capacity on the line in busy periods, two additional signal boxes were provided in June 1934. These were at Wootton Rivers, between Burbage and Pewsey boxes, and Crookwood, between Patney and Lavington.

The year 1936 started badly due to the settlement of the bridge carrying the Andover – Upavon – Devizes road over the main line between Patney and Lavington on 1 January; trains were diverted to other routes, including the Devizes line **(Note 3)**. Fortunately, the weak underbridges on the Devizes line had, in the previous decade, been strengthened with the result that all but the largest GWR locomotives (the "King" class) could use the line.

Rationalisation finally came to the ex-DN&SR line when the loop at the remote station of Litchfield (Hants) was taken out of use and the signal box was removed in 1936. As a portent of things to come, in 1937 part of the Bar End (Winchester) - Shawford Junction section of the line was moved westwards for the construction of the Winchester By-pass.

Between December 1937 and July 1938, the brick arch bridge carrying the Berks & Hants line over the Oxford Road in Reading, immediately north of Reading West station, was replaced with the steel spans that are still in use today. The original shallow brick arch was believed to be sound but clearance for traffic was limited, the double track for tramcars being singled under the bridge. The dip in the road under the arch was prone to flooding and Reading Corporation wished to widen the road and run trolleybuses on it. Maurice Earley's photos "Engineering Work Nos 1, 2 and 3" in his book "Truly the Great Western" (see **Further Reading**) show work in hand under possession on Sunday 20 March and under single line working (up line) on Sunday 26 June whilst the new down line bridge girders were being placed. Demolition of the old bridge under the up line and installation of the up line outside bridge girder took place the following Sunday 3 July, the work being completed early on the Monday morning. Over the following two weeks, including two Sunday 24-hour possessions (occupations of one of the tracks on each occasion), work on the new structure and demolition of the old brick arch continued and was brought to completion. During the course of this work, the points at Oxford Road Junction were moved off the bridge to the north end of the

Carrier John Gould at Newbury Goods Yard (1936) (Kevin Robertson collection)

GWR 'Castle' class 4-6-0 No 4082 'Windsor Castle' heads the London & North Western Railway royal train through Reading West during celebrations for the Silver Jubilee of King George V (May 1935) (National Railway Museum Collection)

bridge; it is also of interest to note that the 10-inch diameter water main (which provided Reading Engine Shed with water from the River Kennet) was temporarily transferred to the up line span and then finally back to its permanent location on the down line span.

Other works known to have been carried out during 1938, which reflect both the age profile of the various structures along the line at that time and the demands of increasing traffic, were:

The pumping plant at Savernake Low Level (water from the canal for railway purposes) was converted to electric operation;

Further extensive works were carried out on the Weymouth Quay tramway, at Ferry Corner;

The bridge over the River Kennet west of Kintbury was reconstructed;

To meet the need for weighing facilities at Midgham

station, a 12-ton cart weighbridge was installed;

A bridge over the Holy Brook, between Theale and Southcote Junction, was reconstructed.

In January 1938, Tile (Tyle) Mill sidings, on the down side of the line about 1½ miles west of Theale, were taken out of use and the signal box, dating from at least as far back as 1876, closed. The final private siding agreement, only made in 1936, had terminated in 1937.

At Hungerford, the two signal boxes, East and West, dating from the realignment of the main lines through the station in 1900, were reduced to one in January 1939. East Box was closed and replaced with a ground frame, whilst West Box, alongside the level crossing, was enlarged and renamed Hungerford. Elsewhere on the Berks & Hants line, Marsh Box, between Midgham and Colthrop, which was opened in 1906 on the diversion of West of England trains to the line, was closed in November 1939.

The GWR's passenger road operations were progressively transferred to its associated road companies in the late 1920s and early 1930s. These included Thames Valley Traction Co Ltd.; in 1939, investment in this company stood at £93,710 and a rate of return of 9.8% was obtained on this sum.

Developments during the Second World War - Preparations and early developments

With the increasing threat of war, main line railways in Great Britain were placed under government control by the Railway Executive Committee under the Emergency (Railway Control) order of 1 September 1939. The authority for this was Regulation No 69 of the Defence Regulations issued in pursuance of the Emergency Powers (Defence) Act given royal assent on 24 August 1939. A state of war was declared on 3 September 1939; Government control continued until the enactment of the provisions of the Transport Act 1947.

An immediate start was made on evacuating children from London and other cities. From London, evacuees were sent to Wessex and the Far West, the majority of the reception areas being between Reading and Penzance, and including Newbury **(Note 4)**. The GWR played a major role in moving its diminutive passengers to their safe havens in the West. These evacuations were part of a massive country-wide operation to move people out of London, other cities and industrial areas to safer locations.

Following the evacuations, a War Timetable came into operation on the GWR on Monday 25 September 1939. All West of England trains were withdrawn from the Berks & Hants line except the night train to Penzance, the diverted trains running via Bristol. Newbury, Westbury and intermediate stations were served by the Weymouth trains, which continued to use the line; however, Channel Islands services from Weymouth ceased at the outbreak of war.

Through services to and from the Southern Railway via Reading were suspended. The provision of restaurant and sleeping cars was completely withdrawn. Wootton Rivers Signal Box, opened in 1934, was closed on 28 September 1939, followed by Bulls Lock Signal Box on 2 July 1940.

From 16 October 1939, restaurant cars were restored on the GWR, the Cornish Riviera Express returned to its normal route via Westbury and was scheduled to run non-stop between Paddington and Exeter; also, a fortnight later, the 1.30pm from Paddington to Plymouth was re-introduced and ran via Westbury. From 5 February 1940, the Westbury route was restored as the main channel of communication between London and the West of England.

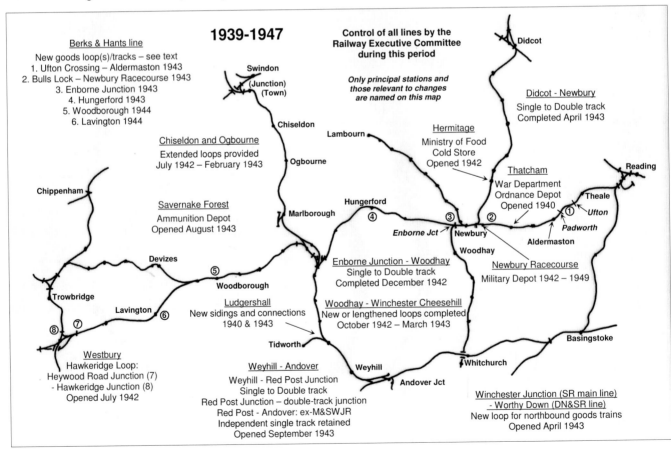

Railway Headquarters move out of London

It was considered advisable, "for the continuance of communication and control", for the GWR to move its headquarters out of London. Six country houses west of Reading were duly adapted to accommodate departments evacuated out of Paddington, as follows:

Beenham Grange, Aldermaston: General Manager, Secretary, Solicitor (Headquarters)

Wharf House, Padworth (near Aldermaston): The Surveyor

Hyde End House, Midgham: Chief Accountant

Wasing Place, Wasing: Chief Accountant's Dept (routine matters)

Crookham House, Thatcham: Chief Goods Manager

The Gables, Cholsey: Registration Office

Another method of providing accommodation outside London was to use excursion coaches, with their open saloons and large windows, as offices. Some of these coaches were based in a siding at Newbury Racecourse.

Newbury Racecourse transformed

Newbury Racecourse was once again used a military depot, no time being wasted in requisitioning the racecourse as soon as war was declared. In 1940, the racecourse was de-requisitioned for six weeks but Dunkirk intervened and the premises were requisitioned again in June, spoiling plans to hold the Derby at Newbury. East of the stands, an RASC (see **Glossary**) main supply depot was installed, a private siding agreement with the Secretary of State for War being made on 5 September 1941. Three widely spaced sidings were laid in, connected to the most southerly of the six existing sidings. Racing was able to continue, however, as the courses were kept clear and in good order, but the whole area was handed over to the American Army in August 1942.

A vast depot and marshalling yard was created which was eventually named G45. Thirty-seven miles of railway track were laid and many concrete roads, obliterating the courses. It was here that petrol was concentrated and dispatched to the American landings in North Africa. Later, a huge quantity of Bailey bridging, landing mats, hutments and much other miscellaneous equipment was assembled for the main invasion of Europe. This equipment included railway locomotives; large numbers of imported USA-built locomotives were processed here before being sent to their military destinations overseas.

Soon after the Normandy landings, most of the stores were transferred across the English Channel and by September 1945, a good clearance was noticeable and it began to look as if use of Marshalling Yard G45 had finished. However, in December, more American equipment and stores were brought in from other depots and this continued until March 1946 when the materials were handed over to the Ministry of Supply for disposal by auction under the American Lend-Lease Agreement.

It was not until June 1947 that the central area which included the courses was released and owing to the slowness of the negotiations, the clearing work was not commenced until August, at which time the Private Siding Agreement was transferred to the Ministry of Works.

Miles of rail and thousands of sleepers as well as hardcore, ashes, concrete and metal all had to be removed before reinstatement of the damaged area to its pre-war condition could begin. The Private Siding Agreement was terminated at the end of 1949, although one of the military sidings laid in 1941 was retained. Racing recommenced in April 1949, but reinstatement of the courses continued well into 1950.

New depots and sidings

During the war, several other additional sources of rail traffic were added between Newbury and Reading. A siding was provided at Theale (East) for the Imperial Tobacco Co and brought into use on 5 January 1940. The private siding agreement, dated 23 January 1940, was amended on 24 December that year when a siding on the access line was converted into a loop. At about this time, the factory was converted to a Royal Ordnance Factory for the duration of the war.

A siding was provided at Padworth for the Ministry of Fuel and Power (Asiatic Petrol Co) with an adjacent tip siding, connected to what was to later become the down goods line immediately east of the station. The sidings were brought into use on 24 February 1942.

At Colthrop, on the up (north) side opposite the Board and Paper Mill, two sidings were added during the war to serve the Royal Naval Victualling Depot established there. The connection with the up main line was located to the west of Colthrop Crossing.

The Thatcham War Department Ordnance Depot was opened in 1940 and was provided with connections into the up main line facing both east and west. In addition to an extensive network of sidings, an up goods loop was provided alongside the length of the depot, a new signal box, Thatcham West, was installed and opened on 19 July 1940, and Thatcham Station Signal Box was extended to handle the additional facilities. Two engine spurs were added within the depot circa 1941.

New Works between Reading and Westbury

In addition to the goods loop at Thatcham, a number of other works were carried out on the Reading - Westbury section in the 1942 - 1944 period to improve capacity and assist with the build up of forces that was necessary. Working westwards as before, these were provided as follows:

ALDERMASTON: Up and Down Goods Loops between Aldermaston and Ufton Crossing (about one mile) were brought into use 14/19 February 1943 and 30 March 1943 respectively. The Down Loop was connected into the sidings already provided at Padworth. A new signal box was provided at Ufton Crossing, opening at the same time as the Up Loop, and replacing the existing box. The 1920-built box at the west end of Aldermaston station was retained; the new signalling arrangements may have used the spare capacity available after the removal from use of the up sidings and connection on 28 March 1940.

NEWBURY RACECOURSE: A double track goods line was provided from the east end of the Racecourse Station to Bulls Lock that was effectively an extension of the two tracks that from 1912 had been available between Newbury and Racecourse stations. The new lines were commissioned between 31 January and 3 February 1943 and were served at the east end by a new signal box called Bulls Lock. An earlier box with the same name, located a mile further east, had been closed in 1940.

*Three views of the works carried out in 1942-1943 east of Aldermaston station. **Above** is a view east from the station looking towards Reading, earthworks having been carried out for the Up Goods Loop. The connecting line to the private sidings at Padworth is seen on the right. Worthy of note is the double line of telegraph poles, reflecting the strategic importance of the railway installations and other facilities in the area served by the line.*

***Opposite, above,** also looking towards Reading, the construction of both Up and Down Goods Loops can be seen to be well advanced. The line to the private sidings, just out of sight on the right, has been connected to the near end of the Down Loop. The wagons on the right are standing on a short spur; the brake van is standing on the down main line. This, together with the various activities in progress, suggests a temporary closure of the Berks and Hants line (maybe a Sunday) – such activities would have been in progress all the way down the line.*

*The **lower** view features the overbridge seen in the far distance in the upper photograph; the view was clearly taken on completion of the Up and Down Goods Loops (GWR)*

ENBORNE JUNCTION: An Up Goods Loop about half a mile in length was provided from immediately west of Enborne Junction towards Newbury. It was possible for an up goods train to enter the loop while a train from the Winchester line was joining the up main line. It was also possible for a goods train from the Winchester line to gain access to the loop; no other movement would have been possible at the same time. Finally, it was possible for up goods trains, having arrived at the loop, to be taken in the Winchester direction using the trailing crossover in the main line. A new frame was installed in the signal box in December 1942, the crossover was available in March 1943 and the loop was brought into use in July 1943.

brought into use in September 1944, together with a new signal box on the up side at the east end. It is worthy of note that the entry and exit points were not opposite each other; due to the location of the goods yard, the Down Loop commenced and ended over 200 yards to the west of the Up Loop, which was created by a western extension of the Up Refuge Siding, dating from the doubling of the line in 1900.

LAVINGTON: An Up Goods Loop about 2½ miles in length was added to the west of the station in August 1944, partially on the site of a military siding dating from 30 years earlier.

Enborne Junction, looking towards Newbury, taken after completion of the Up Goods Loop. As described in the text, this loop was accessible from both the main line and the Winchester line. The signal box replaced one at an adjacent site provided in 1885 for the opening of the Winchester line, and was provided as part of improvements made to the signalling arrangements west of Newbury in 1907 (Adrian Vaughan Collection)

HUNGERFORD: A Down Goods Loop was provided alongside the common between the Dun Mill Lock overbridge and a point east of the connections to the goods yard. It was available for use in October 1943, together with a new ground frame at the goods yard end which replaced that installed in 1939 on closure of the East Box.

WOODBOROUGH: Up and Down Goods Loops were

WESTBURY: a double line connection between the Reading - Westbury line and the Trowbridge - Westbury line, known as the Hawkeridge Loop, was built to enable traffic from the Berks & Hants line to reach the Trowbridge and Bath line and was opened in July 1942. At the east end the junction, situated some 30 chains (3/8 mile) to the west of Heywood Road Junction, was controlled by Heywood Road Junction Signal Box. At the west or north end, however, a new signal box had to be provided; this was situated in the "V" of the new junction and called Hawkeridge Signal Box.

New Works between Didcot, Newbury and Winchester

The Didcot to Winchester line via Newbury was also massively affected by works to improve its capacity and therefore its ability to carry the heavy traffic required in the preparations for D-Day and the subsequent back-up operations.

The entire line from Didcot to Newbury, 18 miles, was doubled. Passenger services were suspended between Didcot, Newbury and Winchester on 4 August 1942; the line was reopened for passengers on 8 March 1943. A substitute bus service was laid on, calling at all stations and at no other points. Double line working was introduced in stages. Newbury to Hermitage was brought into use in January 1943; Hermitage to Hampstead Norris and Upton & Blewbury to Didcot in February; Hampstead Norris to Compton in late March / early April. The last section, Compton to Upton, over the downs, was not opened as a double track until April. From Hampstead Norris to Upton, therefore, was not opened as double track until after the restoration of passenger services.

The line had originally been built for double track, but it was necessary to open out the cuttings, due to fallen chalk. Except where double track already existed, it was necessary to provide for the second track at all underbridges (Note 5). Whilst Churn Halt was reopened (with a new platform) to passengers in March 1943, the doubling had swept away the siding and Churn was officially closed to goods traffic in April 1943. The signal boxes built for the opening of the line were retained and at Hampstead Norris, where the signal box had been replaced by two ground frames in 1912, a new box was provided. A new set of intermediate signals was provided to halve the block section between Compton and Upton, called Ilsley (or West Ilsley) signals.

At Hampstead Norris, a second platform was required as no provision had previously been made for passenger trains to pass. The only other stopping place where a second platform was required was at Pinewood Halt; the original platform was rebuilt. At Hermitage, a Ministry of Food cold store on the south side of the station was opened in 1942. This was served by two lengthy sidings, a similarly lengthy run-round loop / refuge siding (see Glossary) and a headshunt.

Between Newbury and Winchester, the amount of excavation required in the cuttings made doubling the line throughout impractical. Doubling was limited to the 2-mile

section from Enborne Junction to Woodhay, completed in December 1942. For the remaining 23 miles to Winchester, additional passing places were provided and existing loops were lengthened. At some locations, the single line was slewed (moved laterally) to the centre of the formation, particularly under arched overbridges. The line was closed to passengers from August 1942 to March 1943, as recorded above, to enable the engineering work to be carried out. The only exception was a once-weekly train for soldiers from Winchester to Sutton Scotney. Freight traffic was reduced to a once nightly through freight in each direction.

The single-line section commenced at Woodhay where a new signal box was built, opening in October 1942. The centre span of the timber bridge which at that time carried the A34 over the railway, just to the north of Highclere station, was strengthened by the addition of a central timber trestle. Like all bridges spanning the railway, it had been built for double track. Strengthening work was necessary due to the inability of the span to carry wartime traffic and was carried out by the GWR on behalf of the Ministry of War Transport.

Lengthened loops and new signal boxes were provided at Highclere, Burghclere, Litchfield, Whitchurch, Lodge Bridge, Sutton Scotney and Worthy Down. At King's Worthy, a lengthened loop was provided but the existing signal box was retained and moved to a new location at one end of the loop. At the other end of the loop at each of the above stations, the points were worked from the box by a point machine powered by a hand generator and a cabin was provided for the return and issue of tokens. These facilities were completed at various dates between October 1942 and March 1943.

At Burghclere, the private siding agreement for the siding to the lime kilns was terminated in June 1942 and reinstated in July 1943. At Litchfield, the passing loop had been taken out of use in 1936. Locomotive watering facilities were provided at Whitchurch. No loop had previously existed at Lodge Bridge; it was provided to break up the nearly 6-mile section (between centres of stations) between Whitchurch and Sutton Scotney. An unadvertised halt, Barton Stacey, located between Lodge Bridge and Sutton Scotney, was opened during the war.

At Worthy Down, a new island platform was built to replace the previous single platform. Although this station had a loop and sidings, it had not been used for crossing passenger trains before the temporary closure. South of Worthy Down, a new single line connection just over a mile long was built for northbound (up) trains between the station and the up ex-L&SWR main line at Winchester Junction. A junction, with signal box, already existed there for the Alton line. The new line was available for use, for through up ex-LSWR main line freight or troop trains not needing to call at Winchester (Cheesehill) or Bar End Yard, in May 1943 **(Note 6)**. The possibility of building this link had been considered in 1933; however, at that time, it was one of the options for by-passing Winchester Cheesehill station which would have enabled the closure of some five miles of line through Cheesehill to Shawford Junction.

At Winchester, the double line in the station was extended through the tunnel and brought into use in October 1942. No changes were made at the station itself or at Bar End Goods, and the single line remained between the station and Shawford Junction. However, it was necessary to enlarge the station signal box to control the additional facilities.

New Works between Swindon, Savernake and Andover

Investment was also made in the ex-M&SWJR line between Swindon, Savernake and Andover to increase capacity for wartime traffic. On the single line section between Swindon Town and Marlborough, loops at the first-named, and at Chiseldon and Ogbourne were extended between July 1942 and February 1943, whilst the signal box at Chiseldon was extended and that at Ogbourne replaced. As on the ex-DN&SR line, the points at the far end of the loops were so far from the box controlling them that they were worked by a hand-turned generator. No changes were made to the layout between Marlborough and Grafton, which had been rationalised in 1933 to give two independent single lines, one of which joined the Berks & Hants line at Savernake Low Level and left it at Wolfhall Junction. On the other line, which ran via Savernake High Level, a siding into a military facility, a massive ammunition depot in the forest, was opened in August 1943. The connection to the depot was by a connection facing northbound trains about two miles from Savernake and was served by North Savernake Ground Frame.

Double track was already in place between Grafton and Weyhill, so no changes were required on that section. The single line between Weyhill and Red Post Junction was doubled and was available from September 1943, a double junction being provided with the Southern Railway's main line. The independent single line from the junction to Andover was retained.

At Ludgershall changes were made on the Tidworth branch. War Department sidings were added in 1940, and in 1943 a connection was made to the RAOC (see **Glossary**) Central Vehicle Depot and alterations were made at the start of the single line to Tidworth at Perham.

Other wartime events along the line

In 1940, pillboxes and anti-tank obstructions were built by or near the canal, some of which were close to the railway. At Dun Mill Lock, east of Hungerford, not one but two pillboxes were situated on the adjacent railway overbridge and, like many others, they remain there to this day. Near Crofton, anti-tank obstructions have survived on an abandoned canal bridge and can be clearly seen from the train.

The GWR again tried to close the canal in 1941, but was unsuccessful.

On Wednesday 10 February 1943, Newbury was subjected to a low-level bombing raid which caused a great deal of damage, particularly to St John's Church, the almshouses at what is now Fair Close and the Council Primary School, the site of which is now St Nicolas C.E Junior School. Damage to the railway was limited to the roof of Newbury West Signal Box and an adjacent pump house. It is interesting to note that this raid took place during the period of intense activity on track additions and alterations. However, it is thought that the railway was not a primary target; possible targets, together with a detailed analysis of the raid and its aftermath, are described in the referenced locally-published book.

With the completion of loops at Woodborough in September 1944, the wartime works to increase capacity, ease congestion and provide additional facilities on the Reading - Westbury, Didcot - Winchester and Swindon - Andover lines were completed.

Peace returns and heralds the last days of the Great Western Railway

After peace returned in 1945, train services slowly returned to normal. One event worthy of note was the reintroduction of the London – Penzance TPO (Travelling Post Office) on 1 October 1945. Channel Island services restarted in September, with normal service resuming in June 1946.

Opposite, upper - The first of two photographs taken at Hungerford station in 1946. The main station building, on the down platform, dates from circa 1871 and had replaced the ramshackle collection of buildings provided on the opening of the Berks and Hants Railway in 1847, one of which was burnt down in 1867. Changes to the station in the 1898-1900 period, which included a realignment of the tracks through the station, had left the main building somewhat remote from the platform edge. In the same period the up side building and footbridge were provided. Lighting is by gas and the station name on the main building remains blacked out. The second (lower) photograph shows that the signal box has been doubled in size compared with the view on page 96; the work was completed in January 1939. The steps have been incorporated in the building and the name of the box has yet to emerge from its wartime blackout (GWR)

GROUPING TO NATIONALISATION 1923 - 1947

Sidings and goods facilities that had become redundant were closed. Burghclere down side sidings and limekiln private sidings were removed in 1946, and Burbage Wharf station (goods only) was closed as from 11 November 1947.

But much greater changes were on the way. The 1947 Transport Act, which became law on 6 August, spelt the end of the Great Western Railway as a private company and authorised its replacement by the Western Region of British Railways from 1 January 1948.

NOTES

NOTE 1: DATES

"History of the Great Western Railway Volume III" (Nock) gives date as March 1933; "History of the Great Western Railway Volume 2" (Semmens) gives date as 1932; Railway Magazine July 1933 gives the opening date for freight; Great Western Railway Magazine June 1933 gives the opening date for passenger trains; "Track Layout Diagrams of the GWR and BR WR Section 21: Bath and Westbury" (Cooke) gives opening dates of cut-offs and signal boxes at each end as: Westbury 1 January 1933, Frome 2 January 1933. Information on and photographs of these projects may also be found in "Somewhere Along The Line" (Peters).

NOTE 2:

An item in the Railway Magazine May 1938 states that the extensive alterations in the layout of the lines between Grafton South Junction, Savernake and Marlborough were brought into use on 26 February 1933; it also states that these changes resulted in two single lines in the 647yd Marlborough Tunnel and poses the question as to whether there were any other tunnels in the country with two single lines.

NOTE 3:

An excellent photo of this bridge is shown at plate 86 in "Newbury to Westbury" (see **Further Reading**); the location is not identified. The rebuilt part of the bridge can be clearly seen.

NOTE 4:

The specific reference to Newbury is based on an item in the Newbury Weekly News 28 December 1989, under the heading '50 years ago'. References to evacuees being resettled in Berkshire and Wiltshire may also be found in local history sources.

NOTE 5:

Examination of the surviving bridges reveals that generally new concrete deck spans were provided for both tracks, replacing the original steel spans. The abutments were altered as required, in order to comply with the standards applicable at the time with regard to axle loading and clearances.

NOTE 6:

The Railway Magazine May/June 1946, under 'New Works for Wartime Traffic', gives the date of the new line from Worthy Down to Winchester Junction as 5 May 1943.

ACTS

Great Western Railway Act, 4 June 1930, (20&21 Geo V, c. 68) (Westbury and Frome Avoiding Lines)

Transport Act, 6 August 1947, (10&11 Geo VI, c. 49) (nationalisation of Britain's railways)

CHAPTER REFERENCES

Deposited Documents (see Chapter 1 for interpretation of references)

(A1/371/172MS): Great Western Railway: (relevant part) Burbage (1928)

(A1/371/173MS): Great Western Railway: Westbury Avoiding Line (1929)

PUBLISHED REFERENCES

History of the Great Western Railway

Peter Semmens (Guild Publishing /George Allen & Unwin)

Volume 1 Consolidation 1923 – 1929 (1985)

Volume 2 The Thirties 1930 – 1939 (1985)

Volume 3 Wartime and the Final Years 1939 – 1948 (1985)

Kintbury signalman at crossing gate wheel (Kevin Robertson collection)

History of the Great Western Railway Volume III 1923 – 1947

O S Nock (Ian Allan Ltd 1967)

Atlas of the Great Western Railway as at 1947

R A Cooke (First published 1988; Revised Edition 1997)

The Great Western Railway in the 20th Century

O S Nock (Ian Allan 1964 (1971 edition))

The Great Western at Work 1921 – 1939

A Vaughan (Patrick Stephens Limited 1993)

The Last Years of the Big Four

A Earnshaw & D Jenkinson (Atlantic Publishers 1997)

The Bombing of Newbury

Bryan Philpott (Pegasus Publications Newbury 1989)

Somewhere Along The Line

Ivo Peters (Oxford Publishing Co 1976)

GWR Engineering Work 1928-1938

R Tourret (Tourret Publishing 2003)

Railway World

Vol 22 The Development of Rail-Sea Facilities at Weymouth; Part 1 June 1961 p201-5; Part 2 July 1961 p227-232

Vol 26 Reading in the 1920s July 1965 p258

Backtrack

Vol 6 No 4 1992 p207: Railway Interest in Buses - GWR services

Railway Magazine

Vol 54 1924 p241-2 Railway Communication with Weymouth

Vol 55 1924 p470 Marlborough Railway

Vol 56 1925 p147 Speed Restrictions, Reading – Westbury section

Vol 56 1925 p503 Vol 57 1925 p368 & p474: GWR Channel Islands Service

Vol 61 1927 p141 Devizes Line – restrictions on types of locomotives permitted

Vol 63 1928 p248 New halt to be constructed at Wootton Rivers (between Savernake and Pewsey)

Vol 63 1928 p465 Vol 64 1929 p144 & p228 Grafton Curve - origin, purpose and traffic review

Vol 64 1929 p418 New halt at Pans Lane, between Patney & Chirton and Devizes, was opened on 4 March 1929

Vol 66 1930 p298-307 The Main Line Gradients of British Railways XVI – GWR Paddington to Penzance with Basingstoke, Weymouth and Torquay branches

Vol 67 1930 p447 New GWR Rail By-Passes to the West

Vol 69 1931 p74 Automatic Train Control system – "From Whitsun, the whole of the GWR main line to the West of England, from Paddington to Plymouth *via* Westbury and *via* Bristol was brought under the automatic train control system, which is being installed on all the company's main line routes"

Vol 72 1933 p145 Railway Developments at Winchester: mostly historical, but mentions possibility of spurs connecting line south of Worthy Down with L&SWR main line

Vol 72 1933 p377-9 Developments on the MSWJ Section, GWR: describes changes in track layouts brought into use on Monday 6 March 1933; also notes that: the section Wolfhall Junction to Wolfhall Junction MSW (renamed Grafton South Junction) was re-opened for passenger traffic in "early 1932" and that the former GWR engine shed at Marlborough will continue to house the branch engine

Vol 73 1933 p70 GW Summer Services – small savings on new cut-offs until new banks have "settled"; Weymouth portion of the Cornish Riviera Express may be detached at the new junction east of Westbury

Vol 73 1933 p73 New by-pass lines – brought into use at the end of March last - details of testing – freight traffic worked over route "for a considerable period" before any diversion of regular passenger traffic

Vol 73 1933 p123 Effect of opening Westbury cut-off (under Summer Train Services 1933)

Vol 73 1933 p309 Restrictions on types of locomotives used on the Patney to Holt Junction via Devizes route

Vol 75 1934 p454 Channel Islands boat service; fast newspaper trains

Vol 76 1935 p385 Short siding provided at Heywood Road Junction for locomotive taking the Westbury slip portion of the "Cornish Riviera Limited" into the station

Vol 78 1936 p231-2 Services operated by GW diesel railcars; collapse of bridge near Patney (1.1.36) caused diversions via Swindon and Devizes

Vol 82 1938 p235 Closed Branch Lines I; p387: Extensive alterations to layout of lines between Grafton South Junction, Savernake and Marlborough brought into use on 26 February 1933; from that date Marlborough Tunnel has two single lines replacing the previous up and down lines; p399: Closed Branch Lines III – SR Hurstbourne to Fullerton – referenced in Chapter 4 in connection with possible loops at Whitchurch on the Newbury – Winchester line

Vol 83 1938 p216 The Westbury and Frome cut-offs – "due to exceptional settlement problems with earthworks on these cut-offs, maximum speed running has not yet been permitted"

Vol 83 1938 p382 Weymouth Quay Lines improvements

Vol 83 1938 p461 The Devizes Line GWR – reference to the bridge problem near Patney in 1936 and strengthening of underbridges on the Devizes line to permit use by heavier locomotives

Vol 84 1939 p66-7 & p141 Weymouth Tramway - history and present operation

Vol 85 1939 pp295, 311-320, 373-7, 395-404 Articles on changes due to the declaration of war

Vol 86 1940 p181-2 From the timetable changes on 5 February, further restoration of Westbury route as "the main channel of communication between London and the West of England"

Vol 86 1940 p317 The Coley Branch GWR (branch line to Reading Central Goods)

Vol 90 1944 p346 Wartime engineering works Didcot-Winchester works described but location not specified – see further reference: Vol 92 1946 p178-9

Vol 91 1945 p299 Item relating to the use of the term "Berks & Hants" line for the GWR line from Reading to Newbury, Savernake and Devizes and explaining the inclusion of "Hants" in the original company's name

Vol 91 1945 p311 Return of the TPO (Travelling Post Office) – "now resumed on the GWR between Paddington and Penzance" (item in November/December issue)

Vol 92 1946 p178-9 Didcot-Winchester wartime works: information further to that given in Vol 90 (above); new line from Worthy Down to Winchester Junction stated to be available from 5 May 1943

Vol 92 1946 p181 New wartime connection at Westbury, opened 30 July 1942

Vol 92 1946 p386 Slip coaches (see Glossary) restored on the GWR in the 1946 summer timetables; new bracket home signals with "slip distants" (signals) installed at Reading Main Line West Junction (start/end of the Berks & Hants line) to govern traffic approaching Reading in the up direction

Vol 93 1947 p58 "King" Class Locomotives, GWR "Weight restrictions on certain underline bridges prohibit locomotives of the "King" class from working between Patney & Chirton and Holt Junction, even under emergency conditions, but engines of the "Castle" class may use this route"

Vol 93 1947 p178 GWR Loads 40 Years Ago – references to Weymouth and West of England trains

Vol 93 1947 p337 British Transport Commission, Railway Executive and London Transport Executive - events following Royal Assent

Great Western Railway Magazine

January 1932 p30 Work in progress on "avoiding lines" at Westbury and Frome

January 1933 p17 The Engineering Department - Government Schemes -avoiding lines at Westbury and Frome - refers to the Development (Loan Guarantees and Grants) Act of 1929 and to the standard of the permanent way (track) laid on the avoiding lines

June 1933 p235 The GWR Summer Service - into operation on 17 July 1933 -refers to improved times for West of England expresses

July 1933 p281 & August p330 Pier and Harbour Improvements at Weymouth

September 1933 p369-370 Watercress traffic at Bedwyn, Hungerford and Kintbury stations

September 1933 p378 Tidworth Tattoo: GWR ran 43 excursions to Tidworth Station

December 1933 p508 Contract let for extension of Goods Warehouse at Newbury

January 1938 p11 Pumping plant at Savernake (Low Level)

January 1938 p14 & October p413 Curve Improvement Works on Weymouth Quay Tramway

January 1938 p32 Works to be Undertaken: River Kennet bridge, near Kintbury

February 1938 p67 Works to be Undertaken: New cart weighbridge, Midgham

March 1938 p118 Works to be Undertaken: Bridge over Holy Brook, near Theale

July 1938 p282-3 Luxury Transit for Tomatoes – fruit and vegetable traffic from the Channel Islands and France

August 1938 p327-8 Reconstruction of Oxford Road Bridge, Reading

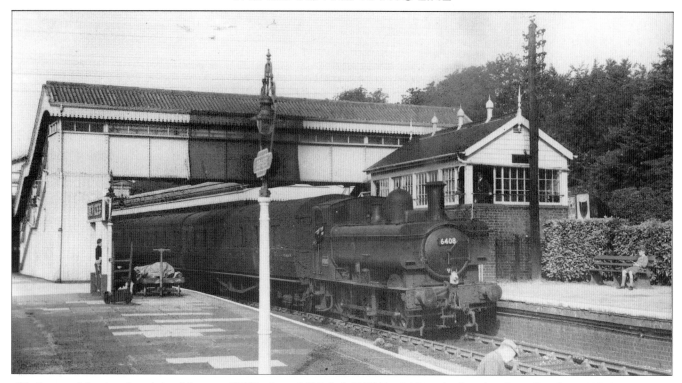

Station architectural variety. **Above -** *GWR class 6400 0-6-0PT No 6408 on a local train at Devizes. Whilst the station footbridge is similar to that at Lavington, the signal box is of a type not featured elsewhere in this book (South Wiltshire Museum, Devizes)*

Middle - *This view of Midgham is from the Newbury end of the down platform – the range of buildings on the up side include the large goods shed, the additional shelter for passengers dating from the Second World War and the main station building which replaced that destroyed in 1888. On the down side is a shelter similar in appearance to that at Bedwyn. Regrettably, all station facilities were swept away during the late sixties/ early seventies, leaving only the platforms themselves and the sign on the up platform. Photograph not dated but the visible evidence suggests late fifties/early sixties (Great Western Trust)*

Lower - *The Berks and Hants Extension Railway station at Pewsey, seen from the approach road side. Clearly alterations have been made at the near end, apparently in order to provide both male and female toilets within the 1862 station. Today the station continues to fulfil its role as the principal station for the town and the Pewsey Vale. Photograph dated September 1965 (Philip J Kelley)*

7
NATIONALISATION TO MODERNISATION
1948 - 1966

1948 - 1954 Reorganisation, rationalisation and a new line

On 1 January 1948, the Great Western Railway became "British Railways (Western Region)" (BR). All the ex-GWR lines in the area, including those absorbed in 1923, were included in the Western Region. The railway and the canal were to be administered by the Region, which in turn was responsible to the Railway Executive of the British Transport Commission (BTC). The canal was soon transferred (on 28 February 1949) to the then newly-formed Docks and Inland Waterways Executive of the Commission.

Reorganisation was inevitable under the new regime. On 26 September 1949, Whitchurch (Hants) on the Newbury and Winchester line was renamed Whitchurch Town to distinguish it from the Southern Region station of the same name, which was renamed

Whitchurch North. On 2 April 1950, boundary changes came into force under which several sections of ex-GWR lines were transferred to the Southern Region. These were the ex-DN&SR line from Enborne Junction to Winchester Cheesehill (renamed Chesil on the same date as Whitchurch), the ex-M&SWJR line from Grafton & Burbage to Red Post Junction and the Tidworth branch, and the ex-Berks and Hants Railway line between Southcote Junction and Basingstoke. The Weymouth - Channel Islands shipping services, previously a joint GWR/SR operation, were also transferred to the Southern Region on that date.

It was also a time for rationalisation; without the previous intensive military traffic such moves were inevitable. On the Winchester line south of Newbury, two facilities installed in 1943 were removed. In March 1951, Lodge Bridge, the passing loop added between Whitchurch and Sutton Scotney, was taken out of use and the signal box closed, restoring the almost six mile

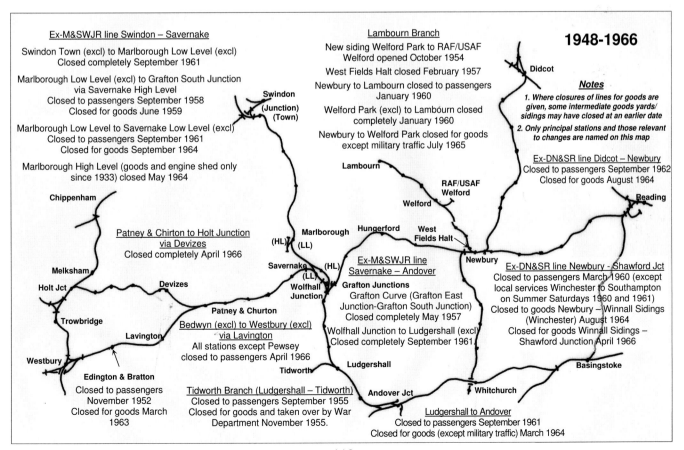

Ex-M&SWJR line Swindon – Savernake

Swindon Town (excl) to Marlborough Low Level (excl)
Closed completely September 1961

Marlborough Low Level (excl) to Grafton South Junction via Savernake High Level
Closed to passengers September 1958
Closed for goods June 1959

Marlborough Low Level to Savernake Low Level (excl)
Closed to passengers September 1961
Closed for goods September 1964

Marlborough High Level (goods and engine shed only since 1933) closed May 1964

Lambourn Branch

New siding Welford Park to RAF/USAF Welford opened October 1954
West Fields Halt closed February 1957
Newbury to Lambourn closed to passengers January 1960
Welford Park (excl) to Lambourn closed completely January 1960
Newbury to Welford Park closed for goods except military traffic July 1965

1948-1966

Notes

1. Where closures of lines for goods are given, some intermediate goods yards/sidings may have closed at an earlier date
2. Only principal stations and those relevant to changes are named on this map

Ex-DN&SR line Didcot – Newbury
Closed to passengers September 1962
Closed for goods August 1964

Patney & Chirton to Holt Junction via Devizes
Closed completely April 1966

Ex-M&SWJR line Savernake – Andover

Grafton Junctions
Grafton Curve (Grafton East Junction-Grafton South Junction) Closed completely May 1957
Wolfhall Junction to Ludgershall (excl) Closed completely September 1961

Ex-DN&SR line Newbury - Shawford Jct
Closed to passengers March 1960 (except local services Winchester to Southampton on Summer Saturdays 1960 and 1961)
Closed to goods Newbury – Winnall Sidings (Winchester) August 1964
Closed for goods Winnall Sidings – Shawford Junction April 1966

Bedwyn (excl) to Westbury (excl) via Lavington
All stations except Pewsey closed to passengers April 1966

Edington & Bratton
Closed to passengers November 1952
Closed for goods March 1963

Tidworth Branch (Ludgershall – Tidworth)
Closed to passengers September 1955
Closed for goods and taken over by War Department November 1955.

Ludgershall to Andover
Closed to passengers September 1961
Closed for goods (except military traffic) March 1964

A railway crane assists with completion of the new bridge over the Kennet Navigation east of Newbury known as Bulls Lock Viaduct, although the new bridge has one span and not three like the previous structure. As described below, John Gould's boats, "Colin" and "Iris" can be seen playing their part in the replacement of the bridge, carried out during closure of the canal in April and May 1953.

long block section (see **Glossary**) between the two stations. In November 1951, the Winchester Junction - Worthy Down curve was abolished as a through line. From the latter date, therefore, all trains from Winchester to Newbury had once again to pass through Winchester Chesil; in practice, however, according to the September 1950 Working Timetable, all regular trains were already routed this way. On the direct line between Grafton and Marlborough, access to the military depot in Savernake Forest was severed when North Savernake Ground Frame was taken out of use in August 1950.

The first closure to passengers was that of Edington & Bratton, on the main line, in November 1952. The station dated from the opening of the Stert and Westbury line to passengers in October 1900. Unlike its neighbour Lavington, opened at the same time, Edington & Bratton was only served by a sparse local service and the level of traffic (no doubt reflecting its small catchment area) clearly did not justify its retention for passengers.

The main line was witness to two encouraging developments during the early years following nationalisation, however. On 18 October 1948, a private siding agreement commenced for a siding to serve Sterling Cables at Aldermaston and in May 1949, Wootton Rivers Signal Box, closed in 1939, was reopened. The closure of Burbage Signal Box in 1948 had created too long a section (well over 5 miles) between Savernake and Pewsey for intensive working. The September 1950 working timetable stated that the box was "open as required".

The short-lived Railway Executive was abolished from October 1953 by the Transport Act 1953. Management of the railways was taken over by the British Transport Commission acting through Railway Boards, the regional structure being unchanged.

Although no longer under the control of the railway, the canal came into the news again in 1953 and in 1954. During late April and early May 1953, the bridge over the Kennet Navigation east of Newbury known as Bulls Lock Viaduct was replaced. An article in the Railway Magazine for June 1953, with accompanying photograph, shows two of the late John Gould's boats, "Colin" and "Iris", assisting with the work. The original three spans were replaced by one larger span of 66 yards and new abutments were provided in front of the existing ones. In 1954, it was reported that the BTC intended to abandon the canal as soon as possible. This was vigorously opposed by those carrying on business on the canal, as well as many other parties, and another 10 years were to elapse before the canal could be considered safe from attempts to close it and could therefore be redeveloped.

Construction of a 2¼-mile long single line rail link between the Lambourn branch and RAF Welford, for the movement of munitions, started in July 1952. Estimated to take 22 months, in fact work was not completed until October 1954, by which time administrative control of the camp had passed to USAF. A junction was made at Welford Park, facing towards Lambourn, and four interchange sidings were provided. The new line crossed the Welford Woods Road, where a new underbridge was built adjacent to that carrying the line from Newbury, and climbed steadily towards the camp, curving to run almost due north and passing through a deep cutting, before reaching the extensive sidings.

In later years, the course of the line was visible from the M4 Motorway; its course at the north end was adapted to become the private slip road giving access to and from the base for military convoys. Construction and operation of the line is fully described in "An Illustrated History of the Lambourn Branch".

1955 – 1957 Modernisation plans and the first closures

In early 1955, the southern section of the Didcot, Newbury and Southampton line, transferred to the Southern Region in 1950, witnessed changes as a consequence of the reduction in the number of trains being operated. At Highclere and Litchfield, the crossing loops were taken out of use and the signal boxes closed, although the loops were not actually removed until 1960 and 1959 respectively. At Kings Worthy, the crossing loop was removed and the signal box closed. Facilities for goods traffic were retained at these stations until 1962. Following this rationalisation, between Enborne Junction and Winchester crossing loops were only available at Woodhay, Burghclere, Whitchurch, Sutton Scotney and Worthy Down.

Another event of 1955 was the withdrawal of the Tidworth branch passenger and goods services in September and November respectively. The line was

View from the road bridge at Little Bedwyn as GWR 'King' class 4-6-0 No 6026 'King John' climbs to the summit at Savernake with the down 'Cornish Riviera Limited', passing under the footbridges provided to replace the erstwhile road crossing here c.1898 and themselves later replaced. The redundant crossing-keeper's cottage has since been demolished (24 June 1956) (E Fry – Rod Blencowe collection)

not closed however, being taken over by the War Department and continuing in use until 1963 for military troop and freight trains. These closures resulted in a potential loss of freight traffic to the Berks & Hants line, such traffic having been previously been routed via Newbury and the Grafton Curve, as described in Chapter 5: New Military Traffic for the Berks & Hants line.

However, dominating all other news or events in 1955 was the publication of a Modernisation Plan. The plan embraced all spheres of railway activity; some of the areas of particular relevance to the Berks & Hants line were:

Programme for renewal of bridges to be stepped up;

Alterations to the track at junctions and sharply curved sections, to eliminate speed restrictions and pave the way for faster trains (speeds of 100mph were contemplated) as well as providing greater line capacity and improved traffic operation;

Strengthening of the track structure by re-ballasting and relaying, which would permit higher speeds and the operation of heavier trains;

Widespread extension of colour-light signalling with the replacement of manually worked signal boxes by a greatly reduced number of power-operated installations;

Considerable extension of track circuiting (see **Glossary**);

Progressive increase in the use of automatic train control (see **Glossary**);

Modernisation of telecommunication systems;

Phasing out of steam locomotives and replacement with diesel or electric power (electrification on a country-wide scale was not considered);

Phasing out of non-corridor compartment coaching stock;

Branch lines to be operated by diesel railcars or multiple units; unremunerative branches to be replaced by road transport;

Improved accommodation and amenities at stations;

Improved working methods in dealing with freight including the closure of inadequate or redundant goods yards and the construction of new depots and marshalling yards;

The fitting of continuous brakes to all freight wagons.

The morning train from Weymouth to Paddington, due at Newbury at mid-day, passes the site of Burbage Goods hauled by GWR 'Hall' class 4-6-0 No 5956 'Horsley Hall'. Seen from the A346 overbridge, the goods shed has survived in private use (21 May 1956) (E Fry – Rod Blencowe collection)

Preserved GWR 'City' class 4-4-0 No 3440 'City of Truro' passes under Rockingham Road Bridge in Newbury on a Southampton train. This locomotive was used on Didcot – Newbury – Southampton trains during the period April 1957 - May 1958. The Lambourn branch line is on the left (Author's collection)

***Above** - GWR '1400' class 0-4-2 No 1444 of Reading Shed, in push-pull mode with an ancient trailer, enters Midgham (for Douai School) station on an up local. Photograph is dated 1960 or earlier as the goods yard closed that year (Great Western Trust)*

GWR railcar W18 sets off from Newbury on the Lambourn branch, the line for which it was designed. The railcar is about to pass under Rockingham Road Bridge, soon after which the line turns northwards towards Speen on the way to Lambourn. On the right is the timber and builders' merchants on the site now occupied by Jewson Ltd. Even in August 1955, when this photo was taken, buddleia was taking over the top of the railway embankment. Car W18 was withdrawn in May 1957 (John Allen collection)

A hybrid GWR diesel train stands in the "Didcot" bay at Newbury station with a departure for Reading. An ordinary coach is sandwiched between two single-ended railcars – on the left W33, on the right W38. The railcars were built in 1942 and 1941 respectively and withdrawn in 1962. The photograph is dated between the introduction of diesel multiple unit green livery (around 1956) and 1961, when the cars were moved away from the area (John Allen collection)

A national event in 1956 was the reduction in the number of classes of accommodation in trains from three to two. The only trains then running with all three classes were some continental boat trains on the Southern Region. The old second class was abolished, third class becoming second class. Many local and branch trains had only one class of accommodation: these therefore became "second class only".

In February 1957, services were withdrawn from West Fields Halt, the first station out of Newbury on the Lambourn branch. The unattended halt platform was a victim of falling patronage and rising maintenance costs. The branch passenger service, however, continued for another three years.

In May 1957, the first of a series of events took place that would eventually lead to the closure of the ex-Midland and South Western Junction Railway system north and south of the Berks & Hants line. The curve connecting the Berks & Hants line just west of Crofton (Grafton East Junction) and the M&SWJR line at Grafton (Grafton South Junction), which had been built by the GWR in 1905, was taken out of use. It was only disconnected at the Crofton end, however, leaving two sidings for wagon storage, a common procedure at the time. It had been little used since the war and in September 1950 had no timetabled trains; the closure of the public services on the Tidworth branch in 1955 would have removed one of the likely sources of occasional traffic. The working timetable for the fore-mentioned month also shows Grafton East Junction

Signal Box as "closed" although all apparatus would have remained in place until official closure of the box in 1957. Grafton South Junction Signal Box was retained, as it controlled the junction between the single lines from Savernake High Level and Wolfhall Junction.

1958-1959 Boundary changes, rationalisation, closures, modernisation commences

The next year also proved eventful for lines in the area. The boundary change of April 1950 on the ex-M&SWJR section was reversed, the section from Grafton & Burbage (inclusive) to Red Post Junction becoming once again the responsibility of the Western Region from February 1958. In September, passenger services ceased to use the direct line from Grafton to Marlborough via Savernake High Level, which crossed the Berks & Hants line and the Kennet and Avon Canal. This direct line, opened in 1898, was singled in 1933 when the earlier rationalisation took place in the area. From 15 September 1958, all Andover - Swindon passenger trains joined the Berks & Hants line at Wolfhall Junction, called at Savernake Low Level and used the original Marlborough Railway line to the point where, from 1933, all trains used the 1898 line to reach Marlborough. Savernake High Level station was closed to passengers, apparently without notice. Articles in the Railway Magazine for February and March 1958 describe these changes with the aid of a very clear map.

North British diesel-hydraulic No D601 'Ark Royal' passing Newbury on the up "Mayflower" 10.30am express from Plymouth. The coach set is in the GWR-style chocolate and cream livery with the exception of an older coach in maroon. This scene has changed almost beyond recognition, the station platforms and the buildings either side of Blackboys Bridge in the distance being the only survivors today of the various buildings and other features that were present when the photograph was taken around 1958. (John Allen collection)

In this west view from the down platform at Savernake (Low Level), GWR '5700' class 0-6-0 Pannier tank No 9740 and train arrives from the Marlborough direction and is signalled into the up main platform. The layout of the double junction to the Marlborough line can clearly be seen, with Savernake West signal box alongside the up main line. Based on the direction of the sun, the train is the 4.52pm Swindon Town to Andover Junction (Summer 1961 timetable). Following previous cuts in the train service, this was the last train of the day to the latter destination. The Marlborough line closed to passengers in September 1961 (see page 127) (John Allen collection)

The retention of goods services through Savernake High Level was short-lived, the line closing to all traffic from 22 June 1959. From this date all traffic between Grafton and Marlborough was operated by the route described above, via the Berks & Hants line and Savernake Low Level. About 5½ miles of single line, the loop, sidings and other facilities at Savernake High Level and the bridges over the canal and over the Berks & Hants line were no longer required and were taken out of use. Grafton South Junction Signal Box remained open as the section of the original M&SWJR line between that junction and Wolfhall Junction on the Berks & Hants was a single line over the canal bridge. At the site of Savernake High Level station, the signal box (closed in 1933), survives today, along with the station building and water tower, in private ownership, concealed from public view by trees.

Meanwhile, elsewhere in 1959, preparations were in hand for the forthcoming diesel operation of both long distance and local services. A diesel refuelling siding was provided in the up sidings at Westbury in April

1959, the steam locomotive shed remaining in use until 1965. At Reading, the steam locomotive shed also continued in use until 1965. On the higher level ground to the south of the shed, the site of the former tip siding and carriage sidings, an area of sidings for the stabling, cleaning and refuelling of the forthcoming diesel multiple units was laid out, to be known as the Triangle Diesel Depot. Access from the Berks & Hants line was provided by facing and trailing connections from the up line between Oxford Road Junction and the locomotive shed connections.

Another event of 1959 was the reconstruction of the 66-yard long Kennet and Avon Canal Viaduct West (Brunsdons Bridge), situated where the main line crosses the canal at a considerable skew between Kintbury and Hungerford. The main line was singled across the bridge, single line working being in force from October to December, enabling the spans under each track to be replaced in turn, commencing with the down line. A temporary signal box was provided, called Brunsdons Bridge.

1960 – 1961 Major closures affect services to and from Newbury

The year of 1960 brought two major events within a few weeks. Hardly had the new year started when the withdrawal of the Lambourn branch passenger service, and complete closure beyond Welford Park, took place as from 4 January. The last trains ran on Saturday 2 January. The line to Welford Park remained open to enable USAF Welford to continue to dispatch and receive military traffic by rail and, for a further five years, the stations at Boxford and Welford Park remained open to deal with goods and parcels traffic.

In early March, passenger train departures westwards from Newbury were further curtailed when passenger services on the ex-DN&SR line were withdrawn between Newbury and Southampton Terminus via Winchester Chesil. The last advertised passenger trains ran on Saturday 5 March, when 250 people travelled on the final southbound train. Freight services south of Newbury lasted for another four years as far as Winnall Sidings (north of Winchester) and for longer further south. It was not the end for Winchester Chesil as a passenger station, however; due to congestion at Winchester City, Chesil was reopened on summer Saturdays in 1960 and 1961 for local services to Southampton.

Continuing the year's trend of retrenchment, Midgham closed to goods traffic in August, the first station on the original Berks & Hants line to lose its goods facilities. In the same month, the section of line between Ludgershall and Red Post Junction on the ex-M&SWJR line was singled and the junction with the Andover - Salisbury line removed. The single line continuing towards Andover carried all traffic; however the signal box at the site of the junction remained in use for a further two years.

The year 1961 proved to be the last year of the ex-Midland and South Western Junction Railway line as a cross-country railway, with one daily (Monday – Saturday) through service each way still surviving between Andover Junction and Cheltenham St James stations (the southbound service continuing to Southampton Terminus). Other trains served intermediate stations, including some linking the two Swindon stations. Double line was still in place between Grafton South Junction and Ludgershall. The entire passenger service was withdrawn as from 11 September 1961 and the line closed completely between Ludgershall and Wolfhall Junction and from Marlborough to Swindon Town. A short section was retained for goods traffic north of Swindon, but that is outside the scope of this book. Goods services were retained between Savernake and Marlborough and the latter station was also kept open for parcels and schools traffic. Savernake Low Level Station was renamed Savernake. The lines serving Tidworth and between Ludgershall and Andover were kept open to serve military establishments at Tidworth and Ludgershall.

The Marlborough goods, parcels and occasional schools traffic was served from the Berks & Hants line via Savernake.

On a beautiful summer's evening, an unidentified GWR 'Hall' class 4-6-0 is mirrored in the canal as it approaches Wolfhall Junction with the Sunday 5.35pm Trowbridge – Reading train (6 August 1961) (Author)

There were three junctions in the Grafton/Savernake area: Wolfhall Junction - **above** - was created on the opening of the Swindon, Marlborough and Andover Railway in 1883. The Midland and South West Junction Railway (M&SWJR) line to Andover Junction leaves the Berks & Hants line, on the left, and crosses the canal, eventually meeting the direct Marlborough - Grafton line (1898), and then the 1905 connection, at Grafton South Junction. The line closed completely in 1961 but the signal box survived until 1964.

Opposite upper - Grafton East Junction. The 1905 connection to the M&SWJR climbs away from the main line and crosses the Kennet & Avon Canal towards Grafton South Junction. The link was closed in 1957, however the signal box remained open, together with Wolfhall Junction, until 1964.

Opposite below - Grafton South Junction. The M&SWJR signal box dates from the opening of the 1905 connection, seen on the right. Despite the closure of the connection, the box remained open until the closure of the M&SWJR in 1961 to control the single-line section over the canal bridge from Wolfhall Junction (all N Simmons)

Left - GWR class 5700 0-6-0PT No 3687 passes Grafton South Junction on a Sundays Only Andover Junction to Swindon Junction train and takes the left-hand line leading to Wolfhall Junction. The right-hand line, clearly disused, was the direct Marlborough - Grafton line of 1898. The junction signal box can just be seen behind the signal post. August 1961 (Author)

Above - *A GWR '4500' class 2-6-2T waits for departure time in the bay platform at Savernake Low Level on a Marlborough train. Date not known, service withdrawn September 1961 (Great Western Trust)*

Below - *SR (ex-SE&CR) 'N' class 2-6-0 No 31818 calls at the up platform on the 1.48pm Cheltenham St James – Southampton Terminus, the only through train between these places. Note the full station name "Savernake Low Level (Change for Marlborough)" (7 August 1961) (Author)*

*Two views of Westbury Shed which provided the locomotives for the Westbury/Trowbridge – Newbury – Reading trains. **Above** – GWR class '5700' 0-6-0PT No 8714 was used on local freight and shunting duties whilst, **below,** GWR class '5600' 0-6-2T No 5689 was employed on banking trains on the steep gradient out of Westbury on the Salisbury line (29 July 1961) (both – Author)*

Above - *A typical local train of the type working in the Westbury/Trowbridge/ Devizes/Swindon area stands in the up island platform at Westbury headed by GWR '5400' class 0-6-0PT No 5416 (29 July 1961). (Author)*

Newbury: **Above -** In June 1961 GWR 'Hall' class 4-6-0 No 4921 'Eaton Hall' calls at Newbury on a Plymouth & Kingswear train, the 5.50pm from Paddington. Through coaches for Weymouth were detached here and taken forward by GWR '4300' class 2-6-0 No 5376 seen in the picture **below** standing in the "Winchester" bay. Built at Swindon in 1920, this locomotive was one of the last survivors of its class, not being withdrawn until September 1963. The station platform and street lighting may be of a similar age! I wonder where those boys are now?

Opposite page, lower - On the same date as the previous Westbury scenes, 29 July 1961, an attractive view of the east end of Devizes station is presented to the photographer as his train, the 7.10pm from Trowbridge, prepares to leave for Reading. "Henshall Hall" is No 7908 of the GWR 4-6-0 'Modified Hall' class and has somehow strayed from its home at Tyseley. The castellated entrance to the tunnel is in harmony with Devizes Castle, out of sight in the trees on the right. It can be seen today at one end of the Station Road Car Park (all - Author)

1962-1964 The Beeching Report published: more closures, de-staffing of stations

The Transport Act 1962 came into force in September of that year and created the British Railways Board from 1 January 1963 to replace the British Transport Commission. Management would be by the Board through Regional Railway Boards.

During the course of 1962, the future trend of freight services became even more apparent and foreshadowed one of the main developments arising out of the "Beeching Report" of 1963, that of reducing the number of small depots handling freight and encouraging the movement of bulk goods between a limited number of locations. Four depots on the Newbury - Winchester line: Woodhay, Highclere, Litchfield and Kings Worthy were closed to traffic during the year. However, three important developments took place on the Berks & Hants line. A new siding layout at Theale West was completed for stone traffic, a siding was provided on the up side at Newbury Racecourse for Shell Mex & BP Ltd and a siding at Westbury Cement Works was brought into use.

In September 1962, the passenger service between Newbury and Didcot was withdrawn. As there were no Sunday trains, the last trains ran on Saturday 8 September. The Newbury Weekly News of 14 December 1961 had recorded that the closure enquiry was in progress the previous day. Six stations and halts were affected: Pinewood Halt was closed completely, whilst Upton & Blewbury, Compton, Hampstead Norris and Hermitage were retained to deal with parcels to be called for or handed in by the public for dispatch and for freight traffic. The list omitted Churn, which was not designated a halt although it had no staff. The first train from Didcot called there and it was available as a request stop on all other trains. The double track line between the two towns was left to survive with the remaining freight and parcels traffic and an occasional diverted or excursion passenger train for another two years.

In terms of passenger traffic, Newbury then reverted to the role it had acquired a hundred years earlier, of an intermediate station on a through line. Now, however, the through line went to Penzance and Newbury retained its role as an important passenger and freight interchange point. To the east, the double track main

The station buildings, canopies and footbridge at Newbury have happily survived to this day. The down side buildings and footbridge are seen in this charming period photograph, also the bookstall on the up platform. The Rover 2000 in the background was registered in 1962, which gives a clue to the date (John Allen collection)

Two views of '2251' class 0-6-0 No 2212 shunting coaching stock at the west end of Newbury station and, in the lower view, masquerading as a Lambourn train. Amongst the many interesting features that have long since disappeared is the small brick building to the left of the lower picture. This housed the pump that raised water to the elevated tank; it replaced the original which was the main casualty of the bomb that fell on the railway on 10 February 1943 (see page 114) (16 February 1962) (both - Author)

Super-power at Kintbury – on 17 March 1962 GWR 'Castle' class 4-6-0 No 5018 "St. Mawes Castle" arrives at Kintbury with the 3.35pm Trowbridge – Reading. This train called at all stations and halts between Devizes and Reading. Classmate No 4086 "Builth Castle", built at Swindon in 1925, accelerates westwards with the 4.36pm Newbury – Trowbridge, also serving all stations and halts to Devizes en route (both – Author)

Above - On 17 March 1962 GWR '4300' class 2-6-0 No 5380 awaits the 5.40pm departure time with the once-weekly steam train from Newbury to Didcot. All other services in the final years of this line were provided by BR-type one-car diesel units. Connection has been made with the 3.35pm Trowbridge – Reading, seen awaiting departure time (5.20pm) in the up platform.

Left - View from the carriage window of the eastern approach to Newbury station and the throat of the goods yard, taken from the only steam train then running from Didcot to Newbury, the Saturdays-only 2.15pm departure, due at Newbury at 2.55pm. Photographs of this train at Newbury are shown on pages 138 and 139, all taken on 25 August 1962, just two weeks before the passenger train service on this route was withdrawn (both - Author)

Above - The Saturdays Only steam train from Didcot has arrived at Newbury station behind GWR '4300' class 2-6-0 No 7327 on Saturday 25 August 1962; the passengers are making their way to the exit or the footbridge and the parcels are being dealt with. At first sight, little has changed about the station, but users of the station will notice many differences.

Below - Seen from the up platform, No 7327 backs its train under the old Cheap Street bridge towards the set of carriages seen in the distance. The movement is controlled by the shunt signal seen at the end of the platform.

Opposite page, top - Later in the afternoon No 7327 is seen stabled on the Lambourn branch line with a motley collection of GWR rolling stock ready to form the 5.40pm to Didcot. At this time the branch remained open for goods traffic to Welford Park and for military traffic to USAF/RAF Welford. The signals on the left applied to the up main line and those on the right to the branch (all - Author)

GWR 'Castle' class 4-6-0 No 5057 "Earl Waldegrave" hurries the down milk empties through Newbury on 25 August 1962. Much has changed since the "Mayflower" was seen passing through (see page 125), indeed in this photograph it can be seen that the antiquated platform gas lamps have already been replaced by modern concrete post type electric lighting. Close examination reveals that in the siding on the left, beyond the erstwhile "Lambourn Bay", is a clerestory coach, whilst on the right the only occupants of the sidings are a van, and a horse box at the horse landing platform (both - Author)

This page, upper - GWR 'Modified Hall' class 4-6-0 No 6990 'Witherslack Hall' passes Reading West on the 4.7pm Reading – Trowbridge on 27 October 1962 (Author)

Below - GWR 'King' class 4-6-0 No 6011 'King James I' approaches Reading West on 'Z11', one of three Newbury Racecourse – Paddington specials on the same day (Author)

Opposite page, upper - Having passed Southcote Junction, GWR '2251' class 0-6-0 No 3219 of Reading Shed heads northwards with a train of fuel tanks. Barrier wagons are marshalled between the tank wagons and the locomotive and also in front of the brake van. The bracket signal reads, from left to right, Coley Branch (to Reading Central Goods), Basingstoke Branch and the Berks & Hants line (M Earley - Kevin Robertson collection)

Opposite page, inset - GWR 'Hall' class 4-6-0 No 6927 'Lilford Hall' is opened up after negotiating the 25mph speed restriction at Southcote Junction to the Basingstoke Branch with the 10.8am York - Bournemouth train (23 March 1963), followed closely *(lower)* by GWR (BR) 'Castle' class 4-6-0 No 7010 'Avondale Castle' on the 4.7pm Reading – Trowbridge via Devizes (both – Author)

line continued to Southcote Junction and Reading. To the west of Newbury, the double track main line ran through to Westbury, whilst the old single line Berks and Hants Extension line/Railway branched off at Patney & Chirton to Devizes, connecting there with the Devizes Branch from Holt Junction. In practice, the entire line from Reading via Newbury and Devizes to Holt Junction was known as the "Berks & Hants Line"; the section from Patney & Chirton to Westbury continued to be officially known as the "Stert and Westbury Line", whilst loco crews at Westbury referred to the latter line as "The Patney".

Further rationalisation took place in 1963. On the main line, the Aldermaston Up Goods Loop and the Newbury Racecourse Goods Loop were taken out of use. Goods facilities were withdrawn from Edington & Bratton station and Wootton Rivers Signal Box finally closed.

Burghclere and Whitchurch stations, on the ex-DN&SR line south of Newbury, were closed for goods traffic in May.

On the ex-M&SWJR line, the Tidworth branch, then served only from Andover, was closed to regular military traffic at the end of July, although the last train did not run until early November.

In Newbury, work commenced on replacing Cheap Street bridge, spanning the through lines, the platform lines, the up island platform and the up bay line at the east end of Newbury station. This steel bridge dated from the reconstruction of the station in 1908-10 and was replaced by a modern concrete bridge for the Newbury North-South Relief Road. Beams for the new bridge were delivered by rail to Newbury Goods Yard, whence they were conveyed to the construction site by an abnormal load specialist, this taking place towards the end of 1964. The provision of the new bridge dictated the need for changes to be made to the signalling equipment in the vicinity of the bridge.

This rather poor quality photograph has been included as it shows both the track layout east of Newbury station and the works for the Newbury North-South Relief Road (A34) bridge. This view was possible because a temporary footbridge had been erected for pedestrians and for the various utilities that crossed the old bridge. Piles are being driven for the retaining wall adjacent to the Railway Hotel. Photograph can be dated to the early part of 1964 (West Berkshire Museum)

The major event of 1963, however, was the publication in March of a report entitled "The Reshaping of British Railways", known then and since as the "Beeching Report" after the man responsible for its production, Dr Beeching. In Part 1, Appendix 2, section 1, the list of passenger services to be withdrawn included that between Patney & Chirton and Holt Junction (partly B&HER and partly WS&WR). Section 2, Passenger Services to be modified, included Reading General to Westbury (Wilts). Section 3, Passenger Stations and Halts to be Closed, included all those eventually closed in 1966, plus Aldermaston, Midgham, Kintbury, Bedwyn and Pewsey. Section 7, Passenger Stations and Halts already under Consideration for Closure before Formulation of the Report, included all intermediate stations between Newbury and Didcot. Similarly, Section 8 of the report, Passenger Services under Consideration for Withdrawal before the Formulation of the Report, included Newbury to Didcot, noting that this withdrawal had already taken place.

Part 2 of the report contained a number of maps. Map 9 showed Didcot - Newbury and Patney - Holt Junction as passenger services to be withdrawn (as at August 1962). Map 10 showed "Proposed Modification of Passenger Train Services" for the Reading - Westbury line. Map 11 showed "Liner Train Routes and Terminals under Consideration" with one route using the Reading - Westbury - Taunton line and with terminals at London, Slough, Reading, Exeter and Plymouth.

The trend of retrenchment, which was to continue until 1967, began in February 1964 with the closure of Sutton Scotney - the last intermediate station between Newbury and Winchester to remain open for goods. On 10 August 1964, the complete closure took place of the ex-DN&SR line from Enborne Junction to (but not including) Winnall Sidings (north of Winchester tunnel), also from Newbury East Junction to Didcot. The goods depots at Hermitage, Hampstead Norris, Compton and Upton & Blewbury survived until closure of the line.

Thus came the end of the Didcot, Newbury and Southampton Railway, with the exception, for the time being, of the freight line from Winnall Sidings at Winchester to Shawford Junction.

With the closure of Ludgershall and Weyhill stations for public goods in March, the Andover - Ludgershall line, the surviving rump of the M&SWJR's southern section, was kept open solely to serve the military depots at Ludgershall.

Wootton Rivers Halt, opened in 1928, looking westwards from the nearby road bridge on 29 September 1962 (see page 148 for a platform level view) (C G Maggs)

The last days of steam at Newbury. **Above -** *An excellent view of the goods yard as GWR class '5700' class 0-6-0 Pannier tank No 3751 takes water at Newbury on its Westbury - Didcot local pick-up trip (2 July 1964)*

Below - *'5700' class 0-6-0 Pannier tank No 8720 leaves Newbury on the Didcot line on the same train a few days earlier (23 July 1964) (both, D Hazell)*

Above - *'2251' class 0-6-0 No 2261 departs Newbury for Reading with empty BP tanks (11 May 1964)*
Below - *Castle' class 4-6-0 No 7008 "Swansea Castle" runs round the breakdown train and goes to Newbury Racecourse for turning prior to returning its train eastwards (24 July 1964) (both, D Hazell)*

Opposite page, upper - *A locomotive with strong local connections, 'Castle' class 4-6-0 No 4089 "Donnington Castle" leaves Newbury with the 3.15pm Westbury - Reading on 5 June 1964 and passes the foundations of the bridge for the Relief Road.*

Opposite page, lower - *Less than four months before complete closure of the Didcot, Newbury and Southampton line, '4300' class 2-6-0 No 6367 passes Newbury on the 12.15pm Washwood Heath - Eastleigh freight (29 April 1964)*

This page, above - *'2800' class 2-8-0 No 2893 arrives at Newbury with pre-cast concrete sections for the Relief Road canal bridge (24 April 1964) (all, D Hazell)*

This page, below*, Haulage contractor Hallett Silbermann prepares to take railway bridge span no 7 from the goods yard to the adjacent construction site (Bill Yates M.I.R.T.E., collection S Wise)*

The remaining goods depots on the main line did not escape attention. In 1964 the depots at Patney & Chirton and Savernake Low Level (May), Pewsey (July) and Bedwyn and Kintbury (both September) were closed for goods traffic and the Up Goods Loop at Lavington was taken out of use. Later that year, in November, it was the turn of Devizes to lose its goods facilities, whilst retaining its passenger services for a further eighteen months.

On closure of the ex-M&SWJR lines in 1961, the line linking the GWR station at Savernake and the M&SWJR station at Marlborough had remained open for goods and Marlborough School special passenger trains. On 1 May 1964, the last school train ran. Later

that month, at the same time as the closure of Savernake to goods, both Marlborough stations were closed for general goods traffic but the Low Level station remained open for coal deliveries until 7 September. On that date, the line from Savernake to Marlborough closed completely, bringing to an end the history of both the ex-GWR branch and that of the M&SWJR in the area served by the Berks & Hants line.

The final act of the year was the removal of all staff from the stations Theale to Bedwyn inclusive, with the exception of Newbury. With effect from the same date, 2 November 1964, the small stations had the word "Halt" added to their names.

Above - *Kintbury level crossing and signal box await the next train on 24 February 1965. The wooden station buildings are believed to be the originals of 1847. Despite being downgraded to a mere 'halt' three months earlier, that suffix has not been added to the nameboards (John Allen collection)*

Left - *A platform view at Wootton Rivers Halt. Although not shown on the nameboard, the word 'Halt' was included in the timetable and correctly conveyed that the station was unstaffed. The signal box was one of the additional ones opened in 1934 (see page 106); its later history is fully described in the text. Date unknown, but appears to be contemporary with the photograph on page 143 (Great Western Trust)*

Top - *Patney & Chirton was a substantial junction station dating from the opening of the Stert and Westbury line in 1900, after which the single line to Devizes was demoted to branch line status. The station was closed in April 1966 (4 September 1965)*

Above - *The equipment at Patney & Chirton for the pick-up of the single-line token for an up train joining the main line from the branch (December 1964) (both, Kevin Robertson collection)*

Right - *This sad photograph, taken on the last day of passenger services, says it all. The authorities couldn't even wait until closure took place before ripping up some of the track. R.I.P. (16 April 1966) (P Strong,)*

1965 – 1966 The end of steam and developments at Reading

In early 1965, five years after its closure to passengers, Boxford was closed to goods traffic, and in July this traffic was discontinued from Welford Park. The ex-Lambourn Valley Railway line from Newbury to Welford Park thereafter remained open solely to serve USAF Welford.

In February 1965, the British Railways Board published a document called "The Development of the Major Trunk Routes". It was generally known as "Beeching Part 2". About 3000 route miles (of the total route mileage of major trunk routes at the time of 7500) were selected for development and were intended to be capable of handling the freight and passenger flows between the main centres forecast for

1984, with a margin for spare capacity. The Reading - Westbury line was not selected, the choice for West of England traffic being the route via Swindon and Bristol.

In Newbury, construction of the Cheap Street bridge for the Relief Road was reported sufficiently far advanced for the bridge to be partially opened to traffic on 28 February. As the parapets had not then been completed, only one lane was available to traffic in each direction and pedestrians had to continue using the temporary footbridge provided in November 1963. Other bridge news of 1965 was the agreement of Newbury Racecourse management to British Railways' suggestion that, due to the high cost of repairs and maintenance, one of the remaining footbridges (No 2, a wooden structure) should be demolished.

Above - An unusual view of Theale signal box, dating from September 1965. By this time it was the first signal box west of Reading on the Berks & Hants line, Reading power signal box having opened in April 1965 (page 153)

Opposite page, upper - GWR 'Hall' class 4-6-0 No 4919 'Donnington Hall' passes Midgham on down milk empties bound for the West Country. The level crossing gates were replaced by barriers in August 1974 and the signal box closed in December 1977 when multiple-aspect signalling was introduced (5 August 1961)

Opposite page, lower - Aldermaston station and signal box from the up platform in September 1965. The original (1847) station buildings are still extant but, regrettably, the main building is obscured by the additional shelters erected during the war for the benefit of railway staff returning eastwards after working at the temporary wartime headquarters offices at Beenham Grange and Wharf House (see page 109) (All P J Kelley)

Above - *Three views of Thatcham station, looking westwards, immediately prior to the demolition of the goods shed and station buildings. The combination of goods and passenger facilities on the down platform was very unusual, if not unique (6 November 1965)*

A slightly later view, looking west under the footbridge, which survived the demolition of the buildings until it was removed in December 1967. On the left can be seen the exit line from the goods yard, with its separate set of crossing gates, passing behind the signal box and joining the down main line in the distance (14 January 1967) (all Stuart Wise)

Opposite page - *A London-bound express passing Woodborough hauled by Type 4 diesel hydraulic No D1050 "Western Ruler". The final symbols of Western Region independence, these locomotives, dating from1961-1963, were replaced by BR standard diesel electrics in the 1970s (4 September 1965) (John Allen collection)*

Meanwhile, at the eastern end of the Berks & Hants, a multiple-aspect (colour-light) signalling (MAS) scheme was introduced in the Reading area, the control centre being located adjacent to Reading Station. On the Berks & Hants line, the scheme included Southcote Junction, the signal box there closing on 25 April 1965, the date of commissioning of the new power signal box. The first signal box on the Newbury line from that date was Theale (see photograph on page 150). Major changes to the track layout at Southcote Junction, however, did not take place until 1971.

The commissioning of the Western Region's (then) latest power box (control centre) at Reading is described in Modern Railways magazine for August 1965. The track plan is of interest as it shows the facilities (as described on page 126) which were accessed from the line between the junction with the main line and Oxford Road Junction, i.e. a single line connection to a Diesel Servicing Depot and another, separate, single line connection to a Diesel Depot (for stabling). Reading steam shed had closed in January of that year.

Westbury Shed, which, in conjunction with Reading shed, supplied steam locomotives for the Reading/ Newbury to Trowbridge/Westbury passenger services as well as for local services and freight, was closed in September 1965.

The elimination of steam haulage of trains on the

Berks & Hants line had been a gradual process starting with the replacement of steam locomotives by diesel-hydraulics on the principal West of England trains from 1958 onwards. On local services, a fleet of 3-car suburban diesel multiple units (dmus) operated from Reading Depot was phased in gradually from 1961 onwards on local trains to Newbury, Hungerford and Bedwyn; these did not, however, displace the steam-hauled Reading – Trowbridge/Westbury trains. By this time, the Lambourn branch had been closed to passengers; the branch trains had been operated at various times by both Great Western diesel railcars and steam trains, although in the final years steam had remained supreme.

The Didcot – Southampton trains passing through Newbury were exclusively operated by steam until the closure of the Winchester line. For the remaining two and half years that passenger trains ran to Didcot, steam held sway until the Summer 1961 timetable when a single diesel car was provided for the daily service; there was an additional train each way on Saturdays, steam-hauled to the end. Freight trains remained in the hands of steam until the final few months leading up the complete closure of the line north and south of Newbury in August 1964.

By this time, diesel traction had a complete monopoly of the West of England trains, whilst steam could still be found on some freight trains and on the few remaining passenger trains running through from

Above - Manningford Halt, between Pewsey and Woodborough, was a typical GWR halt of the inter-war period. Opened in 1932, it was closed when all stopping trains were withdrawn between Bedwyn and Trowbridge/ Westbury in April 1966 (24 February 1965)

Below - Lavington was one of two stations provided on the Stert and Westbury line, the other being Edington & Bratton, which closed in 1952. Lavington was also closed in April 1966, leaving Pewsey as the only station between Bedwyn and Westbury (1 May 1966) (both - John Allen collection)

Trowbridge or Westbury to Reading. The steam-hauled passenger trains were replaced by diesel units operating from Westbury at the start of the summer timetable in June 1964.

Before leaving 1965, a significant development regarding the 3-car suburban dmus operated from Reading depot was the fitting of inter-coach gangways within the units. This improvement was introduced partly to give all passengers toilet access and partly to facilitate the issue of tickets by guards on certain services. The latter measure had become necessary since the withdrawal of staff from all stations served by these trains from Theale to Bedwyn, except Newbury, as previously mentioned.

The year ended as it began. In November, Thatcham station buildings were demolished; in December Aldermaston was closed for goods except private siding traffic.

The Winnall Sidings – Winchester Chesil – Bar End - Shawford Junction section of the DN&SR line, the last remnant of the line to survive (and from Bar End to Shawford Junction, the last to open, in 1891), was closed entirely from 4 April 1966. Goods facilities at Winnall Sidings and Bar End (south of Chesil station) had continued in use since the closure of the line from Newbury to goods in August 1964.

In April 1966 there also took place the most momentous change to the train services on the main line since the opening of the new railway between Stert and Westbury in 1900. The passenger service, which since the opening of the Berks and Hants Extension Railway in 1862 had linked Reading, Newbury and Hungerford with Trowbridge and Westbury via Devizes, was withdrawn. Last trains ran on Saturday 16 April and the closure took effect from Monday 18 April. The line through Devizes, from Patney & Chirton to Holt Junction, was closed completely. All intermediate stations between Bedwyn and Westbury were closed except Pewsey; the title "Berks & Hants line" was in due course taken to mean the entire line from Reading to Westbury.

The stations and halts served by this service and closed from 18 April 1966 (the start of the summer timetable) were: Savernake for Marlborough, Wootton Rivers Halt, Manningford Halt, Woodborough, Patney & Chirton and Lavington on the main line; Pans Lane Halt, Devizes, Bromham & Rowde Halt, Seend Halt and Semington Halt on the Devizes branch; Holt Junction and Staverton Halt on the Thingley Junction - Trowbridge line. Staff had been removed from Savernake, Woodborough and Patney & Chirton stations the previous November.

Also withdrawn from this date (but not served from the Newbury line since 1961) was the remaining passenger service on the Bradford North Triangle, officially known as the Staverton Halt - Bradford Junction (West Junction) line, and services to the other intermediate stations between Thingley Junction and Trowbridge.

Woodborough and Lavington stations had, up to this time, retained their goods depots, however these were closed in August 1966 (Woodborough) and (looking ahead a little) in April 1967 (Lavington).

Although no longer serving passenger trains on the ex-DN&SR line from Newbury (since 1960) or on the ex-M&SWJR line from Savernake (since 1961), it is of interest to note that Southampton Terminus station was closed to passengers on 5 September 1966.

The closure of lines and passenger stations described above were the first "post-Beeching" closures to affect the Berks & Hants line. Previous closures had either taken place before the publication of the Beeching Report, or were under consideration for closure and listed in the Report.

Meanwhile, looking to the future, Newbury Racecourse station attracted some publicity when, on 24 May 1966, the loading of cars on to flat wagons was demonstrated in connection with the opening of the world's first purpose-built car terminal at Kensington Olympia on the same day. An article in the Railway Magazine for August 2005 illustrates this demonstration. The relevant photograph is also of interest as it is taken from one of the footbridges which have since been removed (in 1972) and appears to show that the loop platforms and down platform on the main line had recently had been provided with new coping slabs and new or rebuilt walling.

The bridges over the High Street in Hungerford, which in 1897 had replaced the original single-track bridge built by the Berks and Hants Extension Railway for the opening in 1862, were themselves replaced in 1966. Many other underbridges west of Hungerford, on both the Extension and the Stert – Westbury lines, were rebuilt during this period, new concrete or steel spans being placed on the existing brick abutments. Also, on the Stert – Westbury line, some of the bridges over the line were altered in order to increase clearances, probably to enable the track structure to be strengthened.

In the final chapter, the mostly positive developments that took place on, or affected, the Berks & Hants line over the period up to privatisation are fully described.

PUBLISHED REFERENCES

B. R. Diary 1948 – 1957

Stanley Creer (Ian Allan Ltd 1986)

B. R. Diary 1958 – 1967

John Glover (Ian Allan Ltd 1987)

The Organisation of British Railways

M R Bonavia (Ian Allan Ltd 1971)

The Birth of British Rail

M R Bonavia (Ian Allan Ltd 1979)

British Rail – The First 25 Years

M R Bonavia (David & Charles 1981)

The Last Years of Steam on British Railways

O S Nock (David & Charles 1978)

The Western Since 1948

G Freeman Allen (Ian Allan Ltd 1979)

The Western before Beeching

Chris Leigh (Ian Allan Ltd 1979)

British Rail Track Diagrams 3 – Western Region

(Quail Map Company 1992)

Acts and Government Reports

1955 – January: Modernisation Plan

1962 – Transport Act

1963 – March: The Reshaping of British Railways Part 1 Report, Part 2 Maps   British Railways Board

1965 – February: The Development of the Major Trunk Routes - British Railways Board

British Railways Service Time Tables, Western Operating Area September 1950

British Railways Regional Appendix, Western Region October 1960

British Railways Western Region Timetables May 1948 twice yearly to June 1964

British Railways Western Region Timetables June 1964 annually to May 1974

British Railways Southern Region Timetables various issues

Railway Magazine (RM) and Modern Railways (MR)

RM May/June 1949 "The LSWR at Plymouth" (reference shortest distance London – Plymouth by GWR from 1906)

RM July/August 1949 Kennet and Avon Canal transferred from the Railway Executive to the Docks & Inland Waterways Executive

RM January 1950 Railways at Marlborough (response to query)

RM February 1950 Main Line Companies Dissolved

RM March 1950 "Revision of Regional Boundaries of British Railways"

RM November 1951 & February 1952 "Engineering Works near Westbury" (improvements to track formation on five separate sections of the up line between Patney and Westbury)

RM June 1953 "Bulls Lock Bridge, near Newbury" (reconstruction of bridge over canal during April and May)

RM May 1954 Spur at Winchester Junction

RM November 1954 "The Lambourn Valley Railway" – P W Gentry

RM February and March 1955 "The Didcot, Newbury and Southampton Railway" – T B Sands

RM October 1957 "Railways to Devizes" - T J Saunders

RM January 1958 "Ten Years of British Railways" – "Borderer"

RM February and March 1958 "Savernake, a Railway Crossroads in Wiltshire" – T B Sands

RM April 1958 Further Adjustments of British Railways Regional Boundaries

RM August 1958 Notes and News 635 trains withdrawn by Western Region on June 30

RM December 1958 Notes and News More Railcars for Western Region, including 108 to work suburban services from Paddington (reference introduction of Reading-based units in 1961, page 153)

RM November 1961 "The Passing of the Midland and South Western Junction Railway" – T B Sands

RM May 1963 "The Reshaping of British Railways"

RM January 1965 "By Rail to the Races" (reference place of origin and routes of traffic in 1954)

RM March 1965 "Towards 1984"

RM April 1965 "Looking Twenty Years Ahead"

Modern Railways (MR) April 1965 The Development of the Major Trunk Routes

MR April and August 1965 Major re-signalling scheme based on new power signal box at Reading

MR December 1965 News in Brief Withdrawal of station staff at Savernake, Woodborough and Patney & Chirton from 8 November

RM November 2009 "BR Souvenir Issue Part One: 1948 – 1971"

Newbury Weekly News (NWN): 19.2.48 & 26.8.48 (Newbury Racecourse); 12.5.48, 8.7.48, 22.7.48 (Enborne Valley Reservoir); 23.12.54 (K&A Canal); 28.8.58 (derailment at the Racecourse); 18.6.59, 24.12.59, 10.3.60 (DN&SR south of Newbury); 7.7.58, various dates 1959-61 (Lambourn line closure); various dates 1961-2, 1966-8 and 10.10.85 (DN&SR north of Newbury)

Various dates 1963 – 1965 (new Cheap Street bridge); 16.5.63 (fears of closure of Aldermaston, Midgham and Kintbury stations)

8
MODERNISATION TO PRIVATISATION
1967 - 1993

1967 - 1968 Hope for the future, then a setback

The first significant event of 1967, in March, was the publication of a British Railways Board/Ministry of Transport report entitled "British Railways Network for Development". This identified 11,000 route miles which the government and the Board decided should be retained and developed, "a stable network planned to meet social as well as economic and commercial needs". This network included the line from Reading to Taunton via Westbury and the cross-country routes in the area then still open. The freight only line from Newbury to Welford Park, serving USAF Welford, was shown as open, but was not included in the network for development.

The other events of 1967 all concerned changes to freight facilities. Lavington station closed for goods traffic in April. The Newbury - Welford Park line was leased by the Ministry of Defence from the British Railways Board, the line being required solely for USAF Welford traffic. In November, the sidings to the west of Aldermaston station were removed. These had given access to the goods shed (closed in December 1965), the pump house (redundant since the water troughs ceased to be required) and the Sterling Cable Factory.

The 1968 Transport Act separated the commercially viable railway system from social services which were not self-supporting and created new public bodies, including Passenger Transport Authorities, Passenger Transport Executives and the National Freight Corporation.

In June 1968, it was reported that under the Western Region's future plans, Newbury was to be served by a single-track line with passing places; the possibility that Newbury might be the terminus of the line was also mooted.

1969 – 1975 Modernisation takes effect

At the start of the 1969 timetable, 5 May, the "Halts" from Theale to Bedwyn inclusive ceased to be so called and reverted to the names used before the change in 1964, when they became unstaffed. The change had not affected Newbury, which had retained its staff.

During 1968 or 1969, the level crossing gates were removed from the main line and goods siding at Thatcham, those on the main line being replaced by full lifting barriers operated from the adjacent signal box. The siding crossing the road, which had required the second set of gates, had been taken out of use in

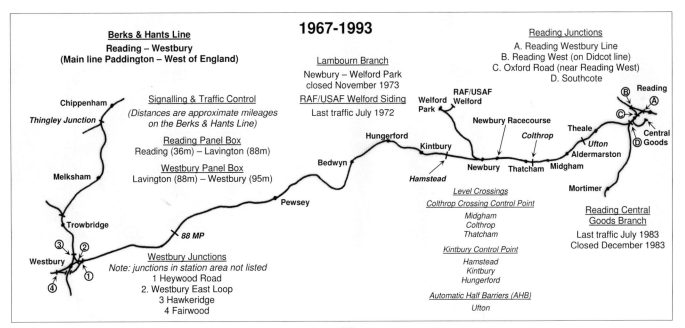

Upper - *A view east from the lineside of the goods shed at Newbury with double-headed 'Warship' class diesel hydraulics on an up Inter-City service (1968) (D Canning)*

Lower - *An unidentified Class 47 on a down West of England service lays a carpet of diesel exhaust fumes as it passes Newbury. The sidings have been taken over by the Permanent Way Engineer. (January 1978) (Author)*

Above - A Class 50 approaches Hamstead Crossing from the Hungerford direction, passing the impressively tall home signal – the height being necessary to give visibility from the maximum possible distance (January 1978) (Kevin Robertson collection)

Left - The level crossing gates at Hamstead Crossing are closed by hand. For pedestrians, a way across whilst the gates were closed was by wicket gates, seen on the right and under the control of the signalman. A colour photograph of the gates and signal box at this crossing can be found on page 161 overleaf (January 1978) (Author)

November 1967. Goods facilities at Thatcham were not withdrawn until July 1970; the sidings east of the road were not taken out of use until November 1976.

Goods facilities were also withdrawn from Hungerford, Padworth sidings (east of Aldermaston) and Theale in 1970. At Padworth and Theale, as at Thatcham (Colthrop), freight trains continued to serve the various private sidings.

In January 1971, it was reported that the future of the local services between Reading, Newbury and Bedwyn could be guaranteed if BR was successful in a bid to secure a contract to transport material for use in the Theale to Winnersh section of the M4 motorway. The importance of the event which took place on the Berks & Hants line in February that year cannot therefore be understated. A significant event in the development of stone traffic, the first train ran in a contract to supply 188,000 tons of Mendip stone for construction of the M4 Motorway. The stone was

unloaded and transferred to road haulage in Newbury Goods Yard.

However, reductions in traffic elsewhere were signified by the termination of the Private Siding Agreement with Reeds Cartons Ltd (formerly Colthrop Board and Paper Mills) in June, followed by the removal of the west-facing connection to the main line. Meanwhile grant aid for 1971 of £188,000 was announced for the Reading - Westbury passenger services.

Remodelling of Southcote Junction was carried out in September and October 1971, the relocation of the adjacent Coley Goods Branch Junction having taken place in January. This area had been incorporated into the Reading MAS scheme in 1965, all signalling being remotely controlled by Reading Power Signal Box. Permissible speeds through Southcote Junction were raised from 40 to 60mph for the main (Newbury) line and from 25 to 40mph for the branch (Basingstoke) line.

Above - *Dramatic scenes at Hungerford station on 10 November 1971 after the derailment of an up loaded stone train during the previous night. The signal box, doubled in size in 1939, appears to have taken the full force of the derailment (L Crosier collection)*

Opposite page, upper - *The replacement signal box at Hungerford (**left**) was very different to the traditional signal boxes such as that at Hamstead Crossing (**right**), a similar design to that destroyed at Hungerford. (both, January 1978) (Author)*

Opposite page, centre - *Colthrop Crossing Signal Box basks in the evening sunshine. From the introduction of the MAS scheme at this location in 1978, the functions of the box were limited to the operation of the crossing barriers and the points to the oil discharge sidings. (July 1995) (Author)*

Opposite page, lower - *An unidentified class 31 is about to pass Kintbury Signal Box on an up train, possibly a holiday relief (Summer 1973) (L Crosier)*

Unplanned changes in signalling took place on 10 November when Hungerford signal box was demolished in a freight train derailment. A replacement signal box, second-hand from its previous site (Bristol East Depot Main Line), was erected on the other side of the crossing and opened for use on 19 March 1972. The level crossing gates and full semaphore signalling were retained, temporary arrangements being made until the new box was ready.

From the beginning of 1972, the MOD locomotive used for traffic to and from USAF Welford was also used on the remaining section of the Lambourn line between Newbury and Welford Park, and it is believed that this locomotive ran right through Newbury station to reach the goods yard with its train. The last movement of MOD traffic to Welford Park took place in July 1972, although the agreement for use of the Newbury - Welford Park line did not expire until a year later. Last trains of any sort ran on 3 November 1973, when four return trips were made with a nine-car train of diesel multiple units for the benefit of local people and rail enthusiasts. It was reported that 3,000 people travelled to and from Welford Park. After this, the line was taken out of use, but a long siding was retained at the Newbury end. The track was not removed until the winter of 1976/7, when it was cut up by contractors and removed in short sections.

Meanwhile, in April 1973, the layout at Colthrop was further rationalised by the removal of the east-facing connection from the down side to the up line, severing the down side sidings from the main line.

The signal box at Aldermaston closed on 31 March 1974 following the removal of the crossover at the west end of the station and the provision of the new layout at the east end. This layout, which maintained access to Padworth sidings, was connected to the main line at Ufton Crossing and controlled by that signal box.

Later in the year, in August and October respectively, full lifting barriers replaced the crossing gates at Midgham and Kintbury. In both cases, control of the crossing remained with the adjacent signal box. These changes left the only remaining crossing gates at Ufton, Colthrop, Hamstead Crossing, Hungerford and Crofton Crossing (worked by hand except Colthrop and Hungerford – worked by a wheel in the box).

The private siding at Theale, immediately to the north of the station, serving Pressed Steel Co. (formerly Imperial Tobacco Co.) was taken out of use in the 1974/75 period.

Four photographs from the British Rail 'Corporate Era' illustrate the bland uniformity of the post-steam age with local trains and locomotives in all-over dull blue and only Inter-City coaches having a relieving grey upper band, later extended to all coaching stock.

Opposite page, top left - An unidentified class 117 DMU departs en route to Bedwyn from the 'Winchester Bay' at Newbury, passing the ancient wooden starting signal with its large spectacle plates. (January 1978)

Opposite page, top right - A recently overhauled class 50 passes Thatcham en route to London in Summer 1977. The tall bracket signal was a reminder of the previous existence of the footbridge, demolished in 1967 and not yet replaced at the date of the photograph.

Opposite page, lower - Class 119 No L586 approaches Newbury from Bedwyn in January 1978. Last used in 1973, the trackbed of the former Lambourn branch can clearly be seen in the background climbing away from the main line.

This page - A rather work-stained class 50 enters Newbury with mixed rake of rolling stock forming an up Inter-City train. So much has changed since this picture was taken (in January 1978) – only the platforms and the buildings in the background in Bartholomew Street have survived to this day. (All: Author)

Above - *The signalboxes shown at the top, Newbury West and Newbury Middle, were two of four provided for the new track layout completed in 1910, the other two being Newbury East and Newbury Racecourse. The main picture was taken on a warm day at Midgham bringing fresh air into the signal box and a boost for the tomatoes. Photographs dated Summer 1977, a few months before closure as a result of the MAS scheme.*

Opposite page, upper - *Class 119 No L582 leaves Newbury for Bedwyn on a frosty morning in January 1978. The station track layout is shown in its final form before reconstruction for the MAS scheme. The rear view of the 'Winchester Bay' starter clearly shows the wooden signal arm which survived to the end.*

Opposite page, lower - *Hungerford station and signal box await the MAS scheme, when the signal box will no longer be required. The new (colour light) signals will all be on the left hand side of the track and the timber goods shed will be just a memory (All, Author)*

Work in hand at Ufton level crossing to install an automatic half-barrier (AHB) type crossing as part of the MAS scheme, which rendered the signal box redundant (Author)

1976 – 1983 Major upgrading, new facilities, new trains and an unwelcome report

Multiple aspect signalling (MAS) was installed from Southcote Junction (exclusive) to Heywood Road Junction, near Westbury (exclusive). Preliminary work on the scheme, estimated to cost £4.5 million, started in 1976. The conversion from semaphore signalling to MAS was staged throughout the period September 1977 to January 1979, working from Theale westwards. Objectives of the scheme were to bring the line up to modern standards and to allow for the introduction of High Speed Trains to the West of England route, which took place in late 1979/early 1980.

Track layouts were changed, fifteen signal boxes closed and the remaining level crossing gates replaced with full lifting barriers. The two exceptions were at Ufton – automatic half barriers (the only ones on the Berks & Hants line) and Crofton – red/green warning light at pedestrian/bridle path crossing. Colthrop Siding Box was retained as a Ground frame, to operate Ufton, Colthrop and Thatcham crossing barriers. Two levers were retained to work the trailing connection into the up line from the heavy fuel oil siding at Colthrop Board Mills. A new ground frame was provided at Kintbury, on the south side of the line, to operate crossing barriers at Hamstead and Hungerford crossings as well as those already in use at Kintbury **(see Note: Hamstead Crossing)**.

Significant changes were made to track layouts west of Theale, east of Aldermaston, at Newbury Racecourse

Above - *Class 33 No 33015 pulls out of Colthrop fuel sidings with empty tanks for Ripple Lane Yard. (D Canning)*

Opposite page, lower - *The Author's youngest son enjoys the Sunday afternoon calm at Pewsey station in Spring 1978. (Author)*

and at Newbury. The entire track layout from the east end of the Racecourse Station to the west end of Newbury station was remodelled, new track being provided where necessary. At the Racecourse Station, track was removed from the line adjacent to the island platform, leaving only one platform available for any special racecourse trains. The line serving this platform remained as an alternative line for down trains, being retained to connect to the down platform loop at Newbury; although available for passenger trains, the track was not replaced and has a speed limit of 25mph. On the up side, the extensive sidings of Newbury Goods Yard were recorded as being complete in 1977, including the spur serving the Newbury Diesel Company whose private siding agreement was formally terminated at the end of 1978. By March 1978, when Newbury East signal box closed, only two sidings remained, accessed by a headshunt connected to the up platform line.

At Newbury station, the main change most visible to passengers was the complete removal of all facilities on the down side at the west end; this had consisted of the "Winchester Bay" and sidings provided for a range of purposes. In latter years, the bay had seen little use, most local trains started at Reading and terminated at Newbury or continued to Bedwyn. However, the

sidings were regularly used for track maintenance machines and wagons. From the train operating point of view, significant improvements included increasing the speed at which trains could enter/leave the platform loops from 25 to 40mph and designing the layout so that down trains could use either up or down platform loops or terminate in the "Didcot Bay". The speed limit for non-stopping passenger trains using the through lines was raised from 90 to 100mph.

At Theale, an additional span was provided to the road bridge at the station to accommodate the new track layout and a footbridge provided adjacent to the road bridge. This footbridge replaced one removed many years previously. Hungerford Down Goods Loop was reduced to a siding and the layout at Bedwyn altered to give a new turn-back siding for terminating passenger trains west of the station. Other works included a new footbridge at Colthrop, part-funded by Reed Paper Mills (February 1978), a new footbridge at Aldermaston, a new lighting system at Kintbury and an extension to the existing car park at Hungerford.

In addition to line speed improvements at Newbury, speed limits were raised throughout the Berks & Hants line from Southcote Junction to the end of the re-signalled section east of Westbury. The line speed was set at 100mph (see **Glossary**), with permanent speed restrictions at: Midgham curve; from Kintbury to west of Hungerford; from Crofton Curve to Savernake; and east of Lavington. At a later date, speeds on certain sections were raised to 110mph; these were from 2 miles west of Thatcham to Kintbury (about 7 miles), another 7-mile section west of Pewsey and an 8-mile section west of Lavington.

Between 1979 and 1982, a number of works were carried out between Theale and Savernake which reflected the changes in operating practices taking place during this period. In September 1979, Theale Down platform was shortened and in March 1980, the Up Goods Loop between Hungerford and Kintbury was brought into use. In June 1981, the present layout at Theale West was commissioned and in the same year a new crossover, worked by a ground frame, was installed at Savernake. In December 1982, the headshunt behind the down platform at Aldermaston was lengthened by 20 yards.

Twenty years after the "Beeching Report", the Serpell Report was published in January 1983. A new attempt to further rationalise the railway system, the most radical of its proposals, Option A, included the closure of the Berks & Hants route, leaving the Paddington - Reading - Didcot - Swindon line as the only main line in Berkshire. Option B retained the Reading - Westbury via Hungerford line but it was not clear how many stations would remain open. Neither option

retained the north - south link between Reading and Basingstoke. The Divisional Manager of British Rail Western Region stated that Option A would lead to an extra 3,500 lorry movements in the region and to a large number of redundancies amongst the 2,500 staff employed in the Reading area. Amongst the lorry movements would be heavy fuel oil from Wales delivered to Colthrop Board Mills, estimated at eight tankers a day.

Fare increases were proposed for commuters. After a public outcry, the proposals were abandoned. With the appointment of a new Secretary of State for Transport, Nicholas Ridley, later in the year, there were firm indications that the Serpell report had been shelved by the Government.

The retention of the Berks & Hants route had been discussed in an article by D. Marshall in Modern Railways for August 1977. Noting the ability of the route to provide the spare capacity which might be required to duplicate the vital Didcot – Wootton Bassett section of the Bristol main line, he states: "In the circumstances it is hardly surprising that the WR (Western Region) regards the retention of the Reading – Westbury section as a strategic necessity, and the decision to extend the Reading multiple-aspect signalling system that far follows logically".

A timely reminder of the use to which the Berks & Hants route was being put came on 16 September

1983, with the operation of the heaviest stone train ever, from Foster Yeoman's quarry at Merehead in Somerset to Acton Yard in West London. A total train weight of 4,500 tonnes included a payload of 3,300 tonnes; the two locomotives and 43 wagons stretched for more than half a mile.

The last closure to affect the Berks & Hants line (other than that of private sidings) took place in December 1983 when the Southcote Junction - Reading Central Goods branch (also known as the Coley Goods Branch) was officially closed. Last traffic had run on 25 July 1983. The facing connection from the main line was not removed until January 1985, concurrent with the lifting of the track on the branch.

1984 -1990 Improvements all the way

The first event of 1984 was the internal reorganisation of the Western Region, which took effect from 20 February. A new regional HQ was created at "125 House" in Swindon, resulting from the amalgamation of the three Divisional Offices and the Regional HQ at Paddington.

The "Open Station" concept was introduced on the Newbury - Taunton line in March 1984, and on the same date on the Bristol – Westbury - Salisbury/ Weymouth line. Ticket collectors were withdrawn from

Newbury, Pewsey, Westbury and Taunton stations, all intermediate stations being unstaffed (except in some cases for the sale of tickets in the mornings).

Modern signalling came to the Westbury area in 1984. Lines north of the station were temporarily taken out of use on 7 April and Westbury North Signal Box closed. A new layout for the station area was commissioned over the period 11 - 14 May 1984. Heywood Road Signal Box was closed with the opening of the new Westbury panel box on 13 May. At the same time, the Hawkeridge Loop was renamed Westbury East Loop.

In the first part of the year, the down side buildings at Newbury station were renovated for lease as offices; their new use began in August. Waiting rooms and toilets were no longer provided on the down side, but the full awning length was retained. At a later date, a conservatory-type building was erected on the platform as a waiting room. The large clocks on each main platform were removed.

Between July and November 1984, in a £200,000 programme, substantial interior changes were made to the up side buildings. Improvements were made to the booking hall and ticket office and a toilet for disabled passengers provided. New clocks and visual display units were provided on each platform. Thirty-one extra car-parking spaces were provided on land formerly

Above - *An up Inter-City HST calls at Newbury as the finishing touches are made to the modernised station, September 1979.*

Opposite page - *The downside buildings and footbridge at Newbury in June 1994. Although little changed in appearance since coming into use in 1910, the buildings had become redundant and were internally renovated in 1984 for lease as offices but were partially returned to railway use in the 21st Century. (Both Author)*

occupied by the Lambourn Bay and adjacent buildings. In November 1984, it was reported that, after discussions with Newbury District Council, the clocks had been returned after renovation and were to be reinstated. In the event, only one was reinstated; this remained in use until 1990.

In February 1985, the line was closed on two consecutive Sundays for bridge work at Kennet and Avon Canal Viaduct East, between Enborne Junction and Hamstead Crossing.

In the same year, extensive works were carried out on the track to enable the maximum speed of passenger trains on about 22 miles of the route to be raised to 110mph; the upgraded sections are listed on page 168. It is understood that this was done in order to achieve a two-hour timing for inter-city trains between London and Exeter from the start of the summer timetable in May of that year.

On 10 June 1986, the former London & South East Sector of British Rail (introduced on the sectorisation of British Rail in 1982) launched its new image as Network SouthEast. Initially, an obvious sign of the change was the new livery for locomotives and coaches; subsequently, all stations in the sector (which extended as far as Bedwyn on the Berks & Hants line) would be repainted and re-signed, major cleaning would be carried out every three months, all waiting rooms would be non-smoking and many of them would have buffet facilities.

Significantly for off-peak services on the line, intensive marketing of spare seats during these periods, and all day on Saturdays, Sundays, and bank holidays was introduced by means of a one-day Capitalcard available in Greater London and on London Regional Transport underground and bus services. Travellers from outside that area would pay 80 pence more than the cheap day return fare to obtain a Capitalcard. In September, a Network Card was introduced enabling other special offers for off-peak travel to be made on Network services.

Network maps were introduced, including one for the London area based on the Greater London Network map first produced in 1965, and these maps were displayed in the trains as well as on stations and on publicity material. Inside the trains, other improvements included litter bins and an increase in no-smoking areas to 85% of the accommodation.

*Above - Class 101 DMU No L835 on a Reading train calls at Newbury Racecourse station, newly opened for regular passenger traffic. **Inset** - Class 47487 'Ruskin College Oxford' heads for Paddington with a 'Network Express'. (both, April 1991, Author)*

Opposite page, upper - Road bridges were provided on each side of Aldermaston station on construction of the Berks and Hants Railway in 1846-1847. The design of the bridge had to take into account the poor soils in the Kennet Valley, hence the provision of side arches and internal arches in the abutments. A steel span has replaced the original centre span and in this form this bridge took all the A340 traffic until replacement in 2013.

Opposite page, lower - Class 37 No 37322 passes under the new footbridge at Thatcham an empty coal working from Westbury on 19 September 1988. (S Wise)

At Thatcham station, a new station building was erected, together with a new shelter on each platform; a new footbridge was also provided. These facilities replaced those removed in 1965; staff were provided again, at least for the purchase of tickets. In addition, the platforms received new surfaces and the down side car park was tidied up and extended. The official opening of the new facilities took place on 8 August 1987.

In 1988 a decision was made to open Newbury Racecourse Station to serve the adjacent trading estate and residential areas, a full service of local trains being provided. For over 80 years, the station had been open only on race days, with special trains from various destinations terminating in its loop platforms and through trains calling there for the benefit of race-goers. The only exception was a two-week period in March 1978 when, during the renewal of the tracks at Newbury station, certain trains started from or terminated there and buses conveyed passengers to and from the main station.

The footbridge and shelters were repaired and repainted, the platforms resurfaced, new lighting and signs erected and a new entrance provided giving access to Hambridge Road. The opening (as an "experimental service") took place on 16 May 1988, the start of the summer timetable, the official opening ceremony following on Tuesday 24 May. The cost was

quoted as £36,000. Earlier in the month it had been announced that a programme of works would be undertaken on the up side buildings at Newbury.

The Bradford North Chord, as it had become known, was "decommissioned" (taken out of use) on 22 March 1990. This line, connecting the Chippenham - Trowbridge line to the Bath - Trowbridge line, had been without a passenger service since April 1966 and was used solely as a diversionary route between Chippenham and Bath. With its closure, it became necessary to divert Paddington to Bath and Bristol trains via the Berks & Hants line if the line was blocked between Chippenham and Bath.

In 1990 it was the turn of the up side buildings at Newbury to be refurbished, following similar work to the down side in 1984 and some interior work on the up side in the same year. The inside was stripped out in stages, dry rot eradicated and new accommodation provided. From the London end, the facilities provided were: ticket office with office/mess room behind, ticket hall, bookstall/mini-buffet with serving counter, waiting rooms, toilets, staff accommodation, and station manager's office. The original station buffet, which had closed in 1970/71 (last shown in 1970/71 timetable), was not reopened; the large room, which had remained disused since the buffet's closure, became the main waiting room.

Opposite page - *Class 56 No 56062 'Mountsorrel' sports the livery of British Rail's Trainload Construction sub-sector as it heads for Bardon's West of England quarries through Reading station's down main platform.*

Above - *Class 60 No 60072 'Cairn Toul' in Trainload Cola sub-sector livery takes the curve to the Berks & Hants line with empty stone wagons returning to the Mendip quarries. June 1994*

Below - *ARC Class 59/1 59104 'Village of Great Elm' in company livery returns empty stone hoppers to Whatley Quarry. June 1994 (all, Author)*

Yeoman's pioneer Class 59 No 59001 'Yeoman Endeavour' hauls aggregates for the construction industry past the site of Patney & Churton station in June 1994 (Author)

The exterior of the buildings received attention and the awning was also renovated, being completely re-sheeted; its entire length was retained. A small building was removed at the end of the site of the Lambourn Bay. Official opening took place on 31 July 1990, when the clock, which had been reinstated in 1984, was presented to Newbury District Council, allegedly for display in the Corn Exchange. The works took 18 months, the total cost being quoted as £664,000, of which £264,000 was spent on the roof.

1991 – 1993 The end of the Western Region, facilities for new local trains and the Railways Act 1993

On 23 June 1991, the Western Region of British Railways ceased to exist after a life of over 40 years. Its functions were taken over, wholly or partly, in the area covered by the book, by the following sectors of the British Railways Board:

Intercity Great Western (previously Intercity)

Intercity Cross Country (previously Intercity)

Thames and Chilterns (previously part of Network South East)

Regional Railways (previously Provincial Railways)

The servicing facilities for the diesel multiple units at Reading Upper Triangle Sidings were destined to become the sole servicing site for the planned fleet of Network Turbo trains, replacing other facilities at Southall and Old Oak Common. A new servicing building and carriage washer were provided adjacent to the Berks & Hants line and the fan of sidings in the triangle equipped to serve the new units. Known as Reading Turbo Depot, reported to cost £8m, it was officially opened on 8 March 1991.

Alterations were carried out to the Reading Maintenance Depot to upgrade the facilities to modern standards and to allow for the longer length of the Turbo trains compared with the units to be displaced. A visit to this depot in April 1993 demonstrated the work in hand amongst a mix of the units which had been in use since 1961 and the new Turbo units. At that time, it was expected that the work would be complete by the time all the Class 165 and 166 Turbo units were commissioned. During the visit, it was noted that the maintenance depot facilities were shared by the Intercity Great Western and the Thames and Chilterns sectors.

During 1991, the platforms at Theale and Thatcham were lengthened in preparation for the future operation of six-car Turbo trains if required. At all intermediate stations, work was done on the platform surfaces and edges (the height being increased if required) and on the provision of shelters. The only "original" buildings at

the small stations left at the end of this period were the down side platform shelters at Midgham and Bedwyn.

For reasons not known, the up platform at Kintbury was not altered at that time, and as a result passengers continued to be faced with a considerable difference in height between platform and train. The original platform fencing and ramp from road level were retained; the latter surfaced with stone setts. At a later date the level was raised throughout and the ramp and platform resurfaced to the standard of the adjacent stations. From the down platform it is possible to see the original length of the up platform prior to lengthening, probably at the time of the general improvements to the line in the 1897–1900 period.

A new Railways Act became law in 1993, its principal purpose being the privatisation of the various functions of the railway, whilst keeping the infrastructure within state ownership. Changes to the infrastructure since 1993 have been modest in nature; however the same cannot be said for the passenger and freight train services, which continue to evolve to cater for the ever-changing needs of the customers of those services that use the Berks & Hants line.

With the onset of privatisation, the story of the Berks & Hants line became infinitely more complex and it is fair to say that an insider's knowledge of the rail industry would be needed to write the story from 1993 to the present day. I therefore decided that, my story having commenced in 1824, nearly 170 years of history of the line from its earliest beginnings to the demise of British Railways would be a viable and worthwhile project on which to base a comprehensive book and a permanent archive.

Top left - *A London-bound InterCity HST in 'Swallow' livery speeds through the Vale of Pewsey in Summer 1994.*

Top right - *Network SouthEast Class 47 No 47547 'University of Oxford' heads for Newbury at Southcote Junction.*

Above - *Beautiful Berkshire: a Class 165 'Networker Turbo' DMU approaches Hamstead Crossing on a local train from Bedwyn to Newbury. (All, Author)*

Above - *'View from Rockingham Road Railway Bridge, Newbury, Berkshire' by Christopher Hall RA (West Berkshire Museum collection)*

Below - *Echo of the Great Western: Preserved GWR 'Castle' class 4-6-0 No 5029 'Nunney Castle' pauses at Reading West on a special train chartered by the Mayor of Newbury on 4 September 1994 (Author)*

NOTE:

Hamstead Crossing – the signal box was due to close and the crossing gates were due to be replaced by automatic half-barriers (AHBs) in 1970 (source: David Canning). However, following the Hixon Level Crossing disaster on 6 January 1968 (see Railway Magazine and Railway World references below), due to the new requirements for AHBs, "it was almost impossible to make a viable case for the conversion of other level crossings from gates to AHB" (reference "Level Crossings" – see below). As noted in the text, the crossing was converted to full lifting barriers as part of the programme of installation of MAS on the Berks & Hants line in 1977-9.

PUBLISHED REFERENCES

B. R. Diary 1968 – 1977

Chris Heaps (Ian Allan Ltd 1988)

B. R. Diary 1978 – 1985

John Glover (Ian Allan Ltd 1985)

The Organisation of British Railways

M R Bonavia (Ian Allan Ltd 1971)

The Birth of British Rail

M R Bonavia (Ian Allan Ltd 1979)

British Rail – The First 25 Years

M R Bonavia (David & Charles 1981)

The Last Years of Steam on British Railways

O S Nock (David & Charles 1978)

Level Crossings

Stanley Hall and Peter van der Mark (Ian Allan Ltd 2008)

Railway World Special The West of England Re-signalling

Adrian Vaughan (Ian Allan Ltd 1987)

The Western Since 1948

G Freeman Allen (Ian Allan Ltd 1979)

British Rail Track Diagrams 3 – Western Region

(Quail Map Company 1992)

The Western before Beeching

Chris Leigh (Ian Allan Ltd 1979)

Government Reports

1967 – March: British Railways Network for Development - British Railways Board

1983 – January: Serpell Report

British Railways Western Region Timetables June 1967 annually to May 1974

British Railways Southern Region Timetables various issues

British Railways All-line Passenger Timetables May 1974 to May 1994

Railway Magazine (RM) and Modern Railways (MR)

RM February, March, June & September 1968 Accident at Hixon Level Crossing, Staffs; changes to requirements for automatic half-barrier level crossings resulting from the accident

The curvature of the Berks & Hants line through the Kennet Valley is illustrated well in this view of class 117 DMU L404 approaching Midgham from Thatcham. The unit is in the white and blue livery given to refurbished units at this time (January 1978)

Railway World (RW) February, April, May, June, July & September 1968 Accident at Hixon Level Crossing, Staffs; changes to requirements for automatic half-barrier level crossings resulting from the accident

RM March 1971 Grant Aid Reading – Westbury

RW January 1977 "The Berks & Hants Line Today" - D E Canning

MR August 1977 "The case for the Berks & Hants – The Strategic Importance of the Berks & Hants route" - D A Marshall

MR November 1982 Railtalk – "Waiting for Serpell"

RM November 1982 "Signalman to Crossing Keeper" - D E Canning

RM November 1983 Heaviest-ever freight train from Merehead Quarry (News and notes)

RM March 1984 "Crossing Keeper 1984" - D E Canning

RM February 1986 Reading: A New Approach

RM February 1986 Reading Central Recollected

RM August 1986 Network SouthEast launched (News & notes)

MR October 1990 "Service Please – Local services on the Berks & Hants"

RM May 1991 Sir Bob opens Reading's £8m Turbo Depot

Steam Days April 1996 Special Traffic – Racing at Newbury - Michael Harris

RM August 2005 "Taking the Car by Train – the Motorail Story" - Keith Hill

RM November 2009 "BR Souvenir Issue Part One: 1948 – 1971"

RM May 2010 "BR Souvenir Issue Part Two: 1971 - 1997"

Newspaper and other references

Letter British Rail Western Region to Newbury and District Rail Passengers Association: 10.2.84 (Internal re-organisation of the Western Region)

Newbury Weekend Newspaper 14.12.84 (Kennet rail crossings plan shelved)

Evening Post (EP) 27.5.88 (Racecourse station), 31.7.90 (Newbury station refurbishment)

Railnews September 1990: (Newbury station refurbishment)

Western Daily Press 30.7.93: Battle to turn West (of England) lines electric

Newbury Weekly News (NWN): 13.2.68, 27.6.1968 (single-track line), 28.8.69 (ammunition trains to Welford, Theale Fuel Depot), 23.10.69 (special train to Welford Park), 15.1.70, 22.1.70 (future of local services), 25.2.71 (M4 stone), 11.11.71 (Derailment at Hungerford), 23.3.72 (future of the line), 8.11.1973 (last trains to Welford Park);

3.2.77, 1.9.77, 15.9.77, 22.9.77, 5.1.78, 28.6.79 (modernisation of track and signalling, Theale to Westbury);

18.2.80 (disquiet over reduced train services), 16.4.81 & 19.1.84 (station announcement system), 26.11.81 (rumoured cut in rural trains denied by BR), 21.8.82 (deliveries of heating oil disrupted by train drivers' strike);

27.1.83 (fare increases), 27.1.83 & 1.12.83 (Serpell Report) 12.5.83 (derailment at Bedwyn station), 7.7.83 (Newbury line to be electrified), 22.9.83 (heaviest train passes), 1.12.83 (BR seeks improved station (Newbury)), 7.2.84 (rail and river bridge at Thatcham), 15.3.84 (freight trains shaking houses) 19.7.84, 2.8.84, 6.9.84, 4.10.84, 8.11.84 & 20.12.84 (Newbury station), 15.11.84 (facilities at station slammed (Thatcham));

14.2.85 (Ufton Crossing Accident), 12.9.85 (BR says 'no' to station footbridge (Thatcham)), 22.9.85 (Incident at Theale depot); 10.10.85 (DN&SR north of Newbury);

25.2.86 (Foster Yeoman to run its own trains), 2.10.86, 16.10.86 (Plans for Thatcham station), 23.10.86 (Old Goods Yard lined up for huge development (Newbury));

14.5.87, 5.5.88 (Newbury station), 18.12.87, 26.5.88 (Newbury Racecourse station);

30.11.89 (Boarding card plan infuriates commuters; west of Newbury rail service criticised);

31.5.90 (Worsening rail service comes under fire again), 2.8.90 (New-look station officially opened (Newbury)), 9.8.90 (More delays for sweating commuters), 18.10.90 (Another price blow for rail commuters), 22.11.90 (BR plans turbo trains for Thames line 1992);

28.3.91 (Crossrail service offers boost for commuters from West Berkshire), 20.6.91 (three men hit by lightning), 29.8.91 (fire crews on alert after tanker derailed (Theale)), 12.9.91 (rail crossing inquest opened (accident at Padworth)), 12.12.91 (vagrants may have lit fires for warmth (Newbury Racecourse));

12.3.92 (Newbury line to have new trains), 23.4.92 (councillors call for new bridge over railway (Thatcham)), May (marking the end of an era – last diesel-hauled locomotive commuter service from Reading to Newbury – 8 May), 16.7.92 (railway bridge plan takes its first step (Thatcham)), (MP says rail changes will bring benefits to users (privatisation)), 30.7.92 (rail users fear cuts in services (privatisation)), 17.9.92, 24.9.92 & 1.10.92 (improved timetable from September based on new turbo trains);

7.1.93 (BR price increases begin to bite; passengers risking their lives (at Kintbury station)), 16.9.93 (Great Bedwyn Parish councillors to meet BR (collection of fares); rail managers come under fire), 21.10.93 (no plans to close village railway station (Bedwyn); BR admits to 'free ride' loophole on local line (under Thatcham news)), 21.10.93 (train fares protest by commuters).

Appendix 1
GLOSSARY

GAUGE

Gauge

The distance between the inner faces of the rails, measured perpendicular to the rails.

Broad gauge

The track gauge of 7ft 0¼in adopted by Brunel for the Great Western Railway. Metric equivalent: 2140mm.

Standard gauge/Narrow gauge

The track gauge of 4ft 8½in adopted by most other railway companies (there were some early exceptions); often referred to as narrow gauge during the life-time of the broad gauge (1835-1892). Metric equivalent: 1435mm. The term 'Narrow Gauge' was, after 1892, and is to this day, used to describe minor railways with a track gauge of less than 4ft 8½in.

Mixed gauge

The combination of broad and narrow gauges on the Great Western Railway, created by laying an additional rail inside the broad gauge rails and thus permitting all types of locomotives and rolling stock to use the track or line.

INFRASTRUCTURE

Automatic Half Barriers (AHB)

Barriers obstructing the nearside half of the roadway at a level crossing, raised and lowered automatically by the passage of trains.

Bridges: Accommodation Bridge

A private bridge over or under a railway provided for the use of the landowner or his tenants when a parcel of land under single ownership has been severed by the construction of the railway.

Bridges: Occupation Bridge

A bridge taking a private road over or under a railway and therefore not a public right of way.

Bridges: Overbridge

Bridge carrying a road, track or canal over a railway line.

Original brick arch accommodation bridge dating from 1847 on the Berks & Hants line just west of Southcote Junction. (Summer 1993)

Bridges: Underbridge

Bridge carrying a railway line over a road or track, footpath, stream, river, canal etc.

Engineer's Line Reference

A code, usually consisting of three letters, sometimes suffixed by a number, used on the national rail network as a unique reference to a section of track or route.

Line Speed

The maximum speed permitted on a specified line of route. This speed may be reduced at particular locations by permanent speed restrictions due to restraints such as line curvature, signal visibility etc.

Lines: Down Line

In general terms, the line carrying traffic from the London direction. On the down line, the distances from London increase. On cross-country lines, the position was as follows: Didcot to Winchester – down line; Swindon to Andover – down line.

Lines: Up Line

In general terms, the line carrying traffic towards London. On the up line, distances to London decrease. On cross-country lines, the position was as follows: Winchester to Didcot - up line; Andover to Swindon – up line.

Lines: Headshunt

A dead-end length of track allowing shunting movements to be made into a siding, or group of sidings, without interruption to traffic on the up or down lines.

Lines: Goods Loops

A loop line connected at each end to the main line normally used only by freight trains, but usable by passenger trains at low speeds in an emergency.

Lines: Loop

This term was used extensively by the GWR to describe a single or double track line connecting two main lines and usually involving a change of direction, for example "Reading West Loop". The term "curve" was also formally used in such a situation.

Lines: Refuge Siding

A siding, entered through a trailing connection, which provides temporary accommodation for slow non-passenger trains out of the way of faster traffic.

Measurements: Miles and chains (still in use in the Twenty-first Century)

The standard method of measurement for railway lines or routes: a mile is divided into 80 chains; 10 chains is a furlong, as still used in horse racing. A chain is equal to 66 feet or 22 yards. Miles and chains are given in the text where taken from original records, followed by the approximate equivalent in miles and quarters of miles. The location of bridges on the Berks & Hants line is marked with the distance from a fixed point (e.g. London terminus) at road/canal level by painted numerals and letters or metal plates (see illustrations).

Measurements: Feet, Yards and Metres

Heights are given in feet, followed by the metric equivalent. Lengths such as bridge spans are given in feet and inches, a foot being approximately 0.3m. Longer distances such as tunnel lengths are given in yards, a yard being approximately 0.9m.

Wagon Turntable

Hand-operated turntable used for turning short-wheelbase wagons from one track to another, avoiding the use of points. A common feature of early station layouts, where shunting of individual vehicles would be carried out using horses or even manual labour. Not suitable for use by locomotives.

Water Troughs

Narrow and lengthy shallow troughs placed between the rails from which water could be scooped up into the tender tanks of steam locomotives whilst on the move (optimum uptake was achieved at around 40mph).

NATIONAL EVENTS

Gauge War 1844-1854

Also known as the 'Battle of the Gauges', the name given to the long war between the supporters of the 'Broad Gauge' and the 'Narrow Gauge'.

Railway Mania

Refers to the rash of schemes proposed in the 1844 - 1847 period; schemes relevant to the book are described in Chapter 2.

NON-RAILWAY

Navigation

Name given to a length of river made suitable for navigation by channels avoiding bends in the river and by the provision of locks to overcome the natural gradient of the river.

Turnpike

Name given to the roads made by the Turnpike Commissioners, paid for by the tolls levied on passing traffic. The turnpike was the actual gate or barrier at the start and end of each section of road.

TRAINS

Slip coach/Slip portion

A coach or coaches capable of being detached from the rear of a moving train. Controlled by its own guard, it was 'slipped' to travel under its own momentum until brought to a stop at its destination platform. Alternatively, as at Westbury from 1935 onwards, the slip portion was detached and brought to a stop on the main line and a locomotive used to bring the coach or coaches into the station. Slip portions enabled places such as Reading, Newbury and Westbury to be served by express trains which made few intermediate stops. Whilst the slipping system was used by many railway companies in early years the Great Western and later the Western Region were the last users.

TRAIN CONTROL AND OPERATION

Automatic Train Control (ATC)

This term is generally understood to describe the system developed by the GWR and eventually extended to all of the company's main lines. Equipment installed on the track and connected to the signals was arranged to activate/deactivate equipment on the locomotive or railcar to give the driver an audible and visual warning of a distant signal at caution ahead or alternatively an audible and visual 'all clear'. In principle, it provided the basis for the British Railways automatic warning system (AWS).

Block Section

A section of track into which only one train is permitted at a time. These sections are controlled by a signal box at each end and apply to the control of traffic on single and double track lines.

Disc and Crossbar Signal

A red disc and crossbar mounted at right-angles to each other on a tall post which would be rotated so as to show either the disc ('all right') or the crossbar ('stop') used, in conjunction with lights shown at night to give the same indications, to control traffic at junctions, stations and tunnels before the introduction of semaphore signals.

Disc Telegraph

An early type of communication between signal boxes for the control of trains using a system of 'dots and dashes' whereby words could be spelt. As a form of shorthand, one word could also be used to describe a specific requirement or description.

Pilotman

Control of the movement of trains by an employee wearing a distinctive armband and allocated to a section of single line (or, more usually, double track temporarily under single line working) who accompanies a train on the single line section, no train being allowed to proceed without him on board, or without his authority.

Running Powers

Formal arrangements which allowed a company, other than that which owned a railway, to exercise a right to operate trains over the owning company's lines in return for a rental payment.

Time Interval System

A crude method of signalling in which a train is allowed sufficient time to clear a section ahead after which a second train can be admitted to the section. In general use in the early days of the railways.

Track Circuiting

An electrical or electronic device used to detect the

absence (or presence) of a train on a defined section of track using the pair of rails as an electric circuit. By this means a signalman can be informed on track diagrams of the presence and progress of a train on any section. Track circuits also enable points to be secured against movement under or in front of an approaching train and, where manual signalling is in use, permit signals or block instruments to be locked or controlled so that signals cannot be moved to 'off' while a train (or part of it) is on the section.

Train Staff

Control of the movement of trains by the use of a visible token of a driver's authority to enter a single line section between crossing places. Before a train can enter, this staff must be held by the driver, and since only one exists for each section, working is thus restricted to alternate trains moving in opposite directions. A variation existed in the form of 'staff and ticket' but was operated under the same strict criteria.

Electric Train Staff

A refinement of train staff working, in which the token of the driver's authority is contained in electrically-controlled and interlocked instruments which allow only one to be released at a time. When this authority is placed in the instrument at the other end of the line, a second token can be taken from the instrument at the beginning of the section, allowing a second train to pass through and so on.

PARLIAMENTARY

Gauge Commission 1845-6

A Royal Commission appointed by the Government to investigate the merits of the rival gauges, and the expediency of enforcing uniformity throughout the country.

Light Railway (Order)

A Light Railway is one purposely built simply and below the engineering standards of normal railways, to reduce the cost of construction and attain economy in working. A Light Railway Order is an order authorising the construction of such a railway. Strict conditions of operation applied.

ORGANISATIONS

NFC

National Freight Corporation; set up under the Transport Act, 1968, to exercise powers, in conjunction with the British Railways Board, to provide, secure or promote properly-integrated services for carriage of freight by road or rail.

PTAs/PTEs

Passenger Transport Authorities/Executives, originally set up in large metropolitan areas (not London) under the Transport Act, 1968.

RAOC

Royal Army Ordnance Corps

RASC

Royal Army Service Corps (now Royal Corps of Transport)

Railway Clearing House (RCH)

An organisation established in 1842 to deal with questions relating to through traffic passing over the lines of different railway companies, apportionment of receipts etc. The RCH published maps which showed details of the junctions between the lines of the various railway companies.

Principal Reference:

The Wordsworth Railway Dictionary, an A-Z of railway terminology.

Alan A Jackson Wordsworth Editions 1992

Supplemented by: Ellis' British Railway Engineering Encyclopaedia.

Iain Ellis Second Edition 2010

Appendix 2
FURTHER READING

Great Western Railway – General *(for Brunel see separate section)*

A History of the Great Western Railway being The Story of the Broad Gauge

G A Sekon (Digby Long & Co 1895)

The Great Great Western

W J Scott (Republished EP Publications 1972; first published 1903)

The Great Western Railway - A New History

Frank Booker (David & Charles 1977, Second Edition 1985)

More Great Westernry

T W F Roche (Town & Country Press 1969)

Tales of the Great Western Railway

O S Nock (David & Charles 1984)

The Great Western Railway - 150 Glorious Years

General Editors Patrick Whitehouse & David St John Thomas (David & Charles 1985)

The Greatness of the Great Western

Keith M Beck (Ian Allan Ltd 1984)

Gone with Regret

George M Behrend (Jersey Artists 3rd Edition 1969)

GWR 150 Vol I: The Royal Road - 150 Years of Enterprise

Philip Rees CCE BR (W) (published BR (W) in association with Avon-AngliA 1985)

GWR 150 Vol II: Western Handbook - A Digest of GWR and WR Data

Geoffrey Body (publisher as Volume I, 1985)

The Great Western Railway - Routes, Statutes, Opening Dates and Other Particulars

(Avon-AngliA 1986)

The Heyday of GWR Train Services

P W B Semmens (Redwood Press, Melksham for David & Charles 1990)

Truly the Great Western (Photos)

M Earley (Oxford Publishing Co (OPC) 1971)

Great Western Progress 1835 - 1935

(David & Charles 1972)

Encyclopedia of the GWR

Edited by William Adams (Patrick Stephens Ltd 1993)

Window on the Great Western

(Wild Swan Publications 1989)

The Great Western Scene (Photos)

M Earley (OPC 1970)

Great Western Railway Halts

K Robertson (Irwell Press 1990)

The Great Western Railway – A Celebration

Tim Bryan (Ian Allan Publishing 2010)

The Great Western at Weymouth – A Railway & Shipping History

J H Lucking (David & Charles 1971)

The GWR Handbook 1923 – 1947

D Wragg (Sutton Publishing 2006)

Great Western Album

R C Riley (Ian Allan 1977)

Great Western Album No 2

R C Riley (Ian Allan 1974)

Great Western Steam in Action

L M Collins (Bradford Barton 1973)

Great Western Steam in Action 2

L M Collins (Bradford Barton 1974)

British Railways Western Region in Colour

L Waters (Ian Allan Publishing 2005)

The Changing Railway Scene – Western Region

L Waters (Ian Allan Publishing 2008)

The Great Way West – The History and Romance of the Great Western's Route to the West

David St John Thomas (David & Charles 1975)

Cornish Riviera Railway World Special

Chris Leigh (Ian Allan Ltd 1899)

Great Western Railway/British Rail Western Region Magazine

Great Western Railway stations

An Historical Survey of Selected Great Western Stations, Volume 1

Bedwyn, Burbage Goods, Devizes, Great Shefford, Hampstead Norris, Hungerford, Kintbury, Patney & Chirton, Savernake Low Level, Upton & Blewbury, Welford Park, Woodborough

R H Clark (OPC 1986)

Volume 2

Aldermaston, Castle Cary, Thatcham

R H Clark (OPC 1988)

Volume 3

Lambourn, Westbury

R H Clark (OPC 1987)

Great Western Branch Line Termini (Combined Edition) Volume 1

Lambourn

Paul Karau (OPC 1977)

GWR Country Stations, Volume 1

Aldermaston, Bedwyn, DN&SR, Hungerford, Kintbury, Lambourn, M&SWJR, Midgham,

Newbury West Fields Halt, Pewsey, Savernake and Theale

Chris Leigh (Ian Allan Ltd 1981)

GWR Country Stations, Volume 2

Burbage Wharf, Highclere, Hungerford, Kintbury, Midgham, Savernake Low Level

Chris Leigh (Ian Allan Ltd 1984)

Great Western Railway signalling

Semaphore Signalling on the Western Region of BR

B P Mills (Permanent Way Institution Journal Volume 110 Part 2 (p209 - 248) 1992)

A Pictorial Record of Great Western Signalling

A Vaughan (OPC 1975)

Signalman's Reflections

A Vaughan (Silver Link Publishing 2004)

Western Region Signalling in Colour

K Robertson (Ian Allan Publishing 2008)

Modern Railways April and August 1965: Major Resignalling Scheme (Reading)

Great Western Railway infrastructure

Track Topics: The Great Western Railway

W.G.Chapman (Reprint of third edition by David & Charles 1939)

Engineering Work 1928-1938

R Tourret (Tourret Publishing 2003)

Great Western Permanent Way

J W Mann (Permanent Way Institution Journal Part 3 (p126-136) 1976)

A Pictorial Record of Great Western Architecture

Aldermaston, Basingstoke, Devizes, Hawkeridge, Hungerford, Lambourn, Marlborough High Level, Midgham, Newbury, Newbury Racecourse, Newbury West Fields, Patney & Chirton, Pewsey, Reading, Savernake Low Level and Westbury

A Vaughan (Oxford Publishing Company 1977)

Brunel

The Life of Isambard Kingdom Brunel – Civil Engineer

Isambard Brunel BCL (Longmans Green & Co 1870)

Isambard Kingdom Brunel – A Biography

L T C Rolt (Book Club Associates 1971)

The Works of Isambard Kingdom Brunel – An Engineering Appreciation

Ed by Sir Alfred Pugsley H of B (ICE London/ University of Bristol 1976)

Brunel - Engineering Giant

Peter Hay (B T Batsford Ltd 1985)

Brunel's Broad Gauge Railway

Christopher Awdry (OPC 1992)

London & South Western Railway

Railway Magazine Volume 79 1936 July, August, October and November

Early Days of the London & South Western Railway I to IV

Railway Magazine Volume 79 1936 December and Volume 80 1937 January

What the Railways are doing: Red Post(s) Junction

'A Royal Road' being the History of the London & South Western Railway from 1825 to the Present Time

Sam Fay at Kingston-on-Thames 1882

The London & South Western Railway - Half a Century of Railway Progress

G A Sekon, published in London 1896

History of the Southern Railway Volume I Part II - The London & South Western Railway

C F Dendy Marshall (Ian Allan Ltd 1963)

The London & South Western Railway – Volume I The Formative Years

R A Williams (David & Charles 1968)

The London & South Western Railway – Volume II Growth and Consolidation

R A Williams (David & Charles 1973)

The L&SWR in the Twentieth Century - Volume III (1900 – 1923)

J N Faulkner & R A Williams (David & Charles 1988)

LSWR – A Tribute to the London and South Western Railway

B K Cooper & R Antell (Ian Allan 1988)

Individual Railways and Lines

Berks & Hants Line (as defined in the book)

Slough to Newbury

Vic Mitchell & Keith Smith (Middleton Press 2000)

Newbury to Westbury

Vic Mitchell & Keith Smith in association with Kevin Robertson (Middleton Press 2001)

The Marlborough Branch

K Robertson & D Abbott (Irwell Press 1990)

Wiltshire Railway Stations

Mike Oakley (The Dovecote Press 2004)

Railway Magazine Volume 151 2004 September, p33-38

The *Short* Way West – the story of the Berks & Hants and how it 'abbreviated' the GWR: Practice and Performance *John Heaton FCILT*

Devizes Branch

The Devizes Branch - A Wiltshire Railway Remembered

Nigel S M Bray (Picton Publishing 1984)

GWR to Devizes

Ron Priddle & David Hyde (Millstream Books 1996)

Didcot, Newbury & Southampton Railway

The Didcot, Newbury & Southampton Railway

T B Sands (The Oakwood Press 1971)

The Didcot, Newbury & Southampton Railway

P Karou, M Parsons & K Robertson (Wild Swan 1984, first published 1981)

The Didcot, Newbury & Southampton Railway Supplement

K Robertson & R Simmonds (Wild Swan 1984)

The Didcot, Newbury & Southampton Railway: a New History 1882-1966 *K Robertson* (Noodle Books 2014)

An Historical Survey of the Didcot, Newbury & Southampton Railway – Layouts & Illustrations

C W Judge (OPC 1984)

Didcot to Winchester

Vic Mitchell & Kevin Robertson (Middleton Press 1998)

Railway Magazine Volume 81 1937 December p469

Items of Interest: Winchester Cheesehill – origin of name

Railway Magazine Volume 84 1939 February p218-9

Southampton's Rival Railway Schemes

Lambourn Valley Railway / Lambourn Branch

An Illustrated History of the Lambourn Branch

K Robertson & R Simmonds (Wild Swan 1984)

Branch Line to Lambourn

Vic Mitchell and Keith Smith in association with Kevin Robertson (Middleton Press 2001)

The Lambourn Branch Revisited

Kevin Robertson (Noodle Books 2008)

Backtrack Magazine Volume 7 No 4 1993 p208-16

"The Lambourn Valley Railway" *Josephine Carter*

Midland & South Western Junction Railway

The Midland & South Western Junction Railway

T B Sands (The Oakwood Press 1959, reprinted 1979)

T B Sands (revised by S C Jenkins) (The Oakwood Press, 2nd Revised Edition 1990)

Swindon's Other Railway – The M&SWJR 1900 – 1985

B Bridgeman, D Barrett & D Bird (Red Brick Publishing Swindon 1985)

The Midland & South Western Junction Railway – The Old Photographs Series

B Bridgeman & M Barnsley (The Chalford Publishing Company 1994)

Andover to Southampton

Vic Mitchell & Keith Smith (Middleton Press 1990)

Midland & South Western Junction Railway: Vol 1

David Bartholomew (Wild Swan 1982)

Railway Magazine Volume 70 1932 March p157-166 (part 1) and April p255-266 (part 2)

The Midland & South Western Junction Railway *D S Barrie*

Lines from Westbury

The Bath to Weymouth Line including Westbury to Salisbury

Colin Maggs (The Oakwood Press 1982)

The Story of the Westbury to Weymouth Line

Derek Phillips (OPC 1994)

Railway Magazine Volume 84 1939 May p380-1

Yeovil and its Railways

Kennet & Avon Canal & Kennet Navigation

Bradshaw's Canals and Navigable Rivers of England and Wales – A Handbook of Inland

Navigation

H Rodolph de Salis (H Blacklock & Co Ltd. 1904 (republished 1969))

The Kennet & Avon Canal

Kenneth R Clew (David & Charles 1988)

The Kennet & Avon Canal (A Pictorial Journey from Bath to Reading)

K & A Canal Trust 1990

The Kennet & Avon Canal: A User's Guide to the Waterways between Reading and Bristol

Niall Allsop (Millstream Books, Bath, 3rd Ed. 1992)

Kennet and Avon Canal Towpath Guides numbers 1 to 12

(Kennet and Avon Canal Trust 1982 – 1987)

The Kennet & Avon Canal

Clive & Helen Hackford (Tempus Publishing Ltd 2001)

Train Services / Loco performance

The Limited - The Story of the Cornish Riviera Express

O S Nock (George Allan & Unwin 1979)

Cornish Riviera Limited

T W E Roche (Town & Country Press Ltd 1969)

Railway Magazine Volume 125 March 1979

Locomotive Practice and Performance: "'Cornish Riviera' – End of an Epoch" (introduction of HST sets on Paddington – West of England services).

Railway World Volume 43 July 1982 p381

Prototype Class 210 driver training at Midgham on 9.05.82 *(photo David Canning)*

Railway Magazine Volume 132 February 1986 p87-91

Locomotive Practice and Performance: "Weymouth for the Channel Isles"

Railway Magazine Volume 132 April 1986

Panorama: "Yeoman Americans arrive" (photos); Traffic & Traction – Western Region: commissioning of Class 59 locomotives

Railway Magazine Volume 132 September 1986

Locomotive Practice and Performance: "Riding a Class 59"; News & notes: "Yeoman locos named"

Regional

The Regional History of the Railways of Great

Britain (Series)

Volume II Southern England

H P White & David St John (5th edition David & Charles 1992)

Volume XIII Thames and Severn

Rex Christiansen (David & Charles 1981)

The Forgotten Railways of Great Britain (Series)

Vol 3 Chilterns and Cotswolds

R Davies & M D Grant (revised edition) (Atlantic Transport Publishers 1984)

Vol 6 South East England

H P White (revised edition) (David St John Thomas 1987)

All Change for the West

G F Gillham (Kingfisher Railway Productions 1980)

Main Lines to the West

Simon Rocksborough-Smith (Ian Allan Ltd 1981)

Rail Routes in Hampshire and East Dorset

David Fereday Glenn (Ian Allan Ltd 1983)

The Railways of Winchester

K Robertson & R Simmonds (Platform 5 1988)

Riviera Express - The Train and its Route

Geoffrey Body (British Rail (Western) and Avon-AngliA 1979)

British Railways Past and Present

No 21: Berkshire & Hampshire

Terry Gough (Past and Present Publishing 1994)

No 22: Wiltshire

Graham Roose & Hugh Ballantyne (Past and Present Publishing 1994)

Maps and Diagrams

Track Layout Diagrams of the G.W.R and BR W.R.

Section 21: Bath & Westbury

Second Edition 1988 *R A Cooke*

Section 22: Midland & South Western Junction Railway

Second Edition 1982 *R A Cooke*

Section 23: Berkshire

Second Edition 1986 *R A Cooke*

Section 24: Lower Thames Valley

1975 *R A Cooke*

Incidents along the line

OFF the RAILS

Bill Bishop (Kingfisher Railway Productions 1984)

Local history

A Popular History of Thatcham

Peter Allen (& R B Tubb) (Millennium Edition 1999)

Village Collection – More Old Tales of Woolhampton, Midgham, Brimpton & Wasing

J Trigg 2000

As We Were 1901 to 1930 : A View of Edwardian and Georgian Woolhampton and Midgham

J Trigg (no date)

Woolhampton 1930 to 1940 – A Time of Change

J Trigg (no date)

Hungerford – A History

The Hungerford Historical Association 2000

The Story of Hungerford

Hugh Pihlens (Local Heritage Books, Newbury 1983)

Reminiscences of Twentieth Century Hungerford

Pam Heseltine (The Hungerford Historical Association 1993).

Kintbury – A Century Remembered 1900 – 1999

Kintbury Volunteer Group 1999

Closed passenger stations and goods depots

Clinker's Register of Closed Passenger Stations and Goods Depots in England, Scotland and Wales, 1830-1977

C R Clinker (Avon-AngliA Publications and Services 1984)

Appendix 3

TABLES OF PRIVATE AND OTHER SIDINGS

READING – WESTBURY

PRIVATE AND OTHER SIDINGS SERVED BY THE BERKS & HANTS LINE

Table One: Berkshire (Reading – Newbury)

Location	Companies and Facilities	Dates
Reading Central Goods (open to traffic 4 May 1908) (last traffic 25 July 1983) (closed December 1983) (see Note 3 for further companies present as at 1961)	Baynes Siding (Baynes (Reading) Ltd) CWS Preserves Factory Esso Petrol siding National Benzole Regent Oil Co H & G Simonds (later Courage) siding Bear Wharf	present 1914; sidings removed 1956-1965 (west), 1972 (east) present 1914; sidings removed 9.1964 added c.12.1930 as Anglo American Oil dates not known in the 1950s present 1914 present 1914
Calcot Mill	Smith Bros Dewe Brothers J T Dewe Holland Bros Siding removed	PSA 5.7.1890 (Note 2) PSA 9.2.1898 PSA 25.3.1905 PSA 1922 1928
Theale East	Private siding into use Imperial Tobacco Co (of GB & I) Ltd Royal Ordnance Factory Pressed Steel Co Ltd	5.1.1940 PSA 23.1.1940 & 24.12.1940 1941-1945? PSA 24.5.1952, PSAT 30.6.1976
Theale West	New Sidings Wraysbury Sand & Gravel Theale & G W Sand & Gravel Co Ltd New Layout Completed: Civil Engineer's Pre-Assembled Track Depot Tip Sidings Layout Changes: Two sidings nearest Theale designated 'Stone Sidings' Nos 1 & 2 (furthest west) removed and replaced by new Murco Oil Siding Further changes: From west to east, private sidings from this date: Murco (as above) Castle Marine Cement (CMC) ARC (Amey Roadstone)	7.2.1929 PSA 27.6.1929 PSA 4.8.1937 30.4.1962 by 1970 PSA 13.5.1971 2.1976 (provided late 1974) Depot opened 1.1.1975, first Cement train 20.1.1975

Location	Companies and Facilities	Dates
Theale West (continued)	New Layout into use	17/19.8.1977, other changes 1980/81
	New arrangements, from west to east:	from 16/29.6.1981
	Company names unchanged	at 1992 (Note 1)
	Murco Petroleum Ltd	PSA 13.5.1971 (as above)
	Foster Yeoman Ltd	PSA 29.1.1982
	Blue Circle Industries	PSA 29.6.1983
	ARC (Amey Roadstone)	No PSA
Tyle (Tile) Mill	Loop from main line and siding to Mill	believed to date from 1876
	Wm Jefferys Strange	PSA 11.9.1885
	F L Smith	PSA 12.8.1901
	(Not known)	PSA 9.7.1908
	(Not known)	PSA 27.1.1910
	Siding to Mill taken out of use	pre-1918
	Sidings adjacent to main line in use	from 1918
	Messrs Baines (Reading) Ltd	PSA 27.7.1918, PSAT 23.5.1929
	Messrs Baines (G C Usher)	PSA 1.10.1936, PSAT 1937 (Note 2)
	Siding by main line taken out of use	20.01.1938
Aldermaston (Padworth)	Ministry of Fuel & Power Siding into use	from 24.2.1942
	Arrangement (from east to west):	by 1975
	Ministry of Fuel & Power (Oil Terminal)	PSA 9.8.1954
		not present 1992 (Note 1)
	C A Goodwin (London) Ltd Padworth Depot (stone)	at 1992 (Note 1)
	Tip Sidings (Civil Engineer's)	possibly present from 1942
Aldermaston (West)	Water Softening Plant and Pump House Pump House siding adjacent to the down main line	Water troughs into use June 1904; date out of use not known (Note 4)
	Sterling Cables Co Ltd	PSA 18.10.1948
	Sidings removed	11.1967
Colthrop North Side	Siding added for Royal Navy Victualling Depot	Second World War
	To Colthrop Board & Paper Mills Ltd	PSA 7.7.1949
	To Reed Board Mills (Colthrop) Ltd	PSA 1.7.1959
	To Reed Paper & Board (UK) Ltd	PSA 11.7.1976
	Main line connection maintained on reduction of Colthrop Siding SB to Ground Frame	14/16.1.1978
	Connection still in use	1983 (photo evidence)
	No siding shown	At 1992 (Note 1)

TABLES OF PRIVATE AND OTHER SIDINGS

Location	Companies and Facilities	Dates
Colthrop Mills	J Henry & Co Ltd To Colthrop Board & Paper Mills Ltd Colthrop Board & Paper Mills Ltd To Reeds Cartons Ltd Terminated Cropper & Co Ltd To Reeds Cartons Ltd To Field, Sons & Co Ltd (formerly Cropper & Co) Field, Sons & Co Ltd at closure	PSA 17.1.1912 (first sidings east end) PSA 22.8.1918 (east end) PSA 21.10.1927 (new layout) PSA 1.7.1959 PSAT 30.6.1971 PSA 7.6.1922 (first sidings west end) PSA 1.7.1959 (west end) PSAT 30.6.1971 Date not known Date not known
Thatcham West	WD Ordnance Depot West end connections to main line East end connection to main line	Open 1940 (No PSA) (newspaper references) Taken out of use 2.1.1966 Present 1992 (Notes 1 & 5)
Newbury Racecourse Sidings	Government Sidings Removed Secretary of State for War Occupied by American Army To Ministry of Supply To Ministry of Works One siding retained, otherwise All wartime sidings removed	First World War by 1923 PSA 5.9.1941 August 1942 March 1946 PSA 5.8.1947 PSAT 31.12.1949 11.1967
Newbury Racecourse (north side)	Shell Mex & BP Ltd BP Marketing Ltd BP Oil Ltd	PSA 11.3.1963 (siding first used 23.11.) from 29.9.1974 14.4.1976 present 1992 (Note 1)
Newbury (Gas Works)	Newbury Corporation Gas Co To Newbury Corporation To Southern Gas Board Adjacent siding for BP Co Ltd Sidings in this area removed	PSA 22.2.1883 PSA 5.10.1937 (and siding extended) PSA 31.12.1949, PSAT 26.1.1961 PSA 15.8.1923 1961 – 1965
Newbury Goods Yard	First siding: R Skinner Second siding: William Skinner Back-shunt from above: Plenty & Son Ltd (Note 3) Second siding: W Skinner & Co (Newbury) Ltd Ditto: To H Baird & Sons Ltd Plenty Siding: Plenty Still Oil Engines Ltd Ditto: To Newbury Diesel Co Second Siding: To Plenty & Son Ltd Newbury Diesel Co siding	PSA 30.10.1868 PSA 26.5.1894 (may have replaced above) PSA 28.3.1903 PSA 12.8.1913 PSA 14.11.1913 PSA 19.7.1928 PSA 22.7.1943 PSA 5.2.1960, PSAT 30.6.1965 PSAT 31.12.1978

Table Two: West of Newbury (Devizes, Seend and Westbury) (to 1992)

Location	Companies and Facilities	Dates
Bromham & Rowde (Devizes – Holt Junction)	Siding to Saw Mills: Partridge Cox & Co Ltd Ditto: To Seend Electric Saw Mills Ltd	PSA 3.12.1941 PSA 14.11.1946, PSAT 30.9.1963
Seend (Devizes – Holt Junction)	Seend Ironworks (branch from station) Use of siding (part of branch): Robbins, Lane & Pinniger Ditto (to) Thos W Ward Noted siding (part of branch) not used for some time Siding east of station (orig. loop): Seend Iron Mines Co. Ditto siding served by aerial ropeway and chute: The Avon Valley Iron Co	Closed 1875 (Ironworks) PSA 28.3.1887 PSA 24.9.1889 at 30.11.1894, removed by 1900 PSA 17.2.1906, PSAT 31.3.1911 PSA 31.8.1919
Westbury (Heywood Road Junction)	Siding to serve Cement Works Westbury Cement Works APCM (Associated Portland Cement Manufacturers) Blue Circle Cement Ditto	Into use 30.9/1.10.1962 Opened 29.4.1963 PSA 13.7.1966 at 1985 at 1992 (Note 1)
Westbury (west side station)	Westbury Iron co Ltd (Iron Works, Coke Ovens etc) To New Westbury Iron Co Ltd Additional Facilities incl. Crusher AE Farr Ltd & Bovis Ltd Bovis Ltd Civil Engineers' siding	PSA 11.6.1870 PSA 13.4.1904 & 28.5.1906 PSA 26.1.1917, PSAT 26.8.1941 PSA 3.9.1943 at 1979 & 1986 at 1992 (Note 1)
Westbury (east side station, north end)	Siding added by Grain Siding: Nitrovit Ltd Siding:	1940 Taken out of use 1.9.1980

Note 1: Reference - British Rail Track Diagrams No 3 Western Region Second Edition January 1992
Note 2: PSA – Private Siding Agreement
    PSAT – Private Siding Agreement Terminated
Note 3: Reading Central Goods - photographic evidence 1961: also present - H&T Timber Ltd.; W W Hall (builders' yard); C&G Ayres, coal merchants.
Note 4: Aldermaston Water Troughs - last use date probably related to last regular use of steam haulage on West of England trains (1962/3)
Note 5: Thatcham Depot closed 1999 – date of last use of rail connection not known
Note 6: Backshunt – a spur to a siding to which access is obtained by a reversal from the siding

Index

INDEX

197

INDEX

THE BERKS AND HANTS LINE

INDEX

INDEX

INDEX OF PEOPLE

THE BERKS AND HANTS LINE

Canning, David	177 (Note)
Carnarvon, Earl of	21,26,50
Chaplin, William James	26
Craven, Lord	26
Forbes, James Staats	50
Fromont, Miss Maria	33
Giles, Francis	18,20,23
Gould, John	120
Grierson, William Wylie	85
Henderson, George, Colonel	18
Hopson, Councillor Joseph	35 (Note 4)
Hore, John	24 (Note 1)
Jessop, William	24 (Note 1)
Lane, Michael	39
Locke, Joseph	18,19,22,25
Macadam, John Loudon	17
Mackarness, Frederick, MP	78
Marshall, D	168
Mayor of Basingstoke	21
Mayor of Newbury	21
Palmer, Henry Robinson	19,21,22
Price, Henry Habberley	18,22
Rennie, John	24 (Note 1)
Ridley, Nicholas	168
Russell, Charles, MP	21,26,32
Saunders, Charles	20,29
Serpell, Sir David	168
Shaw, Benjamin	22
Stephenson, George	18,19,21,22
Stephenson, Robert	18
Stillman, Frank H	19,35 (Note 4)
Taylor, J N	85
Townsend, W H	18
Walker, James	19
Ward, John	24 (Note 1)
Wellington, Duke of	26
Vignoles, Charles Blacker	22

INDEX OF OTHER ORGANISATIONS

INDEX

Note: References to 'Berks & Hants' and 'Berks & Hants Extension' are not listed from Chapter 5 onwards

THATCHAM STATION STAFF 1942/43

J Allen

R Bellinger

R Butler

V Chapman

B Draper

R East

R Mabbutt

M Miles

R Nutley

R Pinnock

J Reid

P Wise